Teach Yourself
Windows 3.1

By Al Stevens

First Printing

ISBN 1-55828-193-2

Printed in the United States of America

10 9 8 7 6 5 4 3 2 1

MIS:Press books are available at special discounts for bulk purchases for sales promotions, premiums, fund-raising, or educational use. Special editions or book excerpts can also be created to specification.

For details contact: Special Sales Director
MIS:Press
a subsidiary of Henry Holt and Company, Inc.
115 West 18th Street
New York, New York 10011

Trademarks

Dedication

To the fond memory of Richard Phillips—one fourth of a happy time.
(I don't believe I understood that, Rich.)

Acknowledgements

Thanks to:

Microsoft for providing me with beta copies of Windows 3.1. Andy Thomas and the other sysops and participants on the CompuServe WINBTU forum.

Table of Contents

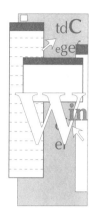

Preface

This book is a tutorial; something like a workbook to teach yourself how to operate Windows 3.1 on your personal computer. Windows 3.1 is an operating environment that adds three features to IBM-compatible PCs. First, a *graphical user interface*—a screen based on pictures, not letters. Second, a user interface that is *similar* in all Windows applications. And third, the ability to *multitask*—to run more than one application at a time. These features are important because they bring the advantages of other kinds of computers, like the Amiga and the Macintosh, to the IBM world.

Windows 3.0, the immediate predecessor of Windows 3.1, was the third version of Windows. Among its improvements over earlier versions was the ability to run DOS programs from within Windows, allowing users to gain the benefits of Windows while gradually upgrading to programs that take advantage of Windows. As a result, users don't have to immediately abandon indispensable older DOS applications.

Windows 3.1 adds several features to the Windows graphical environment and significantly improves its performance. Among the new features are *object linking and embedding*, which allows graphics and text data files to be associated across applications, and support for multimedia devices. Chapter 11, which describes the tools of the Windows power user, explains how to use these new facilities.

This book ignores the earlier versions of Windows and usually refers to Windows 3.1 simply as "Windows."

How to Use This Book

Teach Yourself... Windows 3.1 is a tutorial book. Its purpose is to enable you to learn to operate in the Windows environment with a minimum of fuss. The book assumes that you have a basic understanding of DOS—not necessarily that of a power user, but sufficient knowledge to know how DOS organizes files into directories and subdirectories, what file and directory names look like, and the differences between data files and program files. If you need to learn the fundamentals of DOS, read my book, *Teach Yourself... DOS 5.0* (1991, MIS:Press).

Proceed through the chapters of *Teach Yourself... Windows 3.1* sequentially. This book is not a reference book for looking up a subject and finding everything you need to know about it. It is a set of tutorial exercises designed to expose you to the features of Windows by using subjects already learned to introduce new ones.

As you leaf through the book you will see many illustrations of screens and windows. The exercises in this book do not ask you to imagine what you will see when you try them out. Every exercise is fully illustrated to allow you to read and learn during those times when a computer is not handy and to reinforce your experience when you run the exercises. When what the book shows is what you see on the screen, you know you are doing it right.

Do not expect to learn Windows simply by reading this book. Use the book along with your computer to learn whenever possible. You will need an installed Windows configuration, preferably one that has not been heavily modified and enhanced. Ideally, you should start by installing Windows onto a computer that does not already have it. That way the examples and figures in this book will most closely match the ones you see on your screen.

You may have heard that Windows is a complex, difficult operating environment. It can be, but it doesn't have to start out that way. By learning its basic operations, you can rapidly become a productive Windows user. As you become more proficient, you can move on to Windows' more advanced operations. This book follows that logic by presenting the easy topics first and saving the hard parts until later.

The Windows Graphical User Interface

The Windows graphical user interface (GUI) breaks the bonds of the traditional text-only screen. It presents the software operating environment in pictures—"icons" and other metaphors for computer files and functions—as opposed to the typically terse command-line syntax of DOS. DOS users must necessarily retain mental images of the files, subdirectories, programs, and other DOS resources. The GUI provides these images as pictures on the graphics screen so you do not have to remember them. Many of the cryptic commands and command-line *parameters* that DOS and its applications use are replaced by keyboard shortcuts or point-and-shoot mouse operations under a GUI. Such an interface is more intuitive—obvious just by looking at it—than the DOS command-line interface.

The Windows Consistent User Interface

One of the problems with many computer systems and with DOS in particular is that the user interfaces of the applications differ. A DOS user who runs spreadsheet, word processor, database, electronic mail, and desktop publishing programs must learn the command and data entry languages of each of these programs, all of which might differ substantially. Even the utility programs of DOS itself, such as BACKUP, ATTRIB, and COPY, use command line syntax conventions that differ enough to cause confusion.

Windows users, however, can use programs designed to take advantage of the Windows graphical user interface. Such programs employ command and data entry techniques that emulate those of Windows, including standard menu and dialog formats and use of the mouse to select items from menus, scroll documents on the screen, and move the cursor. Users of Windows programs do not need to learn the basics of a new command language for every new program.

Windows Multitasking

DOS does not exploit the power of most of the computers that run it. If you are running one program, you must terminate it and return to DOS in order to run another. This can be inconvenient. If you run a program frequently, you do not want to constantly save all your work in that program so you can go to other programs—and then repeatedly endure the startup time needed to go back to your main program. Some users run programs that consume time but do not require much attention. These people would also like to run other programs at the same time.

Both groups of users need an operating environment that supports *multitasking*, which allows a computer to run more than one program at the same time.

DOS by itself does not support multitasking. Because of this, software developers have developed techniques for memory-resident utility programs that allow you to load more than one program into memory. When you want to execute one of these programs, you press a "hot key," and the program pops up. The business of switching from one task to another is the responsibility of the memory resident programs. DOS has nothing to do with it. Such a program must record the state of the program it interrupts, establish its own state, coerce DOS into behaving as if the new program is the only one running, and then restore the state of the interrupted program when the user is ready to return to it.

There are many differences between the conditions under which programs operate, not the least of which is the mode of the video screens they have to deal with. Unless every interrupting program is aware of every permutation of video mode, is able to switch to and from all possible permutations, and does it in a way that is compatible with all other programs, chaos will reign. Another disadvantage to the memory-resident programs is that they occupy memory even when they are not doing something. As you add memory-resident applications, the memory available for other tasks decreases. Nonetheless, for years the memory-resident program was the only choice for DOS users who needed multitasking.

Windows is an application and file management shell program that runs on top of DOS. Windows can support true multitasking if your PC has a 386 microprocessor. True multitasking involves running several applications concurrently. While you write a letter with your word processor, the communications program collects your electronic mail, the spreadsheet application computes a large sheet, the database program searches its files to answer a query you entered, and the printer prints the output from the other programs.

Windows can manage the execution of multiple tasks for non-386 users, too. The difference is that even though several programs are loaded and available, only one program is executing at a time. All the applications have access to the entire memory of the computer, however, and users can switch from application to application by letting Windows swap the running tasks in and out. Windows manages the multitasking or swapping of concurrently loaded programs in a way that allows each of them to have the full range of memory normally available to a single program in the DOS environment.

The multitasking environment is not restricted to applications that were developed to run exclusively in the Windows graphical operating environment. Windows can switch between Windows applications and non-Windows DOS applications.

Windows allows applications to exchange data in ways not available under a single-tasking operating environment. You can move data from one application to another, and the two applications do not need to know about one another and do not need to know that the data movement took place. Any Windows application that has a Paste command can receive text from any other Windows application that has a Cut or Copy command as long as Windows is running the application or has run it in the recent past. A Windows application that can accept graphics data and has the Paste command can likewise receive graphics data from any other Windows application that displays graphics data and has a Cut or Copy command. Non-Windows DOS applications can similarly exchange textual data. The user manages these data exchanges by using the Windows Clipboard as the intermediate repository for data values that are to be exchanged.

Some Windows applications have a *dynamic data exchange* (DDE) facility built into them, allowing them to exchange data among themselves without user intervention.

Whence Windows 3.1?

Windows 3.1 is a product from Microsoft Corporation that culminates several generations of products that bore the Windows name. Its predecessors enjoyed less than moderate success for several reasons.

1. The hardware required to run them was expensive;
2. The programs performed poorly;
3. You needed different versions of Windows depending on your processor type;
4. The only applications you could run in the Windows environment were Windows-specific applications; and
5. Prior to version 3.0, Windows had no facility for true multitasking.

The computer industry solved the first problem and Windows 3.1 solves most of the rest. Fast *AT-class* machines (ones with 286 or 386 processors) with mice, high-resolution color displays, and significant amounts of memory are commonplace now. Windows senses what kind of hardware is running and adjusts itself accordingly, so you do not need different Windows versions for different hardware configurations. Windows allows you to install and run non-Windows DOS applications, and, if you are using a 386 machine with sufficient memory, Windows will allow several programs to be executing at the same time.

How This Book Is Organized

Chapter 1 is the introduction to Windows and it is an important one. You will find out what hardware and software you need to run Windows. You will learn how to install, start, and exit Windows. You will learn the basics of using the Windows graphical user interface—subsequent chapters will assume that you understand that interface. Because Windows works with a mouse or a keyboard, most operations can use either one. For example, after Chapter 1 teaches you how to select an item from a menu with either the mouse or the keyboard, other chapters will simply tell you to select the item, assuming that you know how. In Chapter 1 you will learn how the Windows online help system works.

Chapter 2 is about the Windows Program Manager. You will learn how the Program Manager organizes programs into groups and how you can create, organize, and maintain your own groups of programs. You will learn how to operate DOS programs from within Windows and how to operate several programs at one time—how to multitask.

Chapter 3 is about the Windows File Manager. You will learn how to create and delete directories on your hard disk, how to move, copy, and delete files, how to format and copy diskettes, and how to run programs from within the File Manager.

Chapter 4 is about the Clipboard. You will learn how to use the Clipboard to exchange text and graphics data among Windows applications and non-Windows DOS applications.

Chapter 5 is about the Windows Control Panel. You will learn how to use the Control Panel to alter the appearance of the desktop; modify the performance of devices such as the mouse, keyboard, and communications ports; install, select and configure a printer; use the display and input conventions of other countries; set the date and time; and control the Windows beeper.

Chapter 6 is about the Windows Print Manager. You will learn how to print from Windows applications with and without the queuing features of the Print Manager; print from DOS applications; delete and reorder entries in the print queues; and modify the Print Manager's processor priority.

Chapter 7 is about Windows Write, the word processor that comes with Windows. You will learn how to create and modify documents.

Chapter 8 is about Windows Paintbrush, the graphics design program that comes with Windows. You will learn how to create pictures, use graphics elements from other sources, and integrate your designs into your other applications.

Chapter 9 is about Windows Terminal, the communications program that comes with Windows. You will learn how to connect to online services and bulletin board systems, send messages, and upload and download files.

Chapter 10 is about the Windows accessory programs. You will learn how to use the Clock, the Calculator, the Notepad, the Calendar, the Cardfile, and the Recorder.

Chapter 11 contains techniques that you will use when you become a Windows *power user*—someone who modifies Windows in detail to get the most performance out of it. You will learn about the Windows operating modes and when and how to use them. You will learn how to use the Windows PIF Editor to integrate DOS applications into Windows. You will learn how to run applications that were developed for previous versions of Windows. You will integrate a DOS memory-resident program into Windows and run it along with the other programs in your system. You will learn about Object Linking and Embedding and the new features of Windows that support the multimedia devices that you can add to your computer. Finally, you will learn how to use Windows in a network workstation

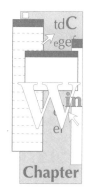

Chapter 1

Introduction to Windows 3.1

This chapter is your introduction to Windows 3.1. If you have never used Windows before and, particularly, if you have never used a graphical operating environment on a computer, this chapter will be a necessary first step. In this chapter you will learn:

◆ How to install Windows on your computer
◆ How to start and exit from Windows
◆ Working with windows and icons
◆ Menus and menu commands
◆ Dialog boxes
◆ The Windows Help system

Following the discussion on "Installation" in this chapter, this book assumes that you have Windows installed in its default configuration. It is best that your Windows configuration not be heavily modified or enhanced when you begin so that the examples and figures in the book will come close to matching those on your screen.

Getting Started

If you are a potential power user—perhaps you were a DOS power user—you will eventually want to customize, modify, and tweak your Windows operating environment to wrest the last ounce of performance from your computer and to personalize its appearance and behavior. There are many ways to do this and many third-party add-on products to enhance or otherwise change the way Windows works. This chapter could not possibly cover all the ways you can customize Windows, nor could the book. Chapter 11 will address some of the ways that you can modify the Windows operating environment. For now, however, the lessons assume that you will install Windows in its simplest configuration, out of the box, up and running.

Required Hardware

You need a certain minimum hardware configuration to run Windows. You might hear that you can run Windows on almost any PC, and to a limited extent that is true. But Windows is a high-end software product that works well if it is given the hardware horsepower it needs. Give Windows less horsepower than it needs and it can become very cumbersome to use and ineffective for the work it was designed to do. The hardware minimums given here are the recommended ones for any reasonable operation of Windows.

Processor

You need a 286 processor at a minimum to run any version of Windows effectively. Even though Windows 3.0 would run on the 8088 (XT) class of machine, most of the advantages offered by Windows are unavailable to that generation of processor, and the typical 8088's processor speed is too slow for reasonable use by Windows. For multitasking DOS and Windows applications, you will need a 386. Processor speed is important even with 286s and 386s. Do not expect to be happy with Windows if you are running a 6Mhz 286. You should have at the very least least a 12Mhz processor. The faster the better. Windows 3.1 will not run on the 8088/XT-type of computer. You need at least a 286.

Memory

Windows needs 640K of conventional and 384K extended memory for a total minimum of 1Mb. You will need 2Mb of extended memory for multitasking or to run in 386 enhanced mode. (You will learn about Windows operating modes in Chapter 11.) The more extended memory you have, the more efficiently Windows will manage multiple tasks.

Disk Space

A Windows installation uses 12.5Mb of hard disk storage. Do not consider installing Windows with less. Beyond this minimum, you will need room for application programs, data files, DOS files, and the working files that Windows builds and uses. The 12.5Mb that Windows uses must be on one disk drive. Applications and DOS can be on other drives if you have them. A good rule of thumb is to install Windows on a system with at least 20Mb of disk storage available. The more the better. You'll also need a 1.2Mb 5.25-inch floppy drive or a 1.44Mb 3.5-inch floppy drive to install Windows.

Video

You need a *graphics adaptor* to run Windows. All PCs have some kind of video adaptor card used to connect a video screen to the computer, but Windows does not run on a machine that has the original IBM Monochrome Display Adaptor (MDA). You need one of the adaptors with graphics capabilities.

Windows works with both Hercules-compatible monochrome adaptors and the Color Graphics Adaptor (CGA), but the display is not very appealing and you will be unimpressed. At a minimum you should have the Enhanced Graphics Adaptor (EGA). The Virtual Graphics Array (VGA) is the recommended adaptor. With that adaptor and a compatible color display monitor, Windows comes alive.

There are several other display adaptors and monitors that you might have that Windows can use. Other hardware vendors will include the necessary software drivers and installation instructions for adding their products to a Windows configuration. Be aware that many such products include drivers for earlier versions of Windows. These drivers might not work with Windows 3.1. Make sure that you get the driver for Windows 3.1.

Mouse

Although it is possible to run Windows without a mouse device, you should have one. Some Windows operations are easier with a mouse. Others lend themselves more readily to keyboard input. Windows is designed to support either mode and a mix of both. Some applications—the Windows tutorial and the Minesweeper game, for example—require a mouse.

Modem

Because Windows excels at multitasking, you might wonder how you would use that facility. The most productive use of a multitasking environment is to let the computer run some program that requires no attention while you use the computer for something interactive. A frequent use for computers and one that executes for long periods of time without operator intervention is communication with other systems over telephone lines. By allowing Windows to run such communications applications in the background while you run an interactive application, such as word processing, in the foreground, you acquire a larger measure of productivity from your computer. Communications programs need a modem. You do not need a modem if you never telecommunicate, but if you do, Windows offers an efficient way to do it.

Printer

Windows is a graphical operating environment, so many graphics-based applications such as desktop publishing, graphics design, and CAD/CAM programs are designed to run with Windows. Laser printers are best able to print the output from these applications. Dot matrix, daisy wheel, and ink jet printers either cannot print graphics, do so at low resolution, or print them very slowly. A laser printer, while not required by Windows, is almost a necessity if you want to derive the maximum benefit from the Windows graphical operating environment.

Required Software

To run Windows you must already have MS-DOS or PC-DOS version 3.1 or higher. Version 5.0 is recommended.

Installation

Windows installs itself. It comes with a package of numbered diskettes. You put the first diskette into a disk drive, log onto that drive, and type SETUP to run the Setup program. Then, for the most part, you follow instructions. To begin with,

Setup asks whether you want to perform the Express or Custom setup procedure. The Custom setup procedure assumes that you are an experienced Windows user, and this discussion assumes that you are not. Otherwise, you would not be reading this book.

This discussion assumes that you are installing Windows 3.1 onto a computer that has no previous version of Windows installed and no compatibility issues to address. (See NOTE.) Select the Express setup procedure. Setup will begin by making sure that there is enough room on your hard disk for Windows. Then it will start copying files from the diskette to the hard disk. At first, Setup displays its progress in the PC's text mode. Soon it switches into a graphics mode and displays the Windows Setup dialog box. You may type your name and the name of your company into the dialog box. When the dialog box has the correct data in both fields, press the Enter key to continue.

N O T E

The worlds of DOS and Windows are complex. There are many varieties of configurations that you might have. There are numerous add-on products that might already be installed in your computer that could affect the installation and operation of Windows. If your computer is a workstation in a network, the versions of the network driver programs might be critical. You should consult with your network administrator before proceeding with the installation of Windows. There are disk compression drivers, such as Stacker and SuperStor, that increase disk capacity by compressing data files. You must be sure that you have the versions of those programs that are compatible with Windows 3.1, and you must be sure that you have them installed with the options that maintain that compatibility. Windows includes some text files that document some of these compatibility issues. However, you need to install Windows before you can read the text files.

The Setup program will proceed by copying more files, and asking you to insert the Windows diskettes one at a time. Sometime during the procedure Setup will display the Printer Installation dialog box. Use the up and down arrow keys to select the printer that you use, and press Enter to choose the current selection. The dialog box will then display a list of the computer ports the printer might be attached to. Choose the port by using the same procedure.

The Setup program now displays the Program Manager window, giving you a preview of what you will see when you run Windows. Setup builds the Program Manager's Main, Accessories, Games, and Startup group windows while you watch. Next, it searches your disk for DOS applications that it can install into the

Applications group window. Setup knows the names of most of these applications. When it finds an application that it cannot determine a name for, Setup displays a dialog box that allows you to select the name from a list.

After Setup is done installing Windows, it allows you to run a brief tutorial on the operation of Windows. You should run that tutorial before proceeding with the lessons in this book.

When you are done with the tutorial, Setup requires you to reboot the computer. Do that by pressing the Enter key when Setup displays the option.

Running Windows

If Windows will always be your primary operating environment, you might want it to execute automatically every time you boot the computer. Use DOS's EDIT, EDLIN or another text editor to add this command to the end of the AUTOEXEC.BAT file in the root directory:

```
WIN
```

If you prefer to execute Windows yourself, do not modify AUTOEXEC.BAT. Instead, type WIN from the command line when you want Windows to run. In either case, when Windows runs you will see a display very much like the one shown in Figure 1.1.

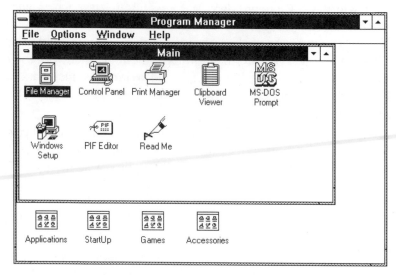

Figure 1.1 *Initial Windows Display*

This display is the Program Manager with the Main application group window opened. The Program Manager is the executive program from which you run all the other applications, utilities, and accessories. It is your introduction to the Windows way of doing things.

Exiting Windows

You can exit from Windows back to DOS in three ways. You can use the mouse or keyboard to select the Program Manager's Control menu and choose the Close command; you can double-click the Control menu selector box in the upper-left corner of the Program Manager window; and you can press Alt+F4 if Program Manager is the active window. The next part of this chapter discusses each of these techniques.

You should always exit from Windows back to DOS before turning power off or rebooting the computer. This ensures that Windows performs an orderly shutdown of everything it is maintaining. It also ensures that all running applications get an opportunity to execute their shutdown procedures.

Regardless of how you tell Windows you want to exit, you will see the dialog box displayed in Figure 1.2.

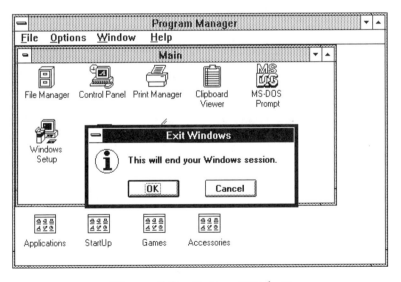

Figure 1.2 *Exiting Windows*

You can exit by pressing the Enter key or by clicking the OK button. To ignore the request and return to Windows, click the Cancel button or press the Esc key. Discussions of the mouse and dialog boxes appear later in this chapter.

When you exit Windows, it saves the condition of the Program Manager desktop to the location of the Program Manager's icons and group windows. When you run Windows the next time, the desktop appears the way you left it. As a result, the illustrations in this book will not always be exactly the way your screen appears when you run the exercises. You will learn how to move things around so that they are the way you want them as you proceed through the chapters that follow. Later, you will learn how to tell Windows not to save the current desktop configuration but to always return to the one you prefer.

Working from the Desktop

Windows operates with the desktop metaphor. Programs and files display themselves on your screen in *windows*, which are rectangular subsections of the screen. Figure 1.1 shows two windows, one titled Program Manager and another titled Main. The windows appear as items on your *desktop*. The metaphor is of documents that lay flat on a desk. You can move the documents around on a desk, and you can move the windows around on the Windows desktop. You can shuffle them, putting current ones on top of others. You can slide them around and make them smaller or make them occupy the entire screen. You can relegate a window to the bottom of the screen as an icon, which is a little picture with a title to remind you that the window is still active but set aside for the moment.

To teach the basics of operating Windows programs, this chapter will use many of the features of the Windows Program Manager. Chapter 2 is about the Program Manager and how it works, but you will get an early look at some of its operations in this chapter. Do not be concerned if you do not completely understand what you see in these examples. The discussions in this chapter are about the Windows user interface—how to get around in any Windows program. The Program Manager is the first program you encounter, and it uses all the components of the Windows user interface. It is, therefore, a good place to begin learning.

Windows

A window can represent a program or a document. A *program* can be an application, one of the Windows utility programs, or a Windows accessory. A *program window* is the rectangular space in which the program operates. *Document windows* display the data and files that programs operate on. Document windows are subordinate to program windows and you cannot move a document outside of the program window that owns it.

The Main window in Figure 1.1 is a document window that belongs to the Program Manager program window. The Program Manager is a Windows utility program. Its Main document window displays some of the data that it operates on, in this case one of the application groups from which you can execute programs. Sometimes, as in the case of a word processor, the program window uses itself to display the document.

Windows and its applications use other window-like display techniques for menus, dialog boxes, and information displays. You cannot move all of these displays around like program and document windows. It will depend on how the application implements the display. You will learn about each of these display types as the lessons proceed.

The Format of a Window

Figure 1.3 shows the window that the Notepad accessory program uses, with the standard window components indicated by labels. Chapter 10 discusses accessory programs and describes the Notepad in more detail. You will use its window here to learn the format of all windows.

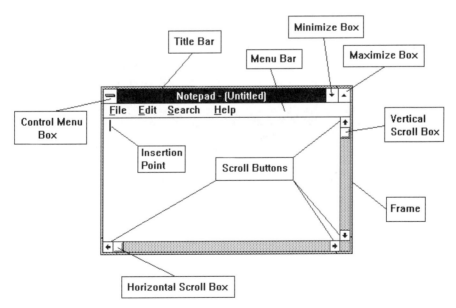

Figure 1.3 *The Components of a Window*

Title Bar

The *title bar* displays the title associated with the window; indicates when the window is active and when it is inactive; and is the means for moving the window—when you point the mouse cursor to the title bar and drag the mouse, you move the window. When a window cannot be moved, it has no title bar. You will learn several ways to move a window in a later exercise.

Frame

The *frame* surrounds the window. When you point the mouse to one of the sides and drag the cursor, you can shrink and expand the window size horizontally. The top and bottom of the frame allow you to shrink and expand the window vertically. When a window cannot be resized, the frame appears as a single solid line. You will learn several ways to resize a window in a later exercise.

Control menu Box

The small box with the horizontal bar in the upper-left corner of the window is the *Control menu box.* It allows you to pop down a *Control menu.* The Control menu is the same for all windows, although at times some of its menu commands are disabled. You select the Control menu by clicking the box with the mouse or by pressing Alt+Spacebar for program windows and Alt+Hyphen for document windows. Figure 1.4 shows the Control menu for the Notepad window.

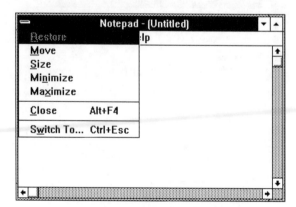

Figure 1.4   *The Control Menu*

Menu Bar

The *menu bar* is the place on a window where the titles of pull-down menus appear. These titles will vary from application to application but certain standards have emerged. You will see File, Edit, and Help menu titles on the menu bars of many applications. A discussion of menu selections appears later in this chapter.

Not all windows have menu bars, because not all windows have operating menu selections for you to execute.

Workspace

The *workspace* of a window is that portion that is inside the frame and under the title bar. This space is also called the "client area." The window displays its data in the workspace.

Minimize/Maximize Boxes

A window can be in one of three conditions of display with respect to its size and placement. It can occupy a section of the desktop or parent window's workspace, it can fill the desktop or parent window's workspace completely, or it can appear as an icon at the bottom of the desktop or parent window's workspace.

You control the window's placement with the Minimize and Maximize boxes in the upper-right corner of the window. Return to the display shown in Figure 1.1. The Program Manager program window and its subordinate Main document window both have Minimize and Maximize boxes. You will learn how these buttons work in a later section.

Scroll Boxes and Scroll Buttons

Often the display of data in the window's workspace extends beyond the area covered by the window. A word processing document is usually much longer than the space displayed by the window. Graphics pictures and many text files can be wider than the window as well. To view the hidden data you must be able to scroll the window horizontally and vertically. The horizontal and vertical scroll boxes and buttons allow you to do this with the mouse.

Mouse and Keyboard

Windows seems to work best when you have a mouse. A mouse is not an absolute requirement because almost everything you can do with the mouse you can do with the keyboard, too. But using the mouse relieves you from having to re-member the different keystrokes that issue the commands. The mouse allows you to point at a visual symbol on the screen and click the appropriate action. The symbols remind you of their purposes. Even the mouse pointer will change its shape to indicate the different effects it can cause.

With the screen still showing the display in Figure 1.1, observe the small arrow. That arrow is the *mouse pointer.* When you move the mouse around on your desk, the mouse pointer moves with it. To get something started, you move the mouse to someplace on the screen where the mouse has an effect, and you press the left button. Sometimes you press it once and release it. Sometimes you press it once, hold it down, and move the mouse. This action usually moves something on the screen and is called *dragging* the mouse. Other times you double-click the mouse to get the desired effect. Sometimes you press and hold the button down, observe its effect, and release it when you are done observing.

You use the keyboard in ways that emulate the mouse. Later you will see that many of the Windows displays tell you which keystroke can emulate what the mouse does. These keystrokes are called *shortcut* and *accelerator* keys. Menus are examples of displays that inform you of these keys.

You must know how to select something in order to use either the keyboard or the mouse.

Selecting and Choosing

Throughout this book you will learn how to use the components of the desktop to issue commands to Windows and the application programs. There are usually two steps in such a procedure. The first step is *selecting* the component. Selecting involves using the mouse or keyboard to point to the item. When you select an item, its display usually changes to tell you that it is selected. For example, a se-lected menu item will display in highlighted colors on the menu to distinguish it from the other, unselected items on the same menu. The second step, *choosing* the item, involves telling Windows to execute the command associated with the selected item. These are important distinctions.

Icons

The display in Figure 1.1 shows an active program window named Program Man-ager and an active document window named Main. You know these windows are active because the top border is made of a dark bar with the window title in white letters. The Main window has some little pictures with descriptive titles. These pictures are called *icons.* The Program Manager window has icons, too, at the bottom of the window. The Main window's icons are all different while the Program Manager's icons are all the same. The Program Manager's icons represent groups of programs. All the icons are the same because each one represents a program group. The Main window's icons are all different because they represent individual programs.

Selecting Icons

When an icon's title is white letters on a dark background, the icon is selected for some following action.

You can use the mouse or keyboard to select icons. Icon selection is the way you specify programs that are to be run. You will use that operation as the first example in learning how to use the mouse and the keyboard.

Selecting Icons with the Mouse

Move the mouse cursor to an icon in the Main window and *click*—press and release—the left button. The title of that icon will show that the icon is selected. Try several other icons.

Now move the mouse cursor to one of the group icons at the bottom of the Program Manager window. Click the left button. If you chose the Accessories icon, for example, you will see the display shown in Figure 1.5.

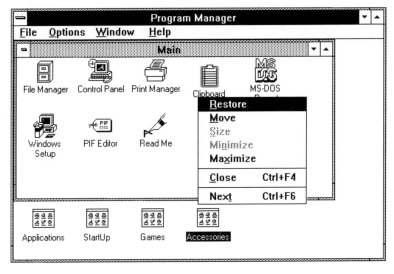

Figure 1.5 *Selecting an Icon in the Program Manager Window*

Figure 1.5 shows you several things. First, the icon that you selected in the Main window is now deselected and the Accessories icon in the Program Manager window is selected. Second, the title bar of the Main window has a light background, indicating that you deselected that entire window as well. You will learn more about that later. Third, there is a new display on the screen, a Control menu window that controls the icon's position and status. You will learn how that menu works later. It contains the same selections as the Notepad's Control menu in Figure 1.4. The menu in Figure 1.5 is for managing the placement and status of an icon. The menu in Figure 1.4 is for managing the placement and status of a window. The two menus are the same because those icons represent program windows for programs that are running but not currently being displayed.

To remove the icon's Control menu for now, move the mouse cursor outside of the Control menu and click the left mouse button. Move the mouse cursor to the inside of the Main window, but not on one of the icons. Click the left button and observe that the Main window is active again, and whichever Main icon you selected last is also active. Click another icon at the bottom of the Program Manager window. Now click a specific icon in the Main window. That will select that icon instead of the icon you had previously selected in the Main window.

Choosing Icons with the Mouse

So far all you have done is select the icons that will be the object of some following action, if any. Now you will actually choose an icon to start running. Move the mouse cursor to the Control Panel icon and *double-click* the mouse by pressing and releasing the left button two times rapidly. If this is the first time you have tried to double-click, don't get upset if nothing happens. You probably just didn't click fast enough. Try clicking faster. You will see the display shown in Figure 1.6.

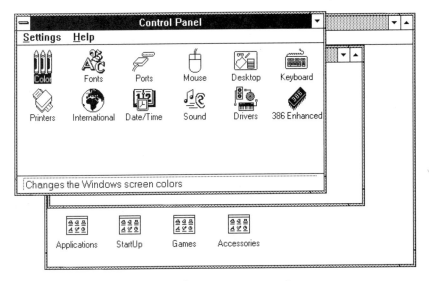

Figure 1.6 *Activating an Icon*

This display shows the Control Panel as a running program with its program window as the active window.

To terminate the Control Panel, move the mouse cursor to the little box with the vertical bar in the upper-left corner of the Control Panel window and double-click the mouse.

Selecting Icons with the Keyboard

If you do not have a mouse or if you prefer not to use one, you can use these procedures to select icons with the keyboard. Start from the display shown in Figure 1.1 again. Use the arrow keys on your keyboard to change the selected icon in the Main window.

Press the Ctrl key and the Tab key at the same time. The active icon moves to one of those in the Program Manager window and the Main window becomes inactive. When you press Ctrl+Tab repetitively, program group icons in the Program Manager window alternatively become active until eventually the program icon that you selected earlier in the Main window is the active one.

Choosing Icons with the Keyboard

Using the technique just described, select the Control Panel icon in the Main window and press the Enter key. You will see the display shown in Figure 1.4. This display shows the Control Panel as a running program with its program window as the active window. To terminate the Control Panel, press Alt+F4. The display returns to the configuration in Figure 1.1.

Moving Icons

You can move some icons around on the screen with the mouse. If the icon represents a minimized window, you can move it with the keyboard as well. You will learn about minimizing and maximizing windows later. For now you have both kinds displayed. The group icons at the bottom of the Program Manager window are minimized icons. The program icons in the Main window are not.

Moving Icons with the Mouse

Move the mouse cursor to one of the icons in the Main window. Hold the left button down and drag the icon around the window. The icon changes to a black-and-white copy of itself without its title for as long as you drag it around. If you try to drag the icon outside of its window, its shape will change to a slashed circle cursor to indicate that you are in forbidden territory. If another group window was displayed, you could drag the icon there to move the application into that group.

Moving Icons with the Keyboard

Press Ctrl+Tab to cycle through the groups until you are at the group icon you want to move. Press Alt+Hyphen to open the icon's Control menu. If you chose the Accessories icon you would see the display shown in Figure 1.5. Press the M key to choose the Move option on the menu. Use the arrow keys to move the icon around on the screen. Press the Enter key when the icon is positioned where you want it.

Note that if you move the Accessories group icon into the Main window, it goes there with no problem. You might think that you are transferring the icon to the Main group. You are not, however. You cannot move a group into another group. If you pressed Enter while the icon was in the Main window, the icon would appear to be properly positioned there. But the first time you select one of the other icons in the main window, the Accessories icon would disappear.

Where could it have gone? It would be under the Main window. You would have to minimize or move the Main window in order to see it. You will learn how to do these things later.

Selecting Windows

The display in Figure 1.1 has two windows, a program window named Program Manager and its document window named Main. The Main window represents one of the program groups that the Program Manager manages. The group icons at the bottom of the Program Manager window represent the other program groups. The example used here has Accessories, Games, Startup, and Applications group icons.

You can have several windows open at one time. From the screen shown in Figure 1.1, choose the Accessories icon. Review "Choosing Icons with the Mouse" or "Choosing Icons with the Keyboard" to see how to do this. You will see the display shown in Figure 1.7. This display shows the Accessories window as the active window on top of the Main window, which remains open but becomes inactive.

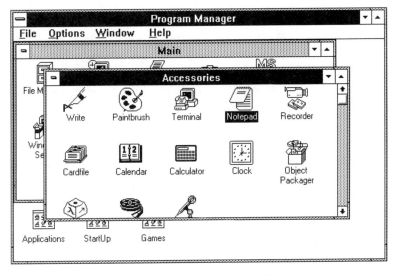

Figure 1.7 *Two Document Windows*

Now choose the Games icon. You will see the display shown in Figure 1.8. This display shows the addition of the Games document window. There are four windows displayed on this screen: the Program Manager program window and the Main, Accessories, and Games document windows.

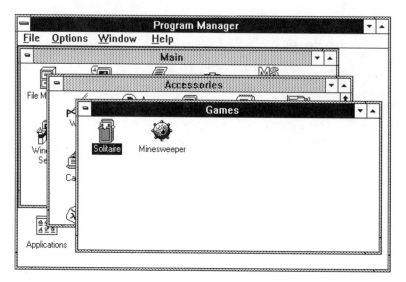

Figure 1.8 *Three Document Windows*

 Do not be confused by the phrases "program window" and "document window." At the moment there seems to be little difference between the two. Most of the windows you have seen so far have been nothing but boxes full of icons. The Program Manager program window does not seem to be an application, and the document windows do not seem to contain documents. In fact, both are what they seem not to be. The Program Manager is the executive program of Windows. Its document windows contain its data items, which consist of the groups of programs that it manages. The Windows lexicon uses "document" as a general reference to all things processed. To further confuse you, some program windows manage their own data from within the workspace of the program window, not using document windows at all.

Suppose that you want to see what is in the Accessories window. It is behind the Games window and its workspace is almost completely obscured. To bring it completely into view, you must select it again.

Selecting Document Windows with the Mouse

Move the mouse to any visible part of the Accessories window and click. You will see the display shown in Figure 1.9.

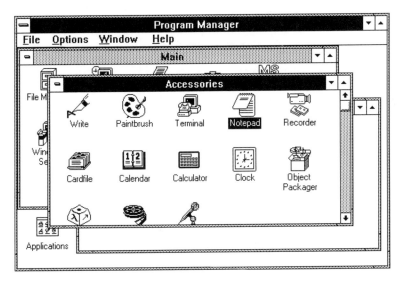

Figure 1.9 *Pulling a Window Forward*

Selecting Document Windows with the Keyboard

Press Ctrl+Tab repetitively until the Accessories window is on top. You will see the display shown in Figure 1.9.

You selected and then chose the group icons to turn them into open group windows. Each time you chose an icon, its window became the active one. The others stayed open but became inactive. Now you can select among the active group windows to make an inactive one the active one.

The Accessories window is now at the forefront and is the active document window. Each of the icons in the Accessories window is an accessory program that you can use any time Windows is running. You will learn all of them in time. For now, choose the Calculator icon by double-clicking it or making it active with the keyboard. You will see the display shown in Figure 1.10.

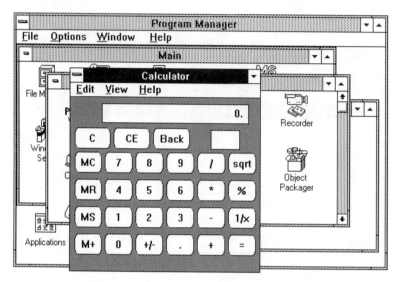

Figure 1.10 *The Calculator Application Window*

When you choose the Calculator icon, you execute the Calculator application. The window at the front is the program window for the Calculator program. You now have two program windows on the screen, the Program Manager window and the Calculator window. The Calculator window is active. When more than one program window is displayed, more than one program is running, although only one of the program windows is active. You can select one of the inactive program windows to be the active one. To select a different program window, you select either the program window or one of its document windows, if it has them.

Selecting Program Windows with the Mouse

Move the mouse cursor to any visible part of the Program Manager window and click. The display will now look like Figure 1.9 again, except that the Calculator icon's title is highlighted. But there is another difference. Even though the display is the same as it was before, the calculator is still running. You cannot see it because its window is completely obscured by the Program Manager. Until you learn how to move windows out of the way with the mouse, you must use the keyboard to get the calculator back.

Selecting Program Windows with the Keyboard

Press Alt+Esc. This key combination cycles through the running programs, making the program window of each the active one in turn. Continue cycling through the program windows until the Calculator is active.

The Calculator window is a dialog box. You can play with it by typing numbers at the numeric keypad or using the mouse to push the number and operator pushbuttons in the Calculator window. You will learn more about dialog boxes in a later lesson.

N O T E

Moving Windows

Sometimes a window gets in the way. Sometimes you cannot see what you need to see on a window that is underneath the active one. You could make the hidden window active but that might not be what you need. Earlier you used the mouse to make the Program Manager active, and the Calculator got hidden. You needed to go to the keyboard to get it back.

Sometimes you need to keep the current active window active while you look at the contents of another window. One way to do this is to move the active window out of the way.

Suppose that you want to look at some of the icons in the Accessory window. The Calculator is in the way. You need to move it.

Moving Windows with the Mouse

Move the mouse cursor to the title bar of the Calculator window, press and hold down the left button, and drag the cursor in the direction you wish to move the window. An outline of the Calculator window will move along with the cursor. When the outline appears where you want the window to be, release the mouse button. The Calculator window now displays in its new location.

Moving Windows with the Keyboard

Press Alt+Space to open the Calculator's Control menu. The Control menu pops down as shown in Figure 1.11. Press the M key. A four-pronged arrow cursor appears. Use the arrow keys to move the window horizontally and vertically. As you press the keys, an outline of the window follows where the window movement will be. When the outline appears where you want the window to be, press the Enter key. The Calculator window now displays in its new location. If you decide to leave the window where it was, press the Esc key.

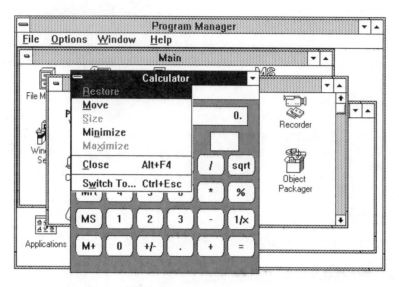

Figure 1.11 *The Calculator's Control Menu*

Figure 1.12 shows the Calculator window moved to the upper-right corner of the screen.

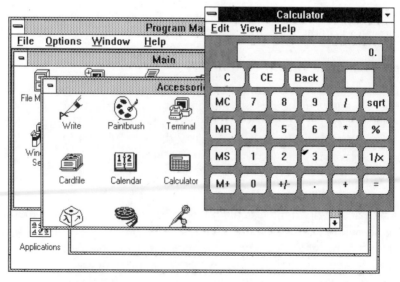

Figure 1.12 *A Window That Has Been Moved*

Moving Document Windows

You can move a document window around inside the program window that owns it, but you cannot move it outside the program window. Select the Accessories window by clicking somewhere inside its frame or by pressing Alt+Esc. The screen will look like Figure 1.13, with the Calculator in the background behind the Program Manager window. By selecting the Accessories window, which is a document window for the Program Manager, you made the Program Manager window the active program window, taking precedence over the Calculator, which is also a program window.

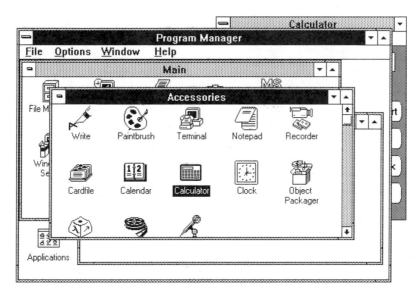

Figure 1.13   *Moving a Document Window*

Use the mouse or the keyboard to move the Accessories window around. Observe that when you move the Accessories window beyond the borders of the Program Manager window, the Accessories window seems to slide under the border and go out of sight. Observe, too, that when this happens the Program Manager window gains scroll boxes and buttons. Figure 1.14 illustrates this behavior.

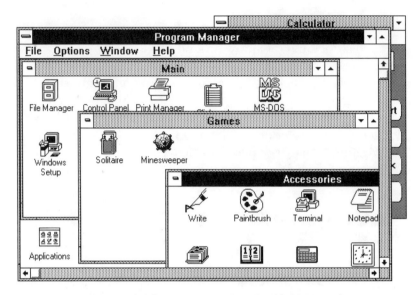

Figure 1.14   *A Document Window Moved*

The Program Manager grew scroll boxes and buttons because the contents of its workspace, in this case the Accessories document window, now exceeds the area of the workspace that can be displayed on the screen.

Resizing Windows

You can change the size of windows that have frames. The Calculator does not have a frame and so its size is fixed. This is usually the case with dialog boxes. The other windows in Figure 1.14 have frames, so any one of them can be *resized*. To resize a window, you must first make it active. The Calculator is a dialog box and you cannot resize it. When in doubt, look to see if the window has a frame. You cannot resize a window unless it has a frame. Another way to tell is to look at a window's Control menu. In Figure 1.11 you see that the Size selection on the Control menu is displayed with a dim intensity. This means that the selection is not available.

Inasmuch as you cannot resize the Calculator, you do not need it for the next exercise. To get rid of it, select it with the mouse or press Alt+Esc. Now terminate it by pressing Alt+F4 or by double-clicking the Control menu selector box in the upper-left corner of the Calculator window.

The display now looks like Figure 1.15 with the Calculator window gone. Move the Accessories window back inside the Program Manager window. The display now looks like Figure 1.9 again, with the scroll boxes and buttons gone from the Program Manager window because all its document windows now reside fully within its borders.

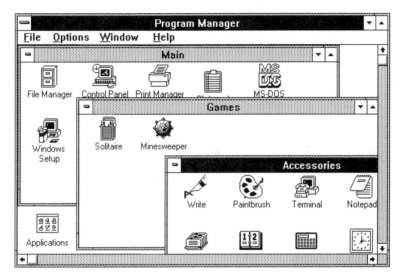

Figure 1.15   *The Accessories Window with the Calculator Removed*

Resizing Windows with the Mouse

Move the mouse cursor to the right side of the Accessories window's frame. The cursor will change to a right-left arrow. Hold the mouse button down and drag the cursor to the right and left. A rectangle will describe the new window-width. When the width is the way you want it, release the button, and the window will display with its new size.

You can do the same thing with the left side, top, and bottom of the window frame, compressing or expanding the window on all sides. The size cursor for the top and bottom of the frame is an up-down arrow.

By pointing the cursor to one of the corners of the window, the cursor will change to a slanted, two-headed arrow, and you can stretch or compress the window on two axes at once.

Resizing Windows with the Keyboard

Press Alt+Hyphen to display the Control menu for the Accessories window. Press the S key to choose the Size command. The four-headed arrow cursor appears in the middle of the window. Press one of the four arrow keys to select whether you are going to move the top, bottom, or one of the sides. The right-left or up-down cursor will appear on the side of the frame you selected. You can use an arrow key to change the position of the selected part of the frame or you can use an arrow key to point to a corner and get the slanted cursor.

Figure 1.16 shows the Accessories window reduced in size on both axes. It has gained scroll boxes and buttons as well because the act of resizing it made its workspace too small to display all its icons. Use the techniques you just learned to make your screen resemble the one in Figure 1.16 for the next exercises.

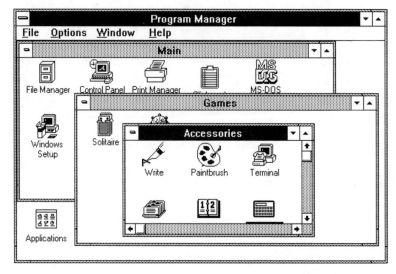

Figure 1.16 *The Accessories Window Reduced in Size*

Scrolling the Workspace

You can now scroll the Accessories window both horizontally and vertically because it has both sets of scroll boxes and buttons.

Scrolling with the Mouse

To scroll the window's workspace up, move the mouse cursor to the scroll button that points down. The scroll button is in the lower-right corner of the window and has an arrow pointing down. Press the left button and hold it down. You will see the window's workspace scroll up and the scroll box move downward. When the scroll box is at the bottom of its travel, the window will appear as you see it in Figure 1.17.

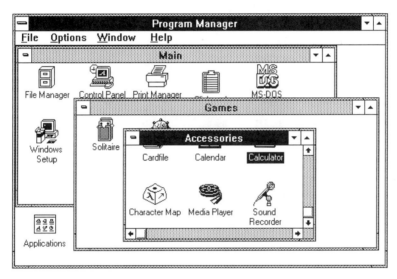

Figure 1.17 *The Accessories Window Scrolled Up*

To scroll the window's workspace to the left, move the mouse cursor to the scroll button that points left. The scroll button is in the lower-right corner of the window and has an arrow pointing right. Use the same procedure to scroll horizontally.

Another way to scroll the workspace is to use the cursor to drag the scroll box along its travel. The scroll box's travel path is proportional to the length or width of the workspace. For larger workspaces, you can point the mouse cursor just ahead or after the scroll box in the scroll bar and click to move forward or back one page.

Scrolling down and to the right work the same way as up and to the left.

Scrolling with the Keyboard

Use the arrow keys to scroll a window in any of its four directions. Use the PgUp and PgDn keys to page through the workspace vertically and Ctrl+PgUp and Ctrl+PgDn to page horizontally. These keys are not as effective in small windows such as the shrunk Accessories window, and they do not always work for scrolling purposes when an application is using the keyboard for its own use. You will learn how to scroll with the keyboard in each application that this book discusses.

Minimizing and Maximizing Windows

A window can be in one of three conditions of display with respect to its size and placement. It can occupy a section of the desktop or parent window's workspace, it can fill the desktop or parent window's workspace completely, or it can appear as an icon at the bottom of the desktop or parent window's workspace.

In Figure 1.17 the resized Accessories window, the Main window, and the Games window occupy a portion of the Program Manager's workspace. Because these windows are child windows to the Program Manager window, they can each occupy some or all of the Program Manager's workspace. The Non-Windows Applications window and the Windows Applications window are there too, but they appear as icons within the Program Manager's workspace rather than as windows. By using the mouse or keyboard you can minimize and maximize the active window, which in this case happens to be the Accessories window.

If you do not have a mouse, you can skip the sections on using it and proceed to those that teach you how to minimize and maximize windows with the keyboard. The keyboard discussions will, however, refer to illustrations shown in the figures that accompany the mouse discussion.

Maximizing Windows with the Mouse

Click the mouse in the Maximize box in the upper-right corner of the Accessories window. The Maximize box contains an up-arrow symbol. The window will expand to occupy the entire workspace of the Program Manager window, as shown in Figure 1.18.

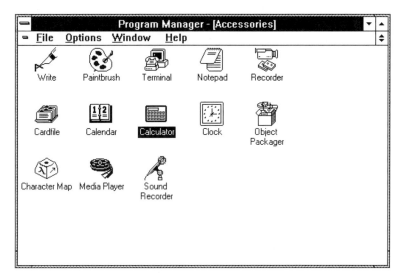

Figure 1.18   *The Accessories Window Maximized*

The title bar in Figure 1.18 now appends the [Accessories] label to its title to indicate that it has dedicated its workspace to the Accessories window. This title bar combines the titles of the two windows.

The Minimize and Maximize boxes to the right of the title bar are for the Program Manager window. The box just under the Program Manager's Maximize box, which contains both up- and down-arrow symbols, is the Restore box for the Accessories window. A *Restore* box restores its window to the size it had before it was maximized or minimized.

Click the Maximize box in the Program Manager's window. This box is the one to the right of the title bar that has an up-arrow symbol. The Program Manager window now occupies the entire screen, as shown in Figure 1.19. Observe that the Program Manager's Maximize box is replaced by the Restore box.

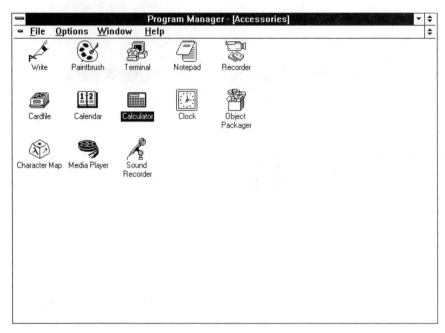

Figure 1.19 *The Program Manager Window Maximized*

Minimizing Windows with the Mouse

Click the Minimize box in the Program Manager window. This box is the one with the single down arrow. The Program Manager window becomes an icon. Because no other programs are running the icon is the only item on the screen, as shown in Figure 1.20.

Figure 1.20 *The Program Manager Window Minimized*

Note that the title of the icon in Figure 1.20 is the same as the one that was in the Program Manager's title bar. Double click the icon to return to the display shown in Figure 1.19. Click the Restore box in the Program Manager's window. There are two of these, one above the other. The one on top is the one you want to click to return the display to that shown in Figure 1.18.

Click the restore box in the Accessories window. The window returns to its prior configuration, that of Figure 1.17. Observe that the Minimize and Maximize boxes are in their own boxes again. Now click the Accessories window's Minimize box, which is the one with the down-arrow symbol. The screen will now appear as shown in Figure 1.21.

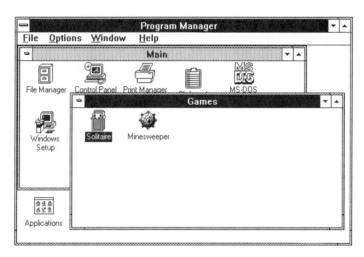

Figure 1.21   *The Accessories Window Minimized*

The Accessories window is now an icon obscured by the Games window, which is now active. Open the Window menu and choose the Accessories window to return to the display shown in Figure 1.17.

Maximizing Windows with the Keyboard

From the display shown in Figure 1.17, press Alt+Hyphen. This command displays the Control menu for the Accessories window, as shown in Figure 1.22.

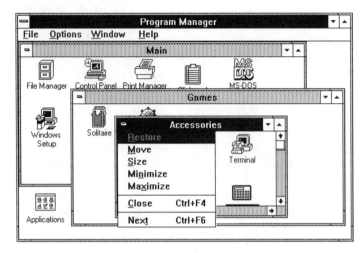

Figure 1.22 *Control Menu for the Accessories Window*

Press the X key to choose the Maximize command from the Accessories window's Control menu. The window will expand to occupy the entire workspace of the Program Manager window, as shown in Figure 1.18.

The title bar in Figure 1.18 appends the [Accessories] label to its title to indicate that it has dedicated its workspace to the Accessories window. This title bar combines the titles of the two windows.

Press Alt+Spacebar. This command displays the Control menu for the Program Manager window, as shown in Figure 1.23.

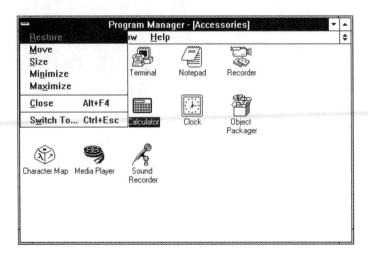

Figure 1.23 *Control Menu for the Program Manager Window*

Press the X key to choose the Maximize command from the Program Manager window's Control menu. The window will expand to occupy the entire screen, as shown in Figure 1.19.

Minimizing Windows with the Keyboard

Press Alt+Spacebar to display the Program Manager window's Control menu, as shown in Figure 1.24. Press the N key to choose the Minimize command. The Program Manager window becomes an icon. Because no other programs are running, the icon is the only item on the screen, as shown in Figure 1.20.

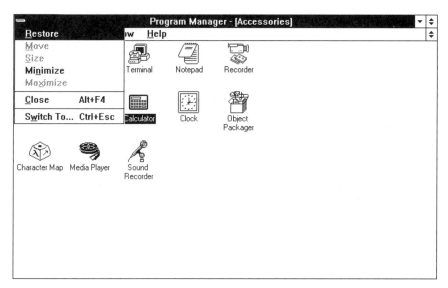

Figure 1.24   *The Maximized Program Manager's Control Menu*

Note that the title of the icon in Figure 1.20 is the same as the one that was in the Program Manager's title bar. To return to the display in Figure 1.19, you must reactivate the Program Manager window. Press the Alt+Space keys. You will see the display shown in Figure 1.25.

Figure 1.25   *Program Manager Icon's Control Menu*

This window in Figure 1.25 is the Control menu for the Program Manager's icon. Press the R key to restore the Program Manager and return to the display shown in Figure 1.19.

Press Alt+Spacebar to display the Program Manager window's Control menu again, as shown in Figure 1.24. Press the R key to choose the Restore command to return the display to that shown in Figure 1.18.

Press Alt+Hyphen to display the Accessories window's Control menu, as shown in Figure 1.26. Press the R key to choose the Restore command to return the display to that shown in Figure 1.17.

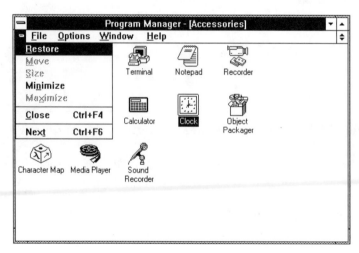

Figure 1.26   *Control Menu for the Accessories Window*

Some Practice

Before proceeding, you must get the display back into its configuration at the beginning of this chapter. One way is to exit from Windows without saving the changes, but you haven't learned how to do that yet. Another way is to apply what you have learned so far to put things back the way they were.

Your display looks like that in Figure 1.17 now. Resize, rescroll, and move the Accessories window so that the display looks like that in Figure 1.13, but without the Calculator window. Bring the Games window to the foreground so the display looks like Figure 1.8. Minimize the Accessories and Games windows to their icons in the Program Manager window so the display looks like Figure 1.1.

Do not worry if your display is not exactly like each figure. Most new subjects in this book begin with the display shown in Figure 1.1, so it is a good idea to use what you have learned so far to get to that configuration each time you exit from Windows. Later you will learn how to make Windows always start with a defined desktop configuration.

Menus

A program that runs in the Windows environment will make extensive use of menus. The Windows menu architecture is consistent across applications and within the Windows programs themselves. This consistency is part of the Windows common user interface.

You have already used one Windows menu. The Control menus in Figures 1.5, 1.11, 1.22, 1.23, 1.24, and 1.26 are typical Windows menus. Applications and other Windows programs have menus as well, and they all work in much the same way. To illustrate this point, begin with the display shown in Figure 1.1. Deselect the Main window by double-clicking the Control menu box or by using the Minimize command in its Control menu. You will see a display similar to that of Figure 1.27, with the Main window minimized to an icon.

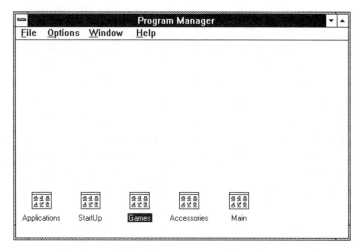

Figure 1.27 *The Main Window Minimized*

The menu bar in the Program Manager window in Figure 1.27 is typical of menu bars for most Windows programs. Remember that the Program Manager is a Windows program itself. It is the executive program that manages the execution of other programs, and because it is a program it uses the Windows conventions for a common user interface. Its menu bar contains four selections. These are the File, Options, Window, and Help menus.

Most Windows applications will have the File menu. It contains the commands to manage document files, print documents, and exit the application.

Many applications will have the Help menu, too. It is the entry to the conventional Windows context-sensitive help system used by both Windows and most Windows applications.

Other menus on a menu bar will depend upon the nature of the application. Virtually every text editor and word processor that operates in the Windows environment includes an Edit menu. The Windows Notepad, Windows Write, and the Clipboard all have Edit menus. You will learn about these programs in later chapters. Graphics programs such as Windows Paint and desktop publishing applications will include View, Font, Style, and other menus.

Regardless of the nature and content of Windows menus, they all work the same way, with a given set of mouse and keyboard operations for navigating and choosing commands from them. There are three menu operations to learn: selecting a menu, moving from menu to menu, and choosing a command from a menu. You can use the menus of the Program Manager to learn these operations.

Selecting a Menu with the Mouse

Move the mouse cursor to the File label in the menu bar and click. You will see the display shown in Figure 1.28. This is a menu. It contains a list of commands and a menu selection cursor, which is a dark bar that extends the length of the selection's name on the menu. Observe the Move and Copy selections. They appear with characters of lesser intensity. This dim display means that in the current context the selections are not available to the user.

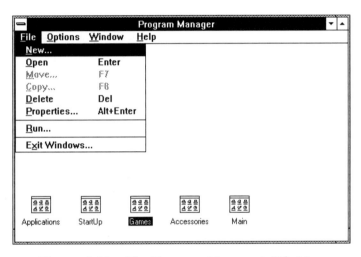

Figure 1.28   *The Program Manager's File Menu*

You can select any menu by moving the mouse cursor to its title on the menu bar and clicking. To deselect the menu, move the mouse cursor outside the menu itself and click. The menu goes away and the screen looks like Figure 1.27 again.

Selecting a Menu with the Keyboard

Observe that each of the menu labels includes an underlined letter, in this case the first letter of the label name. These are the shortcut keys assigned to the menu names. Press Alt+F and you will select the File menu, which will appear as shown in Figure 1.28. Observe the Move and Copy selections. They appear with characters of lesser intensity. This dim display means that in the current context the selections are not available to the user. To select another menu press the Alt+letter combination given for it. Observe that as soon as you press the Alt key, the earlier menu goes away. You can use the Alt key by itself to exit the menu bar and go back to the application.

The keyboard offers several ways to move from menu to menu. Select the File menu again by pressing Alt+F. The display is the same as it was in Figure 1.28. Now press the right arrow key on the cursor keypad. The File menu goes away and the Options menu appears, as shown in Figure 1.29.

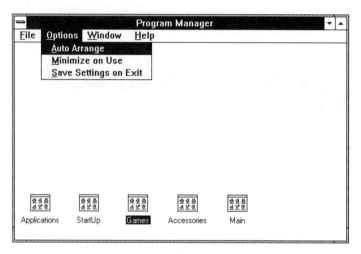

Figure 1.29   *The Options Menu*

Observe the Save Settings on Exit command on the Options menu in Figure 1.29. A check mark next to the command would indicate that the command is a toggled setting and that it is on. You will learn about toggles soon. When you do, you will be able to use this toggle to make these exercises easier. Turn the toggle on, and arrange the desktop into the configuration shown in Figure 1.1. Remember that this is the configuration that you need at the start of most of the exercises in this book. Exit from Windows. Run Windows again, and turn this toggle off. From that point on, every time you exit, Windows will forget the configuration that exists when you exit and always bring up the one that you need to run these exercises.

Use the right and left arrow keys to move from menu to menu. In addition to moving among the menus in the menu bar, these keys move to the Control menu for the Program Manager window and to the Control menu for whichever group icon is current. In this case, the Accessories icon is current. For applications that do not have child windows, there is no corollary to the icon's Control menu, but the Control menu for the application's window will be included in the menu scan.

Press the Alt key (not the Esc key) to return to the display shown in Figure 1.27. Now press the Alt key by itself again and observe that the label for the File menu is highlighted, but the menu itself does not appear. Figure 1.30 shows this behavior.

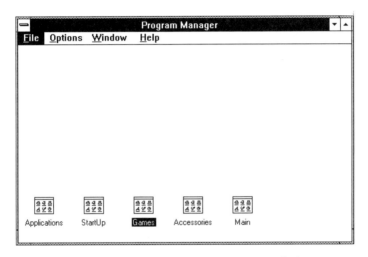

Figure 1.30   *Selecting a Menu Label*

Use the arrow keys to move the label cursor from menu label to menu label. When the cursor is at the label of your choice, press the Enter key to select the menu.

Choosing a Menu Item with the Mouse

Move the mouse cursor to the File menu's label in the menu bar and click so that the display appears as it did in Figure 1.28. The File menu has six possible commands and two that are not available. The unavailable commands are indicated by their displays of less intensity. Move the mouse cursor to the New command on the menu and click. You will see the display shown in Figure 1.31.

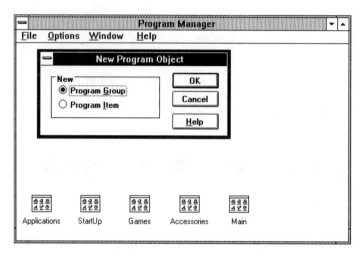

Figure 1.31 *Choosing the File Menu's New Command*

You just used the mouse to choose a command from a menu. The display shown in Figure 1.31 is the result of that command, a Program Manager dialog box that lets you add new program groups and items to those managed by the Program Manager. You will learn about dialog boxes later in this chapter and about the Program Manager in Chapter 2. For now click the Cancel button to exit from this process and return to the Program Manager display shown in Figure 1.27.

Opening Dialog Boxes

When you chose the Run command on the File menu, you opened a dialog box. Commands that have an ellipses (...) following the label are ones that will open a dialog box.

Cascaded Menus

If a menu command shows a dark, right-pointing arrowhead to the right of its title, the command will open a cascaded menu. A cascaded menu pops down along side the current menu. The cascaded menu aligns itself with the menu command that selected it.

Choosing a Menu Item with the Keyboard

From the display in Figure 1.27, press Alt+F to select the File menu, as shown in Figure 1.28. The File menu has six possible commands and two that are not available. The unavailable commands are indicated by their displays of less intensity. There are several ways to choose a command.

Move the menu cursor to the Run command on the menu with the down arrow key. Press Enter. You will see the display shown in Figure 1.32.

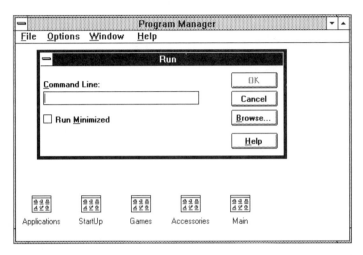

Figure 1.32   *Choosing The File Menu's Run Command*

You just used the keyboard to choose a command from a menu. The display shown in Figure 1.32 is the result of that command, a Program Manager dialog box that lets you run programs by typing their DOS command lines. You will learn about dialog boxes later in this chapter and about the Program Manager in Chapter 2. For now press the Esc key to exit from this process and return to the Program Manager display shown in Figure 1.27.

Menu Command Types

A command on a menu can be one of three types: simple, context-sensitive, or toggled. The two commands you used in the mouse and keyboard exercises were simple commands. Following is a discussion of each of the three command types.

Simple Menu Command

When you choose a *simple* command, you execute the command's action immediately. The command is always the same regardless of the surrounding circumstances. To observe a simple command, use the mouse or the keyboard to move all the group icons into random locations within the Program Manager window's workspace. Figure 1.33 shows how the screen could appear after you do this.

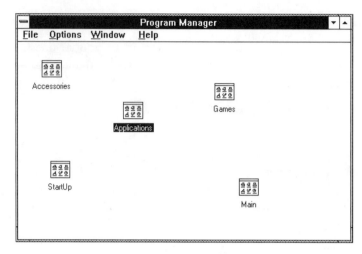

Figure 1.33 *Rearranged Icons*

Open the Window menu as shown in Figure 1.34 and choose the Arrange Icons command. The command rearranges the icons into their original positions. You will see the display return to the configuration it had before you moved the icons around.

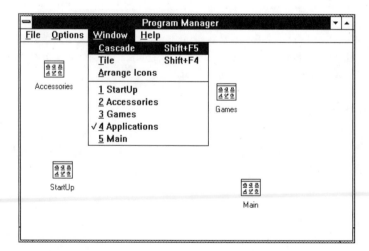

Figure 1.34 *Program Manager's Window Menu*

Context-Sensitive Menu Command

The *context-sensitive* command depends on external variable circumstances. For example, the Open, Delete, and Properties commands on the Program Manager's File menu operate on the currently selected group icon or window. Select the Accessories icon as the current group and select the File menu so that the display appears as shown in Figure 1.35.

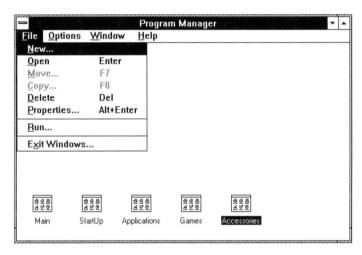

Figure 1.35 *Program Manager's File Menu*

Now choose the Delete command on the File menu. You will see the display shown in Figure 1.36. The dialog box asks if you want to delete the Accessories group. If you had selected a different group as the active one, that group rather than the Accessories group would be up for deleting. You do not want to delete your Accessories group, so press the N key or click the No button.

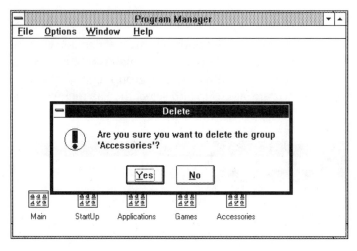

Figure 1.36   *Delete Group Dialog Box*

Toggle Command

A *toggle* command has an on-off setting that affects the behavior of the program. You do not execute a program action when you choose the toggle command. Instead, you reverse the setting of the toggle. The program uses the toggle's setting to determine its subsequent behavior. Select the Options menu to see the display shown in Figure 1.37.

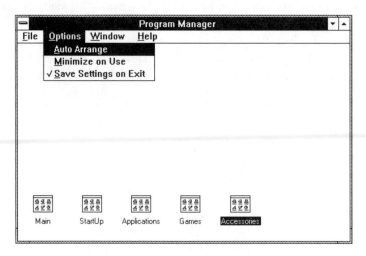

Figure 1.37   *Program Manager's Options Menu*

Choose the Auto Arrange command on the menu. The Options menu disappears and it seems that nothing has happened. But select the Options menu again to see the changes shown in Figure 1.38.

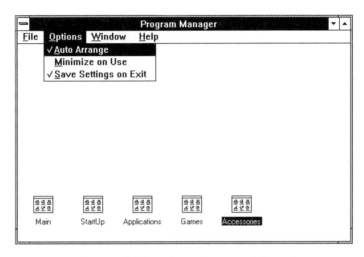

Figure 1.38 *Auto Arrange Selected*

You can see that the Auto Arrange command now has a check mark to its left. That mark indicates that the toggle is set on. Choose the Auto Arrange command again and the toggle will go off.

Menu Item Accelerator Keys

Some menu commands have *accelerator keys* associated with them. An accelerator key allows you to execute the command from the keyboard without opening the menu. Refer to Figure 1.34, which shows the Program Manager's Window menu. The first two commands, Cascade and Tile, have Shift+F5 and Shift+F4 displayed next to the command names. These are the shortcut keys assigned to these commands. You can execute the commands from within the application without opening the menu.

Open all the group windows by selecting their icons one at a time until the screen looks like Figure 1.39. The order and visibility of the windows will depend on the groups you have and the order in which you opened them, so move and resize them to make the screen look as much like Figure 1.39 as you can.

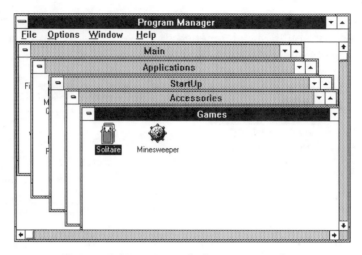

Figure 1.39   *Cascaded Group Windows*

The shortcut key for the Tile command on the Window menu is Shift+F4. Press that key combination and watch the command execute, displaying the screen shown in Figure 1.40.

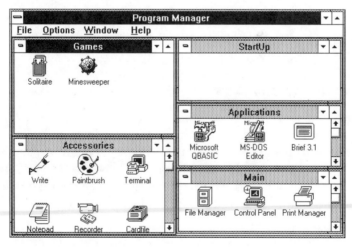

Figure 1.40   *Tiled Group Windows*

The shortcut key for the Cascade command on the Window menu is Shift+F5. Press that combination and watch the windows return to their earlier cascaded configuration. Minimize all the group windows except the Main group to return to the original Program Manager window configuration.

Dialog Boxes

Windows programs use the *dialog box* to allow you to enter the data that the program requires. Data entry follows certain conventions supported by the dialog box.

You have already seen dialog boxes in earlier exercises, although none as complex as the one in Figure 1.41. Figure 1.2 used a dialog box to allow you to exit Windows. Figures 1.31, 1.32, and 1.36 showed dialog boxes used by the Program Manager's Run, New, and Delete commands.

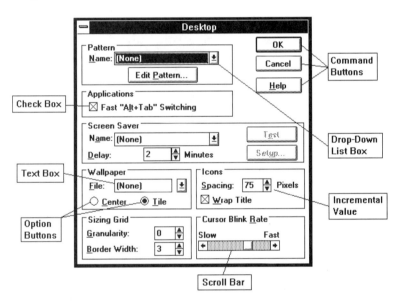

Figure 1.41   *Some Dialog Box Components*

Figure 1.41 shows a dialog box taken from the Control Panel's Desktop command. This particular dialog box allows you to modify the appearance of the desktop by changing certain parameters, and it uses many of the features of the Windows dialog box convention. To display the Desktop dialog box, choose the Control Panel icon from the Main group window and then choose the Desktop icon from the Control Panel window.

You will use the Desktop dialog box to learn about dialog boxes. During the lessons that follow, do *not* press the Enter key or click the OK command button. If you do, the changes you make to the dialog box will take effect whether you want them to or not. You will then have to work with a desktop that looks like whatever changes you made until you learn how to reset it in Chapter 5.

Moving Around the Dialog Box

A dialog box can contain several different data entry fields. At a given time you may enter data into one of them. To change to another field you must move to it. With the mouse you usually click in the field, although this action sometimes changes its value. Pressing the Tab key will move from field to field in a forward direction. Pressing Shift+Tab moves to the previous field.

The dialog box indicates the current field by surrounding it with a dotted line. The Pattern Name field in Figure 1.41 has the dotted line, indicating that it is the current field.

Some fields have names that include underlined letters. You can press the letter to move to the field or to select its value. For example, you can press the G key to select the Granularity field in Figure 1.41.

There is a catch in using the keyboard to move around dialog boxes, however. The first field in the dialog box is the Name field, which uses the keyboard for text entry. You must either use Alt in combination with the desired letter to move to another field, or use Tab to get to the next (non-text-entry) field so you can use the underlined letters to get to another field.

Command Buttons

Most dialog boxes have *command buttons*. The dialog box in Figure 1.41 has several, labeled OK, Cancel, and Help. These buttons are typical; most dialog boxes have them.

Choosing the OK button means that the values in the dialog box are correct and may take effect. When you choose the OK button, the dialog box goes away, and its data values are posted to the application that uses them.

When you choose the Cancel button, the box goes away, and the application ignores any values that you changed.

The Help button runs the Windows Help system described later in the chapter.

You choose a command button by clicking it with the mouse or by pressing the Enter key if the command button has a dark frame. Observe that the OK button in Figure 1.41 has a darker frame than the others. If you want to choose Cancel from the keyboard, you can use the Tab key to step through the entry fields until the Cancel button has the dark frame and then press the Enter key. In the case of Cancel, another way to activate it is to press the Esc key.

When the dialog box needs the Enter key for something other than choosing the command button with a dark frame, the frames of all the buttons have a light frame. Usually, the Enter key is associated with whichever command button has the dark border. Most of the time that is the OK button. Observe that as you tab among the fields the OK button maintains its dark border until you tab cycle through to a different button. This convention allows the Enter key to usually mean that you want to accept the values in the dialog box.

When a command button's label is followed by ellipses (...), the command button will open another dialog box. The Edit Pattern command button is an example of such a button. You will learn more about this button in Chapter 5.

Text Boxes

A *text box* allows you to enter short strings of text data. The dialog box in Figure 1.41 includes a text box named File to name the file that describes the desktop's wallpaper. Once you have selected this field, you can place the cursor at its beginning and type a file name.

Lists

A dialog box can display a list of items from which you can choose. The list displays within a small window. A list has a vertical scroll box and scroll buttons when the length of the list exceeds the window's height. You use them the same way as with other windows. To select from a list, click the entry or use the up arrow, down arrow, scroll box, or Home, End, PgUp, and PgDn keys to move the cursor through the list. Then choose the entry by pressing the Enter key.

You will see an example of a list in the discussion on "File Selection" later on and in the discussion on drop-down lists next.

Drop-Down Lists

The Wallpaper File field and the Pattern Name field in Figure 1.41 both have *drop-down list* boxes. The fields themselves display the current values assigned to the data items. You can type into the Wallpaper File field because it is a text box as well as a drop-down list. The Pattern Name field is not a text box so you must use its drop-down list box. To select the drop-down list click the box with the mouse or tab to the field and press Alt+down arrow. Figure 1.42 shows the Pattern Name field drop-down list after it has been selected.

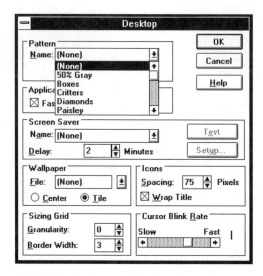

Figure 1.42   *A Drop-Down List*

After the drop-down list has dropped down, it works just like a list except that it goes away after you have made your selection.

Scroll Bars

Figure 1.42 shows how the Desktop dialog box controls the cursor blink rate with a scroll bar. This is one way that programs use the dialog box to allow a user to enter a sliding value where the precise value is not required. In this case you move the scroll box to change the cursor's blink rate. You are concerned only with the relative values between the displayed abstract extremes of Slow and Fast.

Incremental Values

In cases where a range of numbers is required and you must select a specific value, the dialog box uses *incremental value* entries. The Granularity and Border Width fields in Figure 1.42 are examples of this technique. You can enter the specific value by using the left part of the field as a text box or you can step the value up and down. Use the mouse to click the appropriate up or down arrow.

Option Buttons

Option buttons appear in groups where only one of a list of options may be selected. Each of the options has a small circle in front of it, but only the circle in front of the selected option is filled in. Figure 1.42 uses option buttons for the Center and Tile options. These buttons are sometimes called "radio buttons" because they resemble the station selector buttons on older automobile radios, where pressing a button made the one that was already pressed pop out.

You can click a specific button to make it the selected one. You can also tab to the button group and use the arrow keys to change the selected button. When the button labels have underlined letters, you can use those keys with the Alt key to select the option button you want.

Check Boxes

A *check box* functions like the toggled commands on menus. A check box is either selected or deselected, and its setting influences how the application works. The Fast Alt+Tab Switching and Wrap Title fields in Figure 1.42 are check boxes. To select or deselect a check box you can click it with the mouse, press its underlined letter key along with the Alt key, or tab to the field and press the Spacebar.

File Selections

Applications often require that you specify the name and location of a disk file for the application to process. Windows uses a convention for file specifications that allows a dialog box to display a miniature version of the more powerful File Manager from which to select or enter a drive, directory, and file name. Figure 1.43 shows the standard Open dialog box.

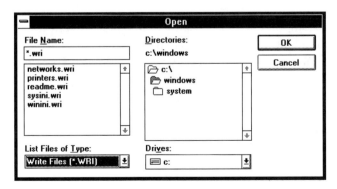

Figure 1.43 *Open Dialog Box for File Selection*

The File Name field in Figure 1.43 is a text box where you can enter an ambiguous DOS path and filename. You can specify the * and ? wild cards in this entry.

The Directories field shows the current subdirectory, and the Drives field shows the current drive. You do not change these fields directly. They change to reflect the changes you make to the other fields.

The list box under the Filename field lists the files in the selected subdirectory that match the filename specification. The Files box is a dialog box list, so you can click to highlight a selection, tab to the list to use the arrow keys to move through it, or double-click it to choose the file name. Moving through the list changes the Filename field value. The list itself changes as you change the drive or directory.

The Directories field shows the subdirectory structure as a hierarchy of folder and document icons. The folders are directories; the documents are files.

The List Files of Type field is a drop-down list box from which you can select file types that the application will accept.

If the application can work with more than one file at a time, you can select a group by holding down the Ctrl key and clicking each of the files or using the arrow keys to select each of the files in the group.

If the dialog box allows you to name a new file to be created, the dialog box title will be Save As, and you must use the Filename text box to type in the new name; the Files box will not show it because it does not exist yet. When the Directory and Filename fields contain the file you want or the group is marked, click OK or press Enter to choose it.

Help

Contemporary computer systems employ online help systems that allow the user to view operating hints and instructions on the screen while the application runs. Windows not only provides such a system, it implements it as a general-purpose help application that is available to other applications. This approach allows the developers of Windows applications to install online help information into their software with a minimum of effort—they simply provide a help database in a format that the Windows Help application can recognize.

A fully developed help database can make user's manuals and reference books unnecessary. A help database that is tutorial in structure can make books such as this one obsolete. However, most software developers prefer not to do away with bound and printed documentation for two reasons. First, the corporate buyers feel more comfortable selecting applications that have a preponderance of expensive-looking documentation. Second, the user's reliance on documentation makes the product less susceptible to piracy. Nevertheless, the time is coming when software will be self-teaching and self-explaining. The Windows Help system is a step in that direction.

Hypertext

Hypertext is a concept for browsing a textual database. While looking at a body of text you can point to a word or phrase and execute a command that tells the software to display other text related to the subject you pointed to. You can browse the text through several such retrieval layers, then retrace your steps if necessary.

The Windows Help system incorporates a form of hypertext. Many of the words and phrases in the help displays are described in a glossary that you can pop up. Others are topics that you can select and view in their entirety.

Context-Sensitive Help

A *context-sensitive help system* is one where the content of the help information depends on what you are doing in the program at the time you run the Help system. Some of the Windows help displays are context-sensitive. Others are constant; you must proceed through the text from a starting point to find what you want. The help files provided with Windows applications might or might not be context-sensitive.

The Help Menu

Most menu bars in Windows applications include a Help selection, usually the right-most command on the bar. The Program Manager's menu bar is an example. When you select the Help command on this menu, the Help menu will pop down, as shown in Figure 1.44.

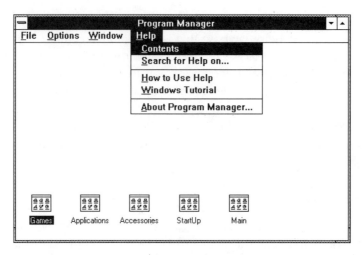

Figure 1.44   *The Program Manager's Help Menu*

The Program Manager's Help menu commands are typical of those found in most Windows applications. The About command is worthy of mention because it provides more information than the About displays in most other applications. Figure 1.45 shows the Program Manager's About display.

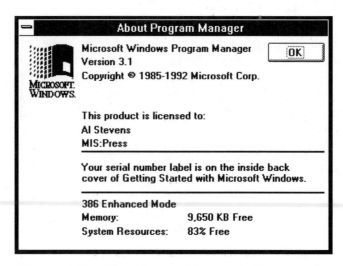

Figure 1.45   *The Program Manager's About Display*

Usually an application's About command gives you a static display that tells you the name of the program, something you already knew, its version, which could be of some use, the copyright date, which you don't care about, and the names of the programmers, which are of interest only to them. The Program Manager's About display goes farther. It tells you the current Windows operating mode, the amount of free memory, and the percent of system resources that are currently available. These values can be useful when you are having problems running programs. If a program will not run, for example, there might not be enough memory for it. The Program Manager's About display might suggest that you should terminate some other programs to free up memory for the new program.

The How to Use Help command on the Help menu instructs you in the use of the Help system itself. This is an example of software that explains itself. When you choose How to Use Help you see the window displayed in Figure 1.46.

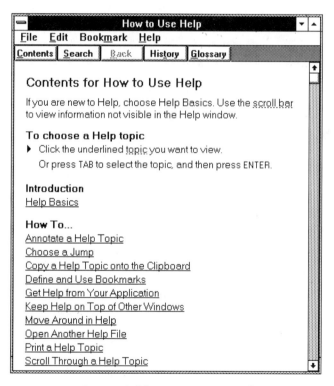

Figure 1.46   *How to Use Help*

The display in Figure 1.46 is typical of the textual help windows that the Help system provides. Remember that the Help system is an application itself, one that runs independently of the application it explains. If you were to minimize the window shown in Figure 1.46, you would see that it becomes an icon, as shown in Figure 1.47.

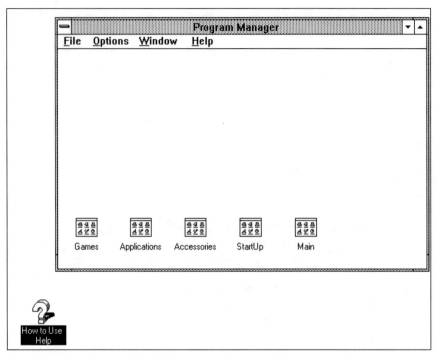

Figure 1.47   *The Help Icon*

Exit from the Help application and choose the Help menu command from the Program Manager's menu bar, as shown in Figure 1.44.

The Help Index

A well-organized Help database begins with an index. You can start with the one in the Program Manager by choosing Contents from its Help menu. You will see the display shown in Figure 1.48. Observe the similarities between Figure 1.48 and Figure 1.46.

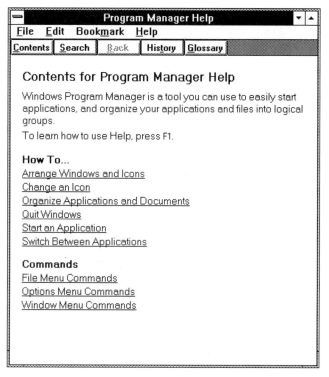

Figure 1.48   *Help Contents*

Cross-References

Several of the lines in Figure 1.48 are underlined. These underlined titles are *cross-reference* items. You can select one of them by pointing the mouse cursor to it. The cursor changes from an arrow to a hand with a pointing finger. Click the topic when the finger is pointing to the topic you want. You can use the keyboard to select a cross-reference topic by pressing the Tab key until the desired topic is highlighted and then pressing Enter. Select the Arrange Windows and Icons topic now. You will see the display shown in Figure 1.49.

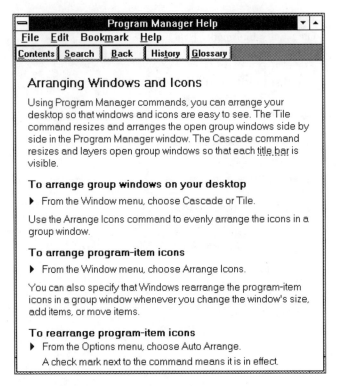

Figure 1.49   *Displaying a Cross-Reference*

Command Buttons

There are five command buttons displayed across the top of the windows in Figures 1.46, 1.48, and 1.49. These buttons work just like the command buttons on dialog boxes, and they allow you to move around in the Help database. When a command button's display is dark, the button is available. When it is light, as is the Back button in Figure 1.48, the button is unavailable. You choose a command button by clicking it or by pressing the letter key that corresponds to the underlined letter in the button's name.

Contents Button

The *Contents button* returns you to the Contents part of the Help database. From the display in Figure 1.49, choose the Index function button. You will be returned to the Contents for Program Manager Help, as shown in Figure 1.48, except that the Back function button is now available.

Back Button

The *Back button* allows you to move backwards through the previous displays in the reverse sequence in which you viewed them. You can choose the Back button repetitively until you get to the first display, shown in Figure 1.48.

The History Button

The *History button* allows you to review a history of the help windows you have viewed. Choose the History button now, and you will see the Windows Help History list box shown in Figure 1.50.

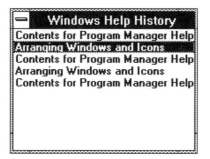

Figure 1.50   *Windows Help History*

The Windows Help History list box is a list of all the help windows you have viewed. You can choose an entry from the list to redisplay that window. If you leave the Windows Help History open, it will update itself as you view additional help windows, and you can return to it by selecting it with the mouse or by pressing Alt+Tab.

Close the Windows Help History window now by pressing Alt+F4 or by double-clicking its Control box.

Search Button

The *Search button* allows you to search the Help database by specifying a key word or phrase. The Search operation uses a predefined list of key values from which you can select. The entries in the list will depend upon the application. Figure 1.51 shows the Search dialog box.

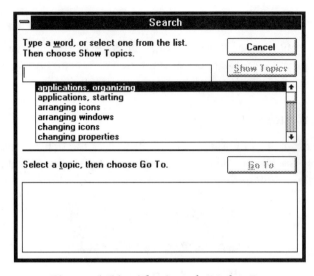

Figure 1.51 *The Search Dialog Box*

You can click on or tab to the key list in the Search dialog box or you can type a key word of your own into the Search For field. As you type letters into the field, the list pointer moves to the entry that most closely matches the field you are typing. The Search process can search only for matches to entries that are in its list. Select the "applications, starting" key phrase and then choose the Show Topics command button. You will see the display shown in Figure 1.52.

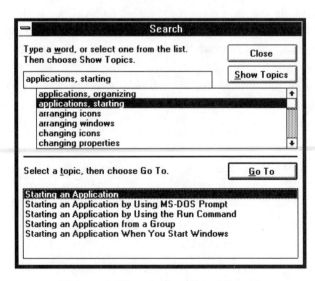

Figure 1.52 *A Completed Search*

Figure 1.52 shows the Search dialog box after the search has completed. In this case there are five entries that match the "opening" key phrase. The list displays the topics that contain the matches. To retrieve the topic for one of the entries in the list, choose that entry by double-clicking it or moving to it and choosing Go To. Choose Starting an Application from a Group to see the display shown in Figure 1.53.

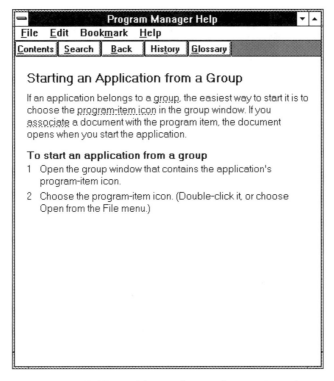

Figure 1.53 *A Topic Chosen from a Search*

The Glossary

When a key word or phrase has a dotted underline rather than a solid one, you can read a description of the item from the Help *Glossary*. The phrases "group," "program-item icon," and "associate" in Figure 1.53 are glossary items. To view the description with the mouse, move the mouse cursor to the phrase. When the cursor changes to the pointing finger symbol, click the left mouse button. To view the description with the keyboard, press the Tab key until the desired item is highlighted and then press Enter. Figure 1.54 shows the Glossary display for the

"associate" item. When you are done viewing the description, click the mouse
button or press Enter.

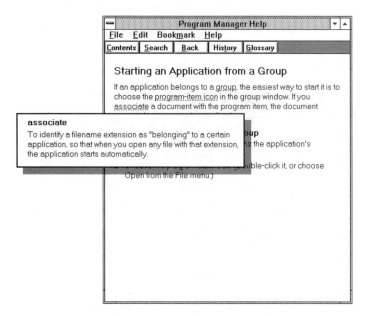

Figure 1.54   *A Glossary Display*

You can view the list of items in the Glossary by choosing the Glossary command
button. Figure 1.55 shows the display that the Glossary command produces.

Figure 1.55   *The Windows Glossary*

The procedures for viewing a glossary item from the list shown in Figure 1.55 are the same as for selecting one from the body of some other Help text. Figure 1.56 shows the "annotate" entry displayed by the Glossary.

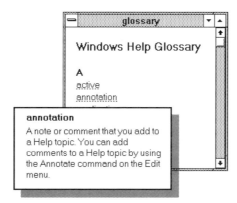

Figure 1.56   *The Glossary with an Item Displayed*

Close the Glossary window by pressing Alt+F4. Return to the display shown in Figure 1.46 by choosing the Contents command.

Bookmarks

You can insert *bookmarks* into a Help textual database. These bookmarks allow you to go directly to a particular topic from anywhere else in the database without searching, browsing, or using the cross-references. Choose the Contents command button and then select the Organize Applications and Documents cross-reference topic. You will see the display shown in Figure 1.57.

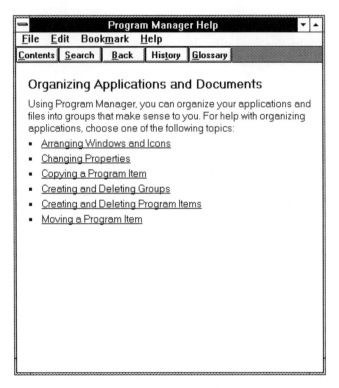

Figure 1.57   *A Topic for Adding Bookmarks*

Now choose the Bookmark command on the menu bar. You will see the display shown in Figure 1.58, which shows the Bookmark menu.

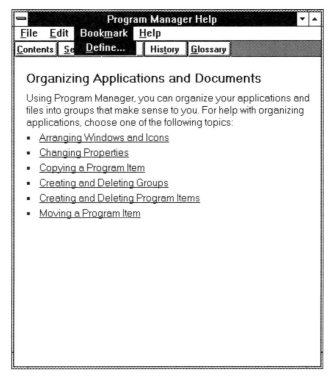

Figure 1.58   *Bookmark Menu*

Setting a Bookmark

The Bookmark menu in Figure 1.58 has only one command, the Define command. When you choose that command, you see the Bookmark Define dialog box shown in Figure 1.59.

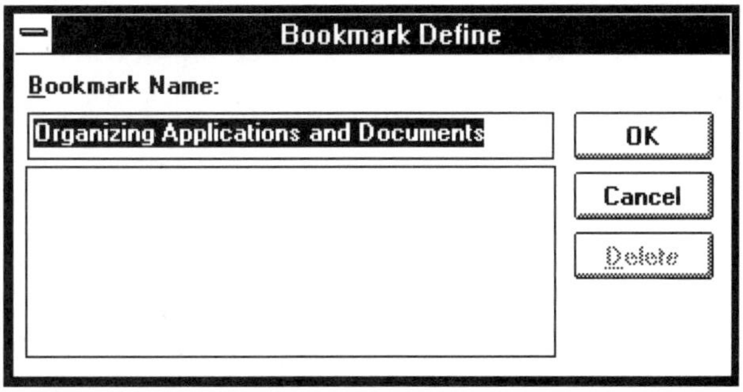

Figure 1.59   *Bookmark Define Dialog Box*

You can accept the name in the Bookmark Name text field or you can change it by entering a different one into the field. The name defaults to the title of the Help topic where you are placing the bookmark. Choose OK to insert the bookmark. Now select the Arranging Windows and Icons cross-reference topic from the display in Figure 1.58 and choose the Bookmark menu command again. You will see the display shown in Figure 1.60.

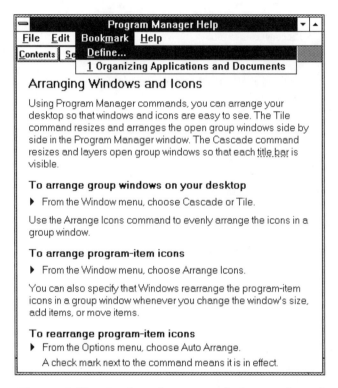

Figure 1.60 *Bookmark Menu with One Bookmark*

Observe that the Bookmark menu now has a second entry, the bookmark that you placed earlier. Choose Define and you will see the Bookmark Define dialog box shown in Figure 1.61.

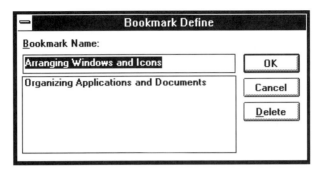

Figure 1.61 *Bookmark Define Dialog Box with a Bookmark*

The Bookmark Define dialog box is the same as the earlier one, except that its default Bookmark Name is that of the Cursor Movement Keys topic, and the earlier bookmark title appears in a list in the lower box. You can choose a name from the lower list box if you wish. For now, choose OK to add the default bookmark. Now when you choose the Bookmark command from the menu bar, you see that there are two bookmarks, as shown in Figure 1.62.

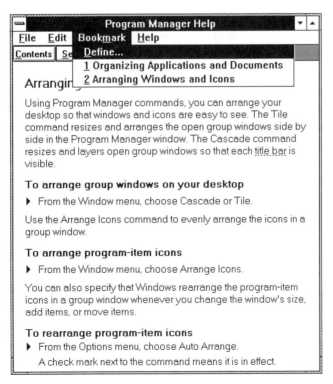

Figure 1.62 *Bookmark Menu with Two Bookmarks*

Whenever you select the Bookmark menu from now on, the two bookmarks will be on the menu. You can choose one of them and proceed directly to the topic that is marked. Observe that the bookmarks are numbered on the menu with underlines. You can key the associated number to select a bookmark.

Use the Contents command button to return to the Contents for Program Manager Help topic, as shown in Figure 1.48.

Deleting a Bookmark

To delete a bookmark, select the Bookmark menu and choose Define. You will see the Bookmark Define dialog box shown in Figure 1.63.

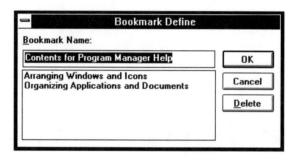

Figure 1.63   *Bookmark Define Dialog Box with Two Bookmarks*

Select the Arranging Windows and Icons entry in the lower list box. Then choose the Delete command button. The entry disappears from the list box, and the bookmark no longer exists in the Help database.

Annotate

You can add your own notes to a Help topic. Use the remaining bookmark to return to the Organizing Applications and Documents topic and select the Edit menu. You will see the display shown in Figure 1.64.

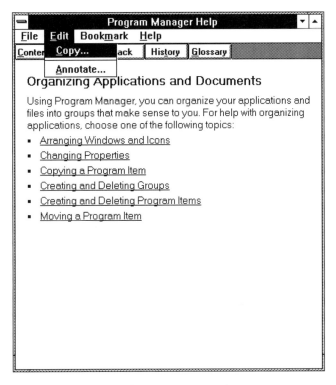

Figure 1.64   *The Help Edit Menu*

Choose the Annotate menu command and observe the Annotate dialog box shown in Figure 1.65.

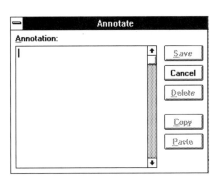

Figure 1.65   *Annotate Dialog Box*

The small vertical bar in the text box is a text cursor. You can type the contents of your annotation into this box. As you type, you can use the cursor keys to move the cursor around in the text. The Backspace key deletes characters to the left of the cursor and the Del key deletes characters to the right of the cursor. You can mark blocks of text by pointing the mouse cursor to a point, holding down the left button, dragging the mouse, and releasing the button when the block is marked. The Del key will delete a marked block. The words will wrap themselves to the next line. Do not use the Enter key to end a line.

Figure 1.66 shows the Annotate dialog box with some text entered.

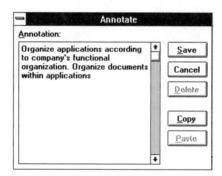

Figure 1.66   *Annotate Dialog Box with Text Added*

When you choose Save on the Annotate dialog box, the annotation is added to the topic, and the topic displays as shown in Figure 1.67.

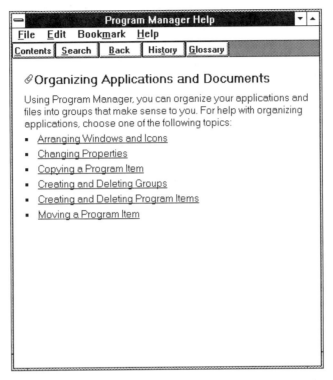

Figure 1.67 *Help Topic with an Annotation*

Reading and Changing an Annotation

Observe the paper clip icon to the left of the topic's title in Figure 1.67. This icon means that the topic has an annotation. To read the annotation, click the icon or tab to it and press Enter. You will see the Annotate dialog box that you saw in Figure 1.66. You can modify the text and save it by choosing Save.

Deleting an Annotation

To delete an annotation, read it by using the procedure you just learned. When the Annotate dialog box displays, choose the Delete command button. The annotation goes away, and the topic displays without the paper clip icon.

Copy and Paste

The Copy and Paste command buttons allow you to copy text from the annotation into the Clipboard and paste text from the Clipboard into the annotation. You will learn about the Clipboard in Chapter 4.

Printing a Topic

You can print the text of the current topic by selecting the Print Topic command from the Help window's File menu, shown in Figure 1.68.

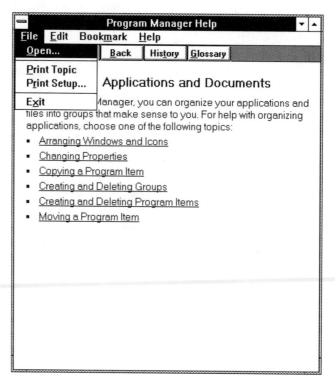

Figure 1.68   *The Help Window's File Menu*

Copying a Topic

You can copy the contents of a topic into another application by using the Copy command on the Help window's Edit menu, shown in Figure 1.64. When you choose the Copy command, you see the Copy dialog box shown in Figure 1.69.

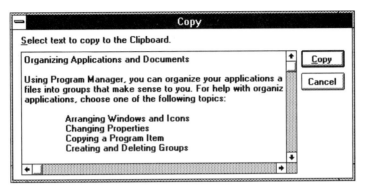

Figure 1.69   *The Copy Dialog Box*

When you mark the text and choose the Copy command on the dialog box, the textual contents of the current topic are copied into the Windows Clipboard. You can subsequently use the Paste command in another application to copy the Clipboard's contents into the application's document. You will learn about the Clipboard and marking text in Chapter 4.

Loading Other Help Files

Windows and its applications have many files in the Help database. You can load a different Help file if you need help with another application. Choose the Open command on the File menu of the Help window. You will see the Open dialog box shown in Figure 1.70. Choose any of the .HLP files from the dialog box to change the active Help file.

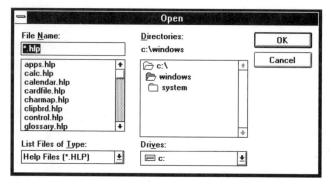

Figure 1.70 *The Help Data Base File Open Dialog Box*

Summary

In this chapter you learned to use the Windows graphical operating environment. You know how to use the mouse and keyboard to move around the Windows desktop. You can execute commands from menus and enter data into dialog boxes. You can rearrange the appearance of the desktop and you understand icons. These lessons are among the most important ones in learning Windows. Beyond this chapter you will see little that will be unfamiliar to you because the applications explained in the following chapters use the same user interface concepts that you learned in this chapter.

You used the Windows Program Manager extensively in this chapter to observe the behavior of the graphical operating environment. Chapter 2 teaches the details of the Program Manager—how you can use it to organize and manage your own system of programs and files.

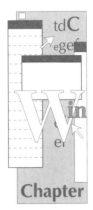

Chapter 2

The Program Manager

This chapter is about the Windows Program Manager, which is the executive program that maintains your applications programs in orderly groups and runs the applications on your command. In this chapter you will learn:

◆ Organizing applications programs into groups
◆ Running Windows applications and non-Windows DOS applications
◆ Running MS-DOS from Windows
◆ Multitasking
◆ Running DOS TSR programs from Windows
◆ Using the Startup group

In Chapter 1 you learned about the Windows graphical operating environment. The exercises in that chapter often used the functions of the Windows Program Manager because the Program Manager is the first application you see when you run Windows. Unless you take steps to change it, the Program Manager runs automatically whenever you start Windows.

The Program Manager is a "shell" program. With it you manage your applications programs by organizing them into manageable groups. Windows begins with an installed set of groups for you to work with. You can use the Program Manager to modify and expand these groups to create a personalized software environment.

Groups, Applications, and Documents

The title of this section represents the view of a computer's work as seen by Windows through the Program Manager. Groups are collections of applications, which are programs that work on collections of documents.

Suppose your work involves report preparation, bookkeeping for your business, and business correspondence. Besides those functions, you use a personal scheduler application, have utility applications to maintain your computer system, and sometimes you knock off for a while and play some computer games. These categories could represent the groups into which you would organize your applications.

You could have a Reports group where you keep your word processor, style checker, paint program, chart program, and desktop publishing applications. Those applications each work on individual documents, the text and graphics that go into the reports you prepare.

You might then have an Accounting group for the general ledger, payroll, tax preparation, and spreadsheet applications. Those applications, too, work on individual documents, the databases and spreadsheet data files.

The Letters group could contain the same word processor application that you use in the Reports group, but with a different set of documents and perhaps different style sheets and default printer settings.

Your Utilities group could contain hard disk management applications.

The Games group, of course, would have computer games you like to play.

The Windows Program Manager provides for your personal control over the software environment you use in ways similar to the model just described. Before you attempt to build your own customized program management environment, take the time to look at the configuration that Windows starts with.

Groups

Figure 2.1 is the starting point for most of the exercises in this chapter and in Chapter 1. It shows the Program Manager as it appears when you start a Windows sessions where little or no customizing has taken place.

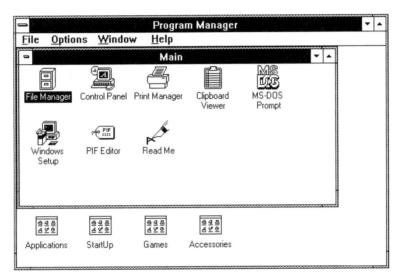

Figure 2.1 *Initial Windows Display*

The Windows display in Figure 2.1 shows five groups: Main, Applications, Startup, Games, and Accessories. Each of these groups contains applications that you will learn about in later chapters. Nothing requires you to preserve the default organization of applications within groups. No doubt you will modify and expand the original configuration. Nonetheless, the next several paragraphs discuss the contents of each of the groups to give you an idea of how applications might be logically arranged.

Opening and Closing a Group Window

When a group window is open, it appears as a document window within the Program Manager's program window. When it is closed, it is an icon at the bottom of the program window. In Figure 2.1 the Main group window is open and the others are closed. To execute an application in a group you must open the group window. When the application is running, you may close the group window from which it came.

To open a group window, you can do one of three things: double-click its icon; tab to the icon and press Enter; or select it from the Program Manager's Window menu. To close a group window you click its Minimize box, double-click its Control menu box, or choose Close from the Control menu itself.

Consider next the various groups in Figure 2.1.

The Main Group

The Main group, Figure 2.2, consists of programs that you use routinely. File Manager, Control Panel, Print Manager, Clipboard, MS-DOS Prompt, and Windows Setup are all utility applications that help you use and manage the Windows operating environment. The PIF editor is a utility program that you use when you integrate non-Windows DOS applications into the Windows environment. The Read Me icon runs the Windows Write accessory application so you can view the file named README.WRI, which contains information about Windows 3.1 that is not in the documentation. You will learn about Windows Write in Chapter 7.

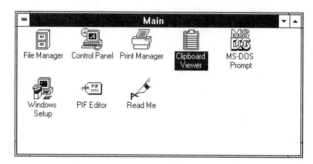

Figure 2.2 *The Main Group*

The Accessories Group

The Accessories group, Figure 2.3, is a set of small applications that by themselves could satisfy the computing needs of many users. Write is a word processor. Paintbrush is a graphical design tool. Terminal is a communications program. Notepad is a small text editor for the occasional memo. Recorder allows you to build keyboard and mouse macros to assign routine data entry functions to a single keystroke. Cardfile is a miniature text database that emulates a 3x5 card file. Calendar is a personal scheduler and alarm clock. Calculator is a desktop calculator utility program. Clock is a time display. Object Packager lets you create an icon that represents an embedded or linked graphics or text object. You can insert the icon into a document. You will learn about object linking and embedding in Chapter 11. Character Map lets you insert extended characters into documents. You can select from the available fonts to see what Alt+number key combinations will insert the characters you want. Media Player and Sound Recorder are multimedia extensions supported by Windows when you have multimedia hardware added to your computer. You will learn about these features in Chapter 11.

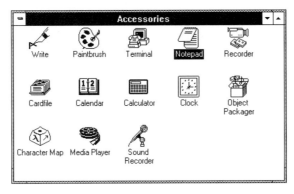

Figure 2.3   *The Accessories Group*

The Games Group

The Games group, Figure 2.4, contains two computer games that are included with Windows. This book will not dwell on them. They are there for your entertainment, and you might use them for a leisurely practice session to become comfortable with the system.

Figure 2.4   *The Games Group*

The Startup Group

The Startup group is empty when you first install Windows. You can add applications to the Startup group by using the procedures you will learn later in this chapter. Any application that you add to the Startup group starts running automatically when you start Windows. Later you will learn how to add the Clock accessory application to the Startup group so that you always have the time displayed when you are viewing the desktop. Figure 2.5 shows the empty Startup group.

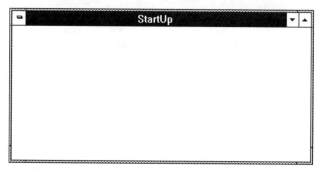

Figure 2.5   *The Startup Group*

The Applications Group

The Applications group, Figure 2.6, shows the non-Windows applications used for the preparation of this book. The applications are typical of non-Windows DOS applications, and the book will use them for examples of that environment. It will not matter that you might not have equivalent programs in your own computer.

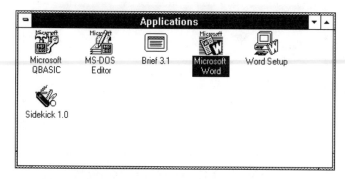

Figure 2.6   *The Applications Group*

Running Applications

There are several ways to run an application from Windows: choosing the application's icon from the group window that contains it; choosing a special copy of the application that is configured to operate with a specific document; using the Run command on the Program Manager's File menu; and running the application from the DOS command line in the DOS window. What happens after you run the application is strictly dependent on what the program does and, in some cases, the mode under which Windows is running.

You can set up a DOS non-Windows application to run in a window if you are running Windows in 386 enhanced mode. Otherwise DOS non-Windows applications must use the full screen. You will learn about Windows modes in Chapter 11.

The File Manager has several more ways that you can run an application. You will learn about the File Manager in Chapter 3.

Running a Program from a Group

You run a program from a group by opening the group window and choosing the program's icon. Open the Accessories group window and choose the Notepad icon. You will see a screen similar to that shown in Figure 2.7.

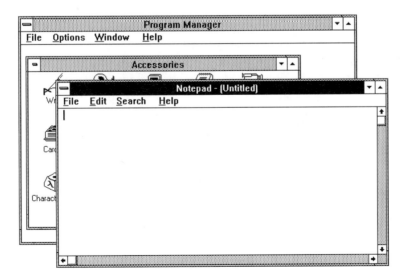

Figure 2.7 *The Notepad Application*

The Program Manager is in the background, and the Notepad application window is active. The Notepad is now a running application. Press Alt+Esc to make the Program Manager active again.

The Run Command

Choose the Run command from the File menu in the Program Manager window. You will see the Run dialog box shown in Figure 2.8.

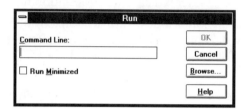

Figure 2.8 *The Run Dialog Box*

To use the Run dialog box, you must know the name and location of the application's .COM, .EXE, or .BAT file—the file that would get it started from the DOS command line. Depending on the application, you might need to know other things about its command line.

You use Run by typing the application's command line in the appropriate text field and choosing the OK command button. If you select the Run Minimized check box, the application will begin its execution as an icon.

You can run either Windows or non-Windows applications with the Run command. Inasmuch as you have several of each kind installed—at least in the example environment set forward in this book—you can try running both kinds of application at this time.

Using Run for a Windows Application

Type the command to execute the Windows Paintbrush program into the Run dialog box. The command is shown in Figure 2.9.

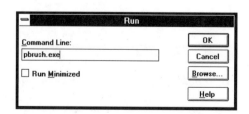

Figure 2.9 *Running PBRUSH.EXE*

Choose OK and the Paintbrush program executes as shown in Figure 2.10. Press Alt+Esc until the Program Manager Window is active again.

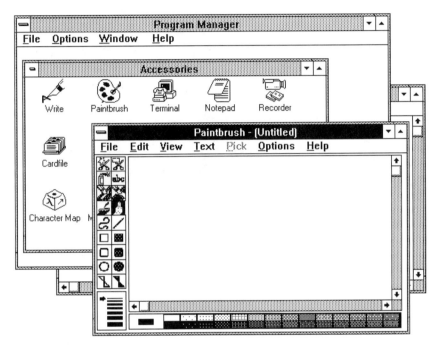

Figure 2.10   *The Paintbrush Application*

Using Run for a Non-Windows DOS Application

For these exercises, assume that the WordStar application, a word processing program, is configured to run in a window, and that you are running in 386 enhanced mode. The command to run WordStar is shown in Figure 2.11.

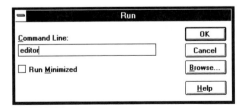

Figure 2.11   *The Command to Run WordStar*

Choose OK and the WordStar program executes as shown in Figure 2.12. At this point the Notepad, Paintbrush, and WordStar applications are running.

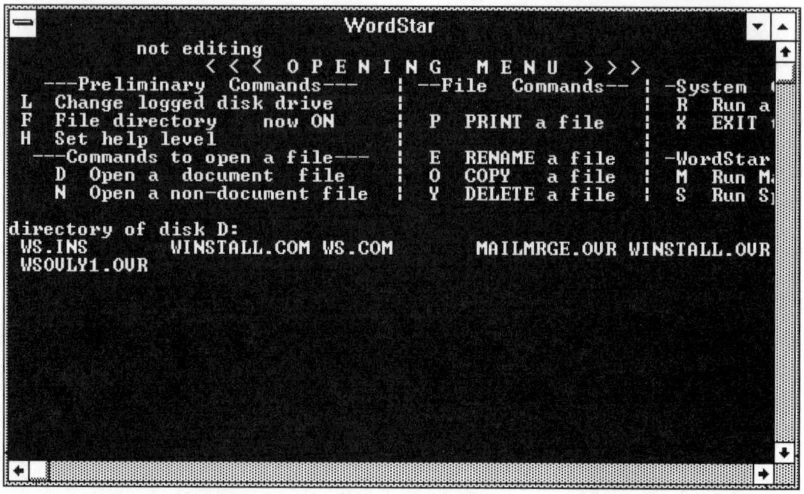

```
┌─────────────────────────────────────────────────────────┐
│ ─                     WordStar                        ▼ ▲ │
│              not editing                                ↑ │
│            < < <  O P E N I N G   M E N U  > > >          │
│     ---Preliminary  Commands---  !  --File  Commands--  ! -System │
│  L  Change logged disk drive     !                      !  R  Run a │
│  F  File directory     now ON    !  P  PRINT a file     !  X  EXIT │
│  H  Set help level               !                      !          │
│     ---Commands to open a file---!  E  RENAME a file     ! -WordStar │
│     D  Open a  document  file    !  O  COPY   a file     !  M  Run M.│
│     N  Open a non-document file  !  Y  DELETE a file     !  S  Run S.│
│                                                           │
│ directory of disk D:                                      │
│ WS.INS         WINSTALL.COM WS.COM        MAILMRGE.OUR WINSTALL.OUR │
│ WSOVLY1.OVR                                                │
│                                                           │
│                                                           │
│                                                           │
│                                                         ▼ │
│ ◆▪                                                      ➡ │
└─────────────────────────────────────────────────────────┘
```

Figure 2.12   *A Non-Windows DOS Application Running in a Window*

The DOS Prompt

For the next exercise, select the Program Manager window and make the Main group the active document window. The other windows will move to the background. The MS-DOS Prompt icon provides a way for you to go directly to the DOS command line from within Windows.

When you choose the MS-DOS Prompt application from the Main group, the entire screen is given over to a DOS session that behaves exactly like a non-Windows DOS computer with respect to running applications. The prompt you see is shown in Figure 2.13.

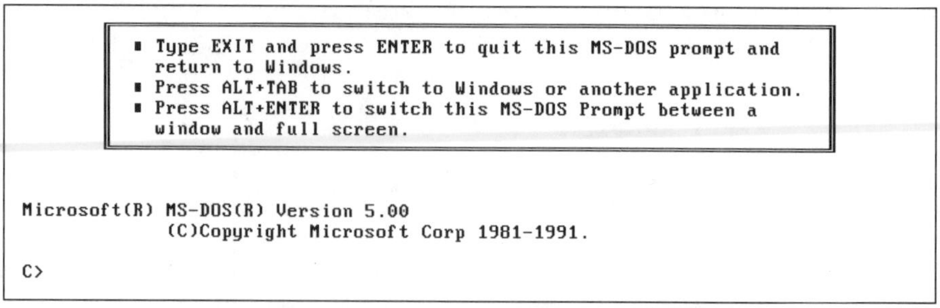

```
┌─────────────────────────────────────────────────────────┐
│   ┌─────────────────────────────────────────────────┐   │
│   │ ▪ Type EXIT and press ENTER to quit this MS-DOS prompt and │
│   │   return to Windows.                            │   │
│   │ ▪ Press ALT+TAB to switch to Windows or another application. │
│   │ ▪ Press ALT+ENTER to switch this MS-DOS Prompt between a │
│   │   window and full screen.                       │   │
│   └─────────────────────────────────────────────────┘   │
│                                                           │
│ Microsoft(R) MS-DOS(R) Version 5.00                       │
│          (C)Copyright Microsoft Corp 1981-1991.           │
│                                                           │
│ C>                                                        │
└─────────────────────────────────────────────────────────┘
```

Figure 2.13   *The DOS Prompt*

The difference between DOS by itself and DOS run from within Windows is that you can switch between DOS and Windows applications without stopping and restarting applications, and you can have more than one DOS session active at a time.

To run a program from the DOS prompt, you run it just as you would from DOS without Windows loaded. Assuming that you have a DOS path to your DOS utility programs, run the DOS program EDLIN by typing its name on the DOS command line with a file name as shown in Figure 2.14. The figure shows the screen after EDLIN has begun running.

```
    ┌──────────────────────────────────────────────────────┐
    │ ■ Type EXIT and press ENTER to quit this MS-DOS prompt and │
    │   return to Windows.                                   │
    │ ■ Press ALT+TAB to switch to Windows or another application. │
    │ ■ Press ALT+ENTER to switch this MS-DOS Prompt between a │
    │   window and full screen.                              │
    └──────────────────────────────────────────────────────┘


Microsoft(R) MS-DOS(R) Version 5.00
          (C)Copyright Microsoft Corp 1981-1991.

C>edlin teach.doc
New file
*
```

Figure 2.14 *Running EDLIN From the DOS Prompt*

Multitasking

If you have followed along with these exercises, you have several applications loaded into your computer, and the DOS Prompt is the current active one. The other applications are the Notepad, the Paintbrush, the WordStar program, and, of course, the Program Manager itself.

If you are running Windows in 386 enhanced mode, the other programs are running now, too, but the screen and keyboard are dedicated to the DOS prompt. If you are not running Windows in 386 enhanced mode, the other programs are loaded and ready to go, but each one must wait for you to switch to it in order to execute. If your computer has enough memory, all the programs are resident at one time. If not, Windows will swap them in and out of its temporary disk swap files as necessary. The mechanics of operating Windows and its applications do not change because you are or are not in 386 enhanced mode. But the overall performance of your computer will be affected. In the case of these particular applications, there is no difference between multitasking and waiting to be switched in. All of them are strictly interactive—they do nothing unless you enter commands with the keyboard or mouse.

Switching Between Applications

Because you have several interactive applications running at one time, you need to be able to switch from one to the other in order to view their results and supply them with their next input. Using Alt+Esc is one way to switch from application to application. You can use Alt+Esc to switch from the DOS prompt of the previous exercise back to one of the windowed applications. Which one comes next will depend on the sequence in which the tasks were last selected. Chances are the Program Manager is next and you would see the screen shown in Figure 2.15.

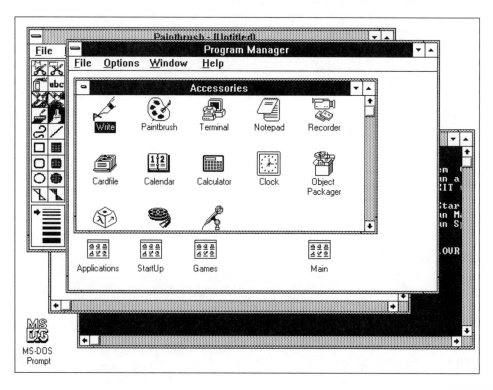

Figure 2.15 *Switching Back into Windows*

Observe the MS-DOS Prompt icon in the lower-left corner of the screen. That icon indicates that a program is running that does not occupy a screen window. The program is, of course, the DOS EDLIN program that you ran from the DOS prompt. Other programs that run as icons might have different icon symbols, but their presence as icons on the desktop indicates that they are running and not using a window.

You can use Alt+Esc to switch from application to application now. When you get to the MS-DOS Prompt, its label becomes highlighted, but the screen does not change to the DOS screen. The Alt+Esc key does not switch an application into a window or onto the screen when the running application is an icon.

To return to the DOS EDLIN program with the mouse, double click the MS-DOS Prompt icon. To return with the keyboard, press Alt+Esc until the MS-DOS Prompt icon's label is highlighted. Then press Enter, or you can press Alt+Spacebar to open the icon's Control menu and choose the Restore command.

You can put the MS-DOS Prompt application—EDLIN in this example—into a Window if you are running in 386 enhanced mode. Press Alt+Enter to toggle DOS applications between window and full-screen modes.

Return now to the windowed applications by pressing Alt+Esc from within the DOS EDLIN session.

The Task List

The Windows task executive software maintains a task list. While not actually a part of the Program Manager, the task list's functions are integral to executing and monitoring the running of applications.

You can view and use the task list in a dialog box by pressing Ctrl+Esc. The Task List dialog box is shown in Figure 2.16. A task in this context is the same as an application.

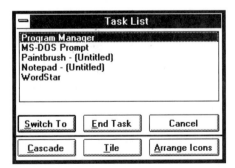

Figure 2.16   *The Task List Dialog Box*

The task list lists all the tasks currently running and provides some commands relative to the tasks. You can move the list box cursor to a task's name and perform several operations on it. If you double-click the task name or choose Switch To when the name is highlighted, the Program Manager switches to the task and the task resumes executing. If you choose End Task, the Program Manager attempts to terminate the task. Cancel closes the Task List dialog box. The Arrange Icons command rearranges the application icons at the bottom of the desktop.

The Cascade command cascades the applications windows so that the screen appears as shown in Figure 2.17. Cascading resizes the windows to a uniform size and stacks them up so that they are all visible.

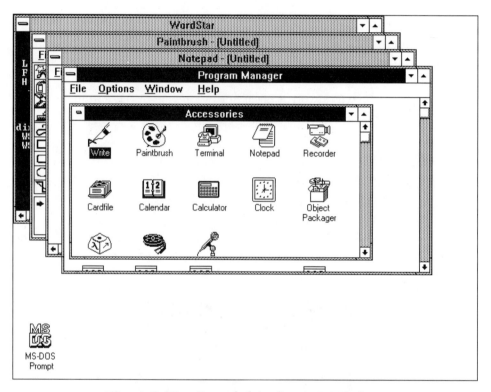

Figure 2.17   *Cascaded Applications Windows*

The Tile command organizes the windows into a tiled configuration, as shown in Figure 2.18. Tiled windows are arranged so that no part of any window overlaps another.

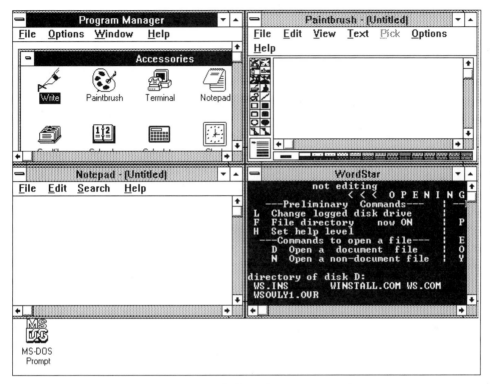

Figure 2.18   *Tiled Applications Windows*

Minimizing an Application

Four of the five applications that are running in Figure 2.18 are running in applications windows. The fifth, the MS-DOS Prompt program, is running as an icon at the bottom of the desktop. You can minimize each running application so that it is an icon. Click the Minimize box for each of the applications or use Alt+Esc to switch to the window, press Alt+Spacebar to call the Control menu, and choose Minimize for each application. When you have minimized all the applications, they are all icons at the bottom of the screen, as shown in Figure 2.19.

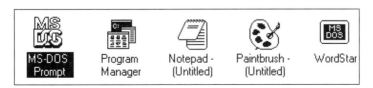

Figure 2.19   *All Applications Minimized to Icons*

You can begin to see the potential for multitasking when you go one step further. Choose the Notepad. You can double-click the Notepad icon, or use Ctrl+Esc to call the Task List and choose it from there. Now resize the Notepad so that it occupies most of the screen but leaves the icons visible, as shown in Figure 2.20.

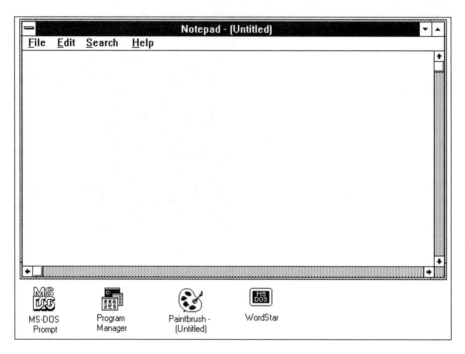

Figure 2.20   *One Application in a Window, the Others as Icons*

The desktop shown in Figure 2.20 represents a typical working environment. You keep the application that you use the most—in this example the Notepad—on the screen in an active window. You keep the applications that you call occasionally running as icons. When you want an application, you choose its icon. When you are done with an application, you minimize it again, returning to an uncluttered desktop with your primary application occupying most of the screen.

The programs from the earlier examples illustrate this point. A more appropriate example is in Figure 2.21. In this example the Write word processing application is the primary one, the Program Manager stands by as an icon at the top of the screen, and your favorite desktop accessories are icons at the bottom. The Clock icon even keeps accurate time. You might arrange your desktop in a similar configuration each morning and work from that baseline throughout the day. Of course, the applications and accessories that you would use would be ones of your personal choice.

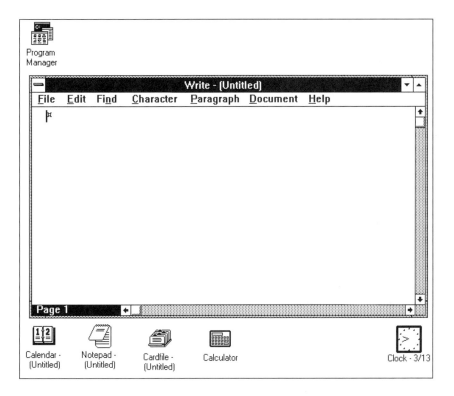

Figure 2.21 *A Typical Desktop*

This environment is very much like the traditional DOS environment, where users often loaded a lot of memory-resident utilities into the computer to pop up over the main application when they needed them—except that with Windows, you do not give up memory to those less frequently used utilities.

Exiting from Applications

Even though an application is an icon at the bottom of the desktop and not using any significant screen space, it is still a running application, and it is using some of the system's resources just to hang around waiting to be needed. In this respect it is very much like the old DOS memory-resident program. It does not diminish the amount of memory that the other applications have available, but it uses time and perhaps extended memory for it to be swapped in and out. Sometimes you can improve system performance just by terminating some of the loaded programs that you do not need at the moment.

Windows applications usually have a File menu with an Exit command. To terminate the application, you can use this command, you can press Alt+F4 when the application is the current window, or you can choose Close from the application's Control menu.

Because an application that is running as an icon has a Control menu too, you can use the Program Manager to exit the application if it is a Windows application. This is a convenience. You do not need to call the application up from its icon into a window in order to terminate it.

Suppose you want to exit from the Paintbrush application in Figure 2.20. The Paintbrush application is an icon. You could double-click it into a window and use the Exit command on its File menu. But if you single click it, its Control menu displays and you can choose Close. And, faster still, if its label is highlighted, you can press Ctrl+F4, and it will terminate. Use one of these techniques to terminate Paintbrush. The screen will look like Figure 2.22, with the Paintbrush icon gone.

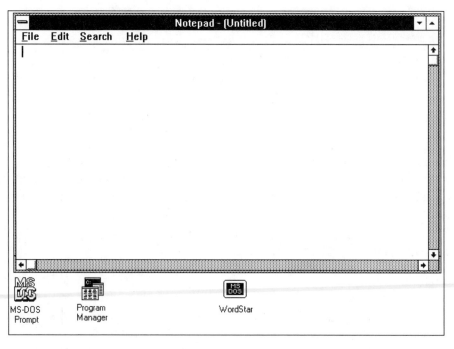

Figure 2.22 *The Paintbrush Application Has Been Terminated*

You could try to terminate the Program Manager in the same way. If you do, it will try to exit from Windows as well. Try that now. You will see the usual Exit Windows dialog box that you learned about in Chapter 1. Choose OK. You will see the display shown in Figure 2.23.

Figure 2.23   *Trying to Exit the Program Manager—and Windows*

The message in Figure 2.23 is telling you that the MS-DOS Prompt application is still active. The MS-DOS Prompt application is the application that you ran earlier to get into DOS so that you could run EDLIN. That program is still running. Its icon is in the lower-left corner of the screen. Choose OK, and you will return to Figure 2.22.

Now open the Control menu for the MS-DOS Prompt icon. It looks like the one in Figure 2.24.

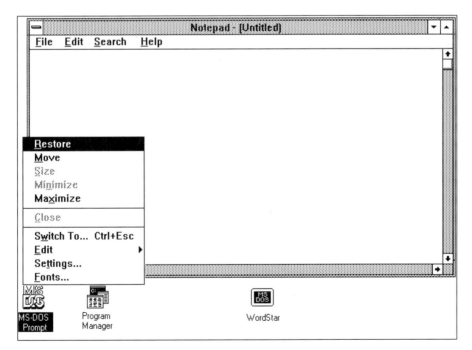

Figure 2.24   *MS-DOS Prompt Icon Control Menu*

The Close command on the Control menu in Figure 2.24 is not available. You can tell because the command's title is displayed in a font of lesser intensity than the available ones. The only way to terminate this application is to switch into it and use its own facilities for terminating it.

With the Control menu displayed as in Figure 2.24, press Enter to choose Restore. Type Q, EDLIN's quit command, and Enter, then answer Y and Enter to the question, and finally type EXIT and Enter to terminate the DOS session. This command sequence is shown in Figure 2.25.

```
■ Type EXIT and press ENTER to quit this MS-DOS prompt and
  return to Windows.
■ Press ALT+TAB to switch to Windows or another application.
■ Press ALT+ENTER to switch this MS-DOS Prompt between a
  window and full screen.


Microsoft(R) MS-DOS(R) Version 5.00
          (C)Copyright Microsoft Corp 1981-1991.

C>edlin teach.doc
New file
*q
Abort edit (Y/N)? y
C>exit
```

Figure 2.25   *Terminating the EDLIN and DOS Session*

After you have terminated EDLIN and DOS, the MS-DOS Prompt icon goes away. Now you want to terminate WordStar. Remember that WordStar is a non-Windows DOS application that runs in a window. Also remember that you might not have a copy of WordStar installed, so you will have to follow this discussion in the book rather than run the exercise on your computer.

Like the MS-DOS Prompt icon, the WordStar icon has a Control menu, but the Control menu's Close command is unavailable. You will have to activate the WordStar window in order to terminate the application. Choose Restore from the menu. The WordStar application window will open, as shown in Figure 2.26. Type the WordStar X command to exit from the application. The WordStar window will close.

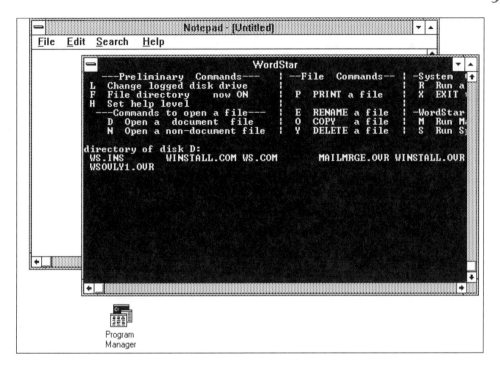

Figure 2.26   *Quitting WordStar*

The only two applications remaining are the Notepad and the Program Manager. The Notepad is still a window, and the Program Manager is the only icon left at the bottom of the desktop, as shown in Figure 2.27.

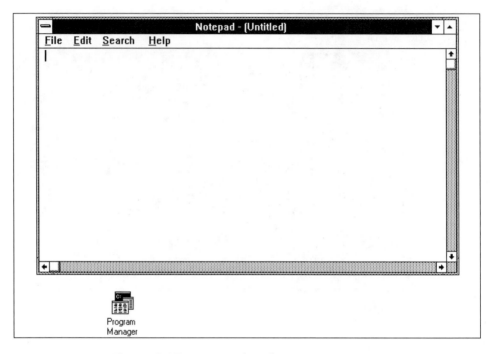

Figure 2.27 *Notepad and Program Manager*

Terminate the Notepad and open the Program Manager so that the display is about what it was in Figure 2.1, at the beginning of this chapter. You might need to move and resize the Program Manager window. With all the shuffling of windows it is unlikely that it will be restored to its original configuration. You can try moving things around, or you might want to exit from Windows and restart it for the next series of lessons.

Managing Groups

The default Windows installation starts you out with the groups of applications that you have been working with here and in Chapter 1. It is unlikely that you will find this particular configuration suited to your taste or needs. To allow you to build your own custom organization of applications, the Program Manager supports the addition, modification, and deletion of groups and applications.

Begin with Figure 2.1 at the start of the chapter and minimize the Main group to clear away some workspace. The Program Manager will look like the display shown in Figure 2.28.

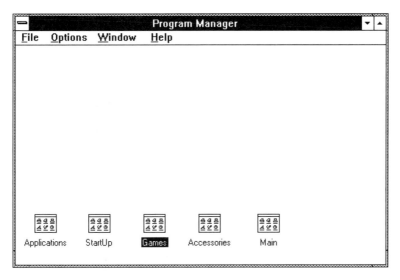

Figure 2.28 *Beginning to Organize*

Adding Groups

Suppose that you keep records for a local civic organization and you want to organize the software you use for this purposes. You have decided that you need a CIVIC group in your Program Manager. Open the Program Manager's File menu and choose the New command. You will see the dialog box shown in Figure 2.29.

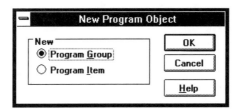

Figure 2.29 *New Program Object Dialog Box: Groups*

The Program Group option button is already selected, so you choose OK. Figure 2.30 shows the next display, the Program Group Properties dialog box.

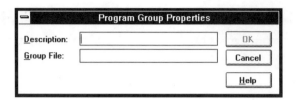

Figure 2.30   *Program Group Properties Dialog Box*

You enter the name of your new group, Civic, into the Description field. You do not need to specify a Group File. Windows will assign a file name and remember it for you. Choose OK, and the Program Manager creates the new Civic group and opens its window, which is empty, as you can see in Figure 2.31. Minimize the Civic group to an icon.

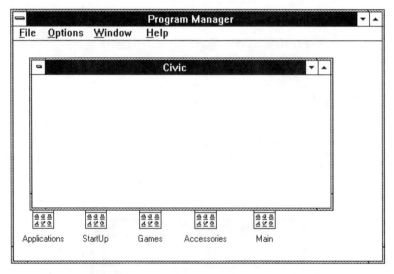

Figure 2.31   *A New Empty Group Named Civic*

Deleting Groups

Suppose now that you decide that you do not need the Games group in the Program Manager. You want to delete it. Select the Games icon so that its label is highlighted and its Control menu is not displayed. Then press Del or choose Delete from the Program Manger's File menu. You will see the dialog box shown in Figure 2.32.

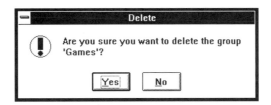

Figure 2.32   *Delete Dialog Box*

Choose Yes or No depending on whether you really meant to delete the group. For now choose No. You can delete the group later if you wish.

Adding Applications

The new Civic group still has no applications. For a group to be of use, you must install some applications into it. You can install existing Windows applications, new Windows applications that are not installed anywhere yet, non-Windows applications that are already installed in another group, and new non-Windows applications.

Adding Windows Applications

Suppose that one of your jobs for this local civic organization is to maintain a list of members. You may decide that the Cardfile is just the application to handle the membership list. To add an application to a group, first you must activate the group's window. Open the Civic group window now. Next choose the New command from the Program Manager's File menu. You will see the dialog box shown in Figure 2.33.

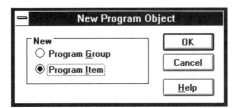

Figure 2.33   *New Program Object Dialog Box: Applications*

The dialog box is the same as the one in Figure 2.30, but the Program Item option button is selected. Choose OK, and you will see the Program Item Properties dialog box, as shown in Figure 2.34.

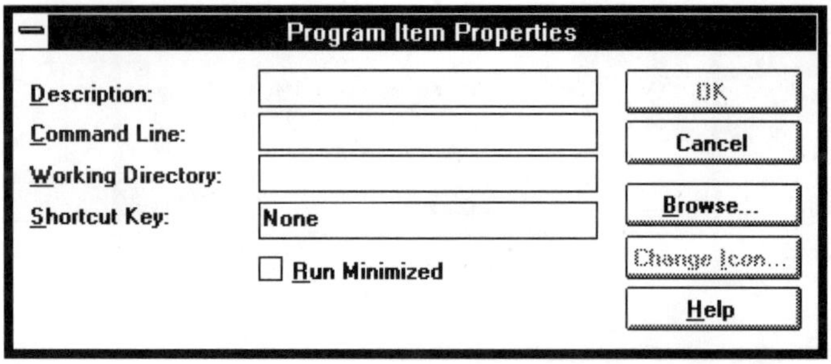

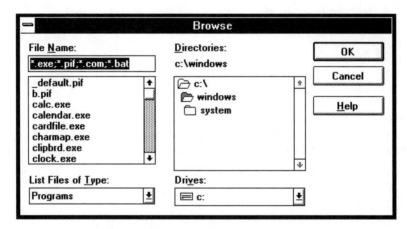

Figure 2.34   *Program Item Properties Dialog Box*

You can enter the Description field as "Membership Roster," but you do not know the command line necessary to execute the Cardfile application. The Program Manager will help you with that. Choose Browse from the dialog box. You will see the Browse dialog box, as shown in Figure 2.35.

Figure 2.35   *Browse Dialog Box*

The Browse dialog box resembles the standard Open dialog box you learned about in Chapter 1. For this example, you do not need to search the disk system for the program you want to install. The CARDFILE.EXE file is in clear view.

Choose the file by double-clicking its name or by moving the cursor to its name and choosing OK. The file's path and command now appear in the Command Line field of the Program Item Properties dialog box, as shown in Figure 2.36.

```
┌─────────────────────────────────────────────────────┐
│ ▬            Program Item Properties                 │
├─────────────────────────────────────────────────────┤
│  D̲escription:      ┌─────────────────────┐  ┌──────┐ │
│                    │ Membership Roster   │  │ ⸴OK⸴ │ │
│  C̲ommand Line:     ├─────────────────────┤  └──────┘ │
│                    │ C:\WINDOWS\CARDFILE.EXE│ ┌──────┐│
│  W̲orking Directory:├─────────────────────┤ │Cancel││
│                    │                     │  └──────┘ │
│  S̲hortcut Key:     ├─────────────────────┤  ┌──────┐ │
│                    │ None                │  │Browse...│
│                    └─────────────────────┘  └──────┘ │
│                    ☐ R̲un Minimized           ┌────────┐│
│                                              │Change I̲con...│
│                                              └────────┘│
│                                              ┌──────┐ │
│                                              │ Help │ │
│                                              └──────┘ │
└─────────────────────────────────────────────────────┘
```

Figure 2.36   *Program Item Properties Dialog Box Filled In*

In some cases you will add parameters to the Command Line field. In this example you might add the name of your planned Cardfile database, "Membership Roster." More on that later in this Chapter.

The Working Directory field is used to specify the default drive and subdirectory that will be used when you run the application. In this example you can leave it blank; the current directory will be used by default.

You can assign a shortcut key to the application by selecting the Shortcut Key field and pressing a key. That key, if pressed in combination with the Ctrl and Alt keys, will be a shortcut key that runs the application whenever the Program Manager is the active window.

Most Windows applications already have icons assigned to them. The Cardfile is no exception, and after you finish this exercise you will see that the Membership Roster application—the renamed Cardfile application—uses the Cardfile's default icon. You can change the icon by choosing the Change Icon command. You will learn about that later, when you add a non-Windows DOS application to the group. For now, choose OK. The Program Manager adds the Cardfile application to the Civic group, but with the name Membership Roster, as shown in Figure 2.37.

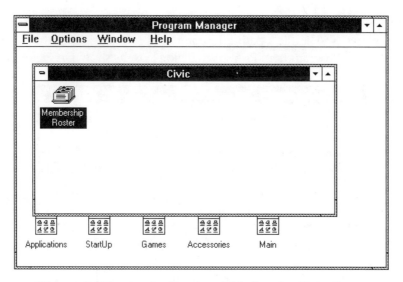

Figure 2.37 *An Application Added to the Civic Group*

You must realize that even though you added the Cardfile application to the Civic group, it still exists in the Accessories group. These are not redundant records of the same application. This operation did not make a copy of all the program's files. It simply added a pointer to the program from within another group, which is a natural way to organize software. You could conceivably add the Cardfile application to several groups: one for sales leads; one for family names, addresses, and birthdays; one for maintenance records on your cars, boat, and appliances; one for recipes.

Later you will learn how to customize these duplicate applications so that when you start an application it opens the data file that pertains to the group where you started it from. It is even possible to have two copies of the same application running in the same group for two different purposes.

In this exercise you added an application that already existed in another group. Normally you need to add applications only to the first group. After that you simply move and copy applications between groups. You will learn that technique later.

Adding Non-Windows DOS Applications

Another of your jobs for the civic organization might be that of editor and publisher of the newsletter. You prefer to use Windows Write and Paintbrush to publish the newsletter, but many of the members submit articles written in their dependable old Wordstar program. To import and edit their work, you will need Wordstar installed into your Civic group. If you have Wordstar installed as a DOS application on your hard disk, installing it is almost the same as installing a Windows application. If you do not have Wordstar, simply follow these exercises in the book.

First you must activate the Civic group's window as you did before. Next, choose the New command from the Program Manager's File menu. This is the same dialog box shown in Figure 2.33. Choose OK to see the same Program Item Properties dialog box shown in Figure 2.34.

Type WordStar in the Description field and choose Browse from the dialog box. You will see the same Browse dialog box shown in Figure 2.35.

For this example, you will need to search the disk system for the Wordstar program. In this example, Wordstar is on the C: drive in the \WS subdirectory. Refer to Figure 2.35 and choose the C:\ entry in the Directories field. This moves you to the root directory. Now select the WS entry to move to the \WS subdirectory. You will see the display shown in Figure 2.38.

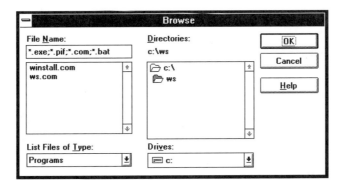

Figure 2.38 *The WordStar Subdirectory*

Select the WS.COM entry and then choose OK. The WordStar path and command appear in the Command Line field of the Program Item Properties dialog box, as shown in Figure 2.39.

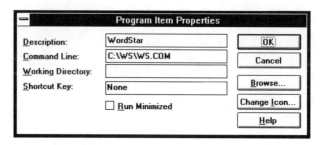

Figure 2.39   *WordStar Ready to be Installed*

Choose OK, and you will see the Wordstar program installed into the Civic group, as shown in Figure 2.40.

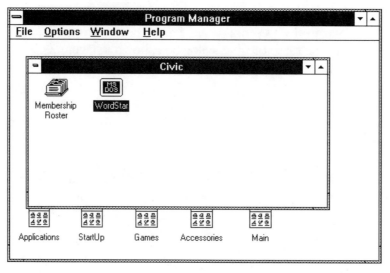

Figure 2.40   *WordStar Added to the Civic Group*

Deleting Applications

That Games group might still be bothering you. How much of it do you really need? Minimize the Civic group and activate the Games group window (shown in Figure 2.4) to see what is in it. You decide that you might want to play Minesweeper from time to time, but that you do not need Solitaire, so you decide to delete it. Choose the Delete command from the Program Manager's File menu. You will see the Delete dialog box shown in Figure 2.41.

Figure 2.41   *Delete Dialog Box*

This dialog box is almost the same as the one in Figure 2.32, where you started to delete the Games group. What is more, both of them are displayed by choosing the Delete command on the File menu or by using the Del key. The difference is that when you chose Delete this time, there was a group window active. When you chose Delete before, no group window was active, but a program item was selected.

When a group window is active, the Delete command refers to the application in that window that is currently highlighted. When no group window is active, the Delete command refers to the group icon that is currently highlighted. This is an important distinction. It would not be difficult to delete one thing when you intended to delete something else, particularly when the dialog boxes are so similar.

You can delete either of the games if you wish. No further exercise depends on them. The illustrations in the book will continue to show the icon, however. You can minimize the Games group at this time.

Moving Applications Between Groups

To produce the civic organization's newsletter, you decide to move the Write and Paintbrush applications into the Civic group. First activate the Civic window and then activate the Accessories window. Move the Accessories window down and to one side so that you can see enough of the Civic window to hold two more icons. Figure 2.42 shows how that might look.

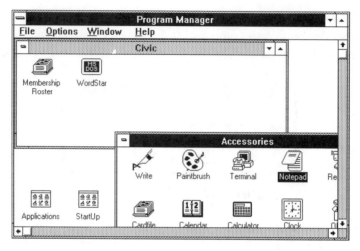

Figure 2.42   *Preparing to Move Applications*

Moving an Application with the Mouse

Place the mouse cursor on the Write icon and press and hold the left button. Drag the icon from the Accessories window onto the Civic window. Release the button, and the screen will look like Figure 2.43, with the Paint icon absent from the Accessories group and newly resident in the Civic group window. Release the button, and the screen will look like Figure 2.43, with the Paint icon absent from the Accessories group and newly resident in the Civic group.

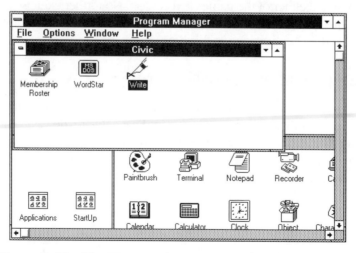

Figure 2.43   *The Write Application Moved to the Civic Group*

Moving an Application with the Keyboard

Press Ctrl+Tab until the Accessories group window is active. Select the Paintbrush icon in the Accessories group by pressing the arrow keys. Open the Program Manager's File menu by pressing Alt+F, and then choose the Move command. You will see the Move Program Item dialog box, as shown in Figure 2.44.

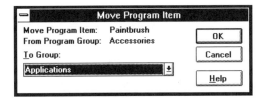

Figure 2.44   *The Move Program Item Dialog Box*

The To Group field is a drop-down list. When you select it, a list of all the groups drops down, as shown in Figure 2.45.

Figure 2.45   *The To Group Drop-Down List*

This drop-down list allows you to move the application to a different group than the one displayed in the To Group field. For this exercise, select the Civic group on the list and choose OK. This command will move the Paintbrush application from the Accessories group into the Civic group, and you will see the display shown in Figure 2.46.

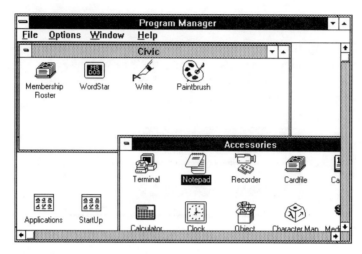

Figure 2.46 *The Paintbrush Application Moved to the Civic Group*

Copying an Application to Another Group

Moving the two applications has set up the Civic group the way you want it, but now you see a problem. You still want the applications in the Accessories group for other uses, and you just moved them out. The answer, of course, is to copy them back into the Accessories group.

Copying an Application with the Mouse

You copy an application with the mouse the same way that you move it, except that you hold down the Ctrl key while you drag the icon. Try that now by dragging the Write icon from the Civic group to the Accessories group with the Ctrl key held down. Drag the icon to the lower part of the Accessories window that is visible in Figure 2.46. You will observe that as you drag the icon, you are dragging a copy. The original stays in place.

Copying an Application with the Keyboard

Select the Paintbrush icon in the Civic window. Next choose the Copy command from the Program Manager's File menu. Everything works much like moving an application. You will see the Copy Program Item dialog box, as shown in Figure 2.47.

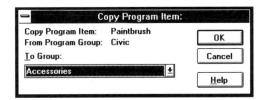

Figure 2.47 *Copy Program Item Dialog Box*

The Copy Program Item dialog box works like the one for moving an application. Choose OK, and the Paintbrush icon is copied to the Accessories window. It might not be in view, so maximize the window and arrange the icons to your liking. Most likely the order will not be the same as before. Do not worry about that. Minimize the Accessories window to an icon and return to the Civic group window.

Changing Properties

You are not stuck with the way an application works or the way its icon appears in the group window just because you copied it from another group. You can change its description, its icon, and its command line by modifying its properties.

Changing the Icon Description

The Write and Paintbrush icons in the Civic group are not very descriptive as to their purpose. You installed them in Civic to support the newsletter but nothing in the displays of their icons tells you that. You can change an icon's description by changing the application's properties. Select the Paintbrush icon so that its label is highlighted. Choose the Properties command from the File menu. You will see the Program Item Properties dialog box shown in Figure 2.48.

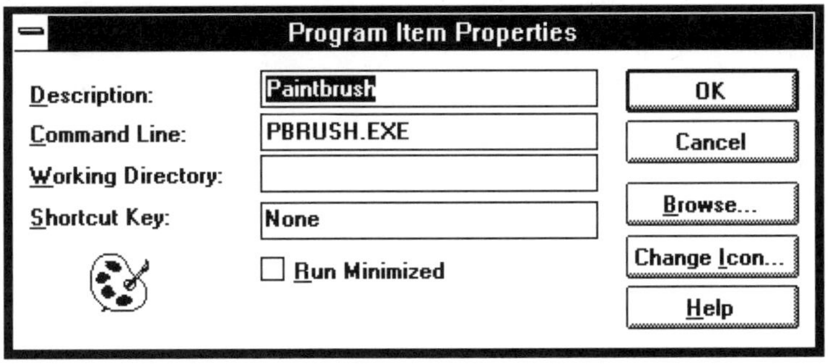

Figure 2.48 *Program Item Properties Dialog Box*

Type Newsletter Graphics in the Description field and choose OK. Use the same procedure to change the label on the Write icon to "Newsletter Text." With the icons renamed, the Civic group now appears as shown in Figure 2.49.

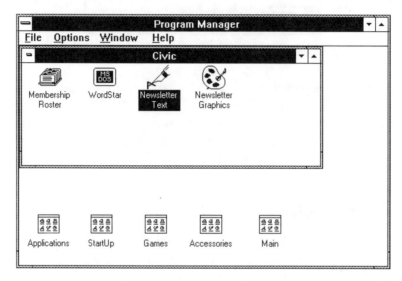

Figure 2.49   *Civic Group with Renamed Icons*

Changing the Icon

Most Windows applications are bound to an icon that the application developer designed and installed into the program. The Cardfile, Write, and Paintbrush applications all have fixed icons. The Wordstar application does not, however, because it is a DOS application. Few developers were thinking about icons and graphical operating environments when Wordstar was first designed in the 1970s.

The MS-DOS icon assigned by Windows to Wordstar merely indicates that the program is a DOS application. But there are other icons available for DOS applications, icons that describe the nature of the application rather than the environment in which it runs. You can change the icon of a DOS application from the Program Item Properties dialog box.

Select the MS-DOS Wordstar icon and choose the Properties command from the File menu. Choose the Change Icon control button from the Program Item Properties dialog box. You will see the Change Icon dialog box shown in Figure 2.50.

Figure 2.50 *Change Icon Dialog Box*

You can select from the many icons available to the Program Manager. Choose the OK command to see the Change Icon dialog box show the icons that the Program Manager can use, as shown in Figure 2.51.

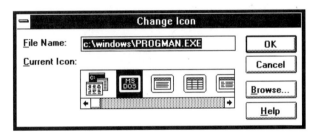

Figure 2.51 *Application Icons*

You can select from the icons in the list by clicking the scroll bar or by tabbing to the icons and using the arrow keys to select one. You can choose the Browse command to select from other Windows applications or icon files to borrow one of their icons for this DOS application. For now, move through the Program Manager's icons until you find the one that looks like a typewriter. Select that icon and choose the OK command. The icon will be added to the lower-left corner of the Program Item Properties dialog box, as shown in Figure 2.52.

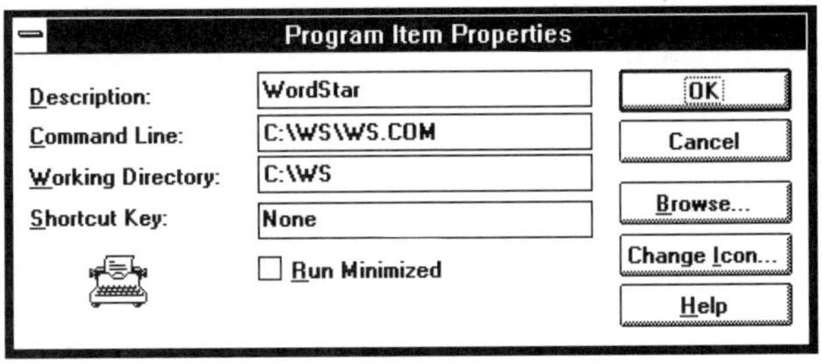

Figure 2.52 *Program Item Properties with an Icon*

Choose OK on the Program Item Properties dialog box. The icon for the Wordstar application is now changed, as shown in Figure 2.53.

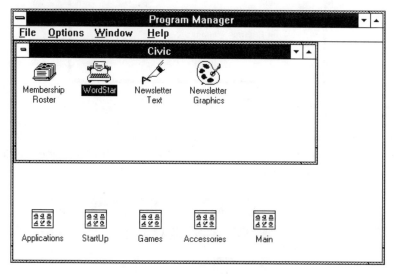

Figure 2.53 *WordStar Icon Changed*

Running an Application with a Named Document

If you were to run the Membership Roster Cardfile application from the Civic group now, it would begin with no database in place. You would need to use its File menu to locate and load the database that represents your membership roster. Rather than do that every time, you can configure the Membership Roster Cardfile to always load the appropriate database when you start the application.

Most Windows applications and many DOS applications allow you to specify a file name on the command line when you run the program. By adding the file name to the Command Line field in the Program Item Properties dialog box, you tell the Program Manager to run the program with the specified file. Select the Membership Roster icon and choose the Properties command on the File menu. Add the filename "members" to the Command Line field, as shown in Figure 2.54.

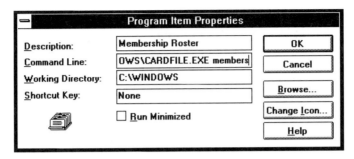

Figure 2.54 *File Name Added to a Command Line Property*

Choose OK. Now, when you run the Membership Roster Cardfile application, it will look for a file named MEMBERS.CRD. Because that file does not exist yet, the program will not load one. You will need to create the file from within the Cardfile application. Chapter 10 includes a section on the Cardfile accessory application.

Running DOS Memory-Resident Utilities (TSRs)

Most DOS users know about memory-resident programs, also called the TSRs, for "Terminate and Stay Resident." A TSR is a program that remains resident in DOS memory so you can execute it by pressing a hot key. The TSR interrupts the program that is currently running and pops up over it. When you exit from the TSR, it returns you to the program that it interrupted.

The TSR's two primary disadvantages are that it occupies memory even when you are not running it, and the fact that there is no standard way of implementing it, resulting in many incompatibilities among different TSRs and the programs they interrupt. Nonetheless, some TSR programs have value to users who do not want to give them up when moving to the Windows graphical operating environment. Until the purveyors of those programs release Windows-compatible versions, the old TSRs must remain.

There are three ways to run a TSR from Windows. The first way is to load the TSR into memory before you run Windows. The disadvantages to this are: 1) the TSR's memory is not available to Windows; 2) many TSRs will not pop up when the screen is in a graphics display mode, which is always the case when you are running Windows; and 3) some TSRs behave in ways that are incompatible with Windows.

The second way to run a TSR is to open the DOS Prompt icon from the Main group, load the TSR, pop it up, and return to Windows by pressing Alt-Esc. The TSR is now a DOS Prompt icon at the bottom of the desktop. You can click it on whenever you want it. In this configuration the TSR uses Windows resources to remain loaded in the same as any other minimized program.

The third and recommended way to run a TSR is to install it as a non-Windows DOS application the same way you did in the section titled Adding Non-Windows DOS Applications earlier in this chapter. Figure 2.5 showed the Sidekick application installed into the Non-Windows Applications group. Sidekick is a TSR. If you have Sidekick, the Setup program could have installed it for you. If not, install it now to run the next exercise. If you do not have Sidekick, perhaps you have some other TSR you use—you can install it instead.

Open the Non-Windows Applications group and select Sidekick or another TSR to run. Windows will switch to a DOS full-screen session, load Sidekick or the other TSR, and in the case of Sidekick, display the screen shown in Figure 2.55.

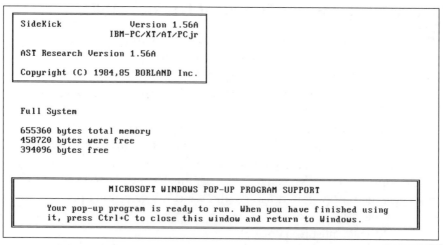

Figure 2.55   *Running a DOS Memory Resident Program*

You can execute the TSR by pressing its hot key. You can return to Windows, keeping the TSR running, by pressing Alt-Esc. If you are finished with the TSR and do not want to commit Windows resources to keeping it resident, pop it down and press Ctrl+C.

Using the Startup Group

Earlier you learned that the Startup Group window is where you put applications that you want executed as soon as you start Windows. Later on you learned how to copy applications from one group window to another. Using those techniques, copy the Clock accessory program from the Accessories group to the Startup group. The Clock accessory will now always start running as a minimized icon, but its icon is different than most in that it changes—it always displays the current time and date. Now, whenever you start Windows, the clock icon will be at the bottom of the desktop, as shown in Figure 2.56.

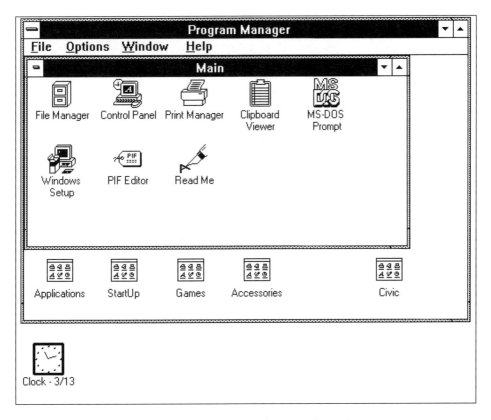

Figure 2.56 *The Clock Accessory Running from the Starting Group*

Summary

With the completion of this chapter, you have learned enough of Windows to use it in many different ways. By understanding the operations of the common user interface and the Program Manager, you are ready to install and use other applications.

Chapter 3 is about the Windows File Manager, an alternative shell to the Program Manager. You can use the File Manager to view the structure of your hard disk's subdirectories and to move, copy, and delete files. You can also use it to execute programs and format and copy diskettes.

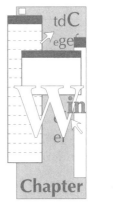

Organizing Data: The File Manager

This chapter is about the File Manager, which is the Windows application that provides a graphical user interface to the DOS file system of directories and files. In this chapter you will learn:

- ◆ Running applications from the File Manager
- ◆ Creating subdirectories
- ◆ Moving, copying, and deleting files
- ◆ Searching for files
- ◆ Printing files
- ◆ File attributes
- ◆ Copying, labeling, and formatting diskettes

In Chapter 2 you learned to organize your applications into functional groups and to install different copies of the same application to operate on different documents, depending upon the nature of the group. This chapter will teach you to organize your document and program files.

The File Manager is the tool that allows you to manage your hard disk system. It provides visibility into the subdirectory structure of your disks, allowing you to navigate from drive to drive and among the subdirectories and files of each drive. It includes commands that move, copy, and delete single files, single subdirectories, selected groups of files, and selected groups of subdirectories. You can rename any file, and any subdirectory. You can search for files, copy diskettes, format diskettes, and view and change the attributes of files. As an alternative to using the Program Manager, you can use the File Manager to execute applications. You can associate document files with applications so that when you select the document or any document with the associated file name extension, the File Manager automatically executes the associated application.

Subdirectories and Files

A DOS disk system consists of files and subdirectories. A DOS disk has the basic structure of a root or originating, or top-level directory with subordinate subdirectories. Any subdirectory can contain files as well as subdirectories of its own. The File Manager provides a windowed user interface for the management of the DOS subdirectory and file structure.

An Analogy: The File Cabinet

Think of your disk system as a file cabinet. The drawers are disk drives. You can remove some of the drawers (floppy disks), while others (hard drives) are fixed in the cabinet. A drawer can contain folders, which are analogous to the subdirectories of the root directory. You can toss paper files into the drawer without placing them in a folder. These paper files are like the files that you can store in the root directory along with the subdirectories. A folder (subdirectory) can contain paper files and other folders.

Some of the paper files in a file cabinet are forms, letters, ledgers, etc. These files are analogous to the document files in a disk subdirectory. Other paper files might be operational procedures, analogous to applications files in your system.

Managing the Files

Just as you can throw things into a file cabinet without order or organization, you can create subdirectories and files on a disk system without much thought to their location and purpose. The File Manager makes your file system easier to examine and provides the tools to move, copy, delete, and rename things in it. The File Manager cannot force you to be orderly, but if you decide that you want to get organized, the File Manager provides the means to do it.

In Chapter 2 you learned to organize your applications into functional groups. You learned to install different copies of the same application to operate on different documents depending upon the nature of the group. This chapter will teach you to organize your document and program files.

If you never pay any attention to where you store your document files, chances are you will always store them in the Windows subdirectory. Recall that in Chapter 2 you built your first Membership Roster Cardfile file—MEMBER.CRD. Because you specified its filename only, Windows assigned it to the current subdirectory for the current drive, which happened to be C:\WINDOWS. That practice is acceptable for these exercises, but continue it into your routine business and your filing system will lack order and organization.

Running the File Manager

The File Manager is a Windows application installed in the Main group. To run it you open the Main group window and select the File Manager. You will see a display similar to that shown in Figure 3.1.

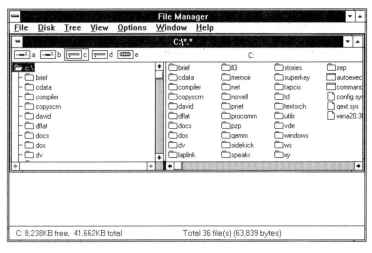

Figure 3.1   *The File Manager Applications Window*

The File Manager display shows the File Manager application window with the Directory document window. This display is the one you will see each time you execute the File Manager. Initially, the disk drive selection will be the drive from which you run Windows. In Figure 3.1 that is the C: drive. Its icon is marked with a box that surrounds it. The directory names in the Directory window will be the names of the directories on your disk system, and so they will, of course, be different from the ones you see in Figure 3.1.

Exiting from the File Manager

You exit from the File Manager the same way you exit from any Windows application. Double-click the Control menu box or press Alt+F4, for example.

The File Manager Window

The File Manager application window has the File Manager menu bar at the top and will contain all of the File Manager's document windows and icons. The Directory window is always present, either as a window or as an icon.

Status Bar

The bottom line of the File Manager has the status bar, which tells you the space available on the selected drive, the drive's total space, and the space on the drive that is occupied by files. You can use the status bar toggle command on the Options menu to turn the status bar on and off. When you have a lot of directory document windows displayed, you might need that extra line at the bottom of the window.

The Directory Window

The Directory window displays the subdirectories and files of the selected drive. The top line of the window has icons that represent the drives installed on your system.

Disk Drives

The floppy disk drives A and B in Figure 3.1 use icons that look like a diskette drive with its diskette slot. The hard disk drives C and D in Figure 3.1 use icons that look like the front of a hard disk drive. The E drive is a RAM disk, and its icon resembles an integrated circuit.

The current disk drive, C in Figure 3.1, is selected. You can change the current drive by clicking a different icon. To change drives with the keyboard, press Tab to select the drive list. The current drive icon will be surrounded by a dotted box to indicate that you are selecting a drive. Use the left and right arrow keys to move the dotted box to the drive you want to choose and press Enter. The File Manager will read the directories for the new drive and display them in the Directory window.

The Tree

The Tree is on the left half of the Directory window. The Tree shows the subdirectories under the root directory of the selected disk. The selected directory is highlighted. In Figure 3.1, the root directory is the selected one.

The Directory

The Directory is on the right half of the Directory window. The Directory shows the files in the selected directory. The files are depicted with different icons depending on the file type. The subdirectory files are shown as folder icons. Executable program files are application icons, such as the AUTOEXEC.BAT icon in Figure 3.1. The application icon resembles a tiny window with a title bar. Document files use the icon that resembles a page with the corner turned down, such as the CONFIG.SYS icon in Figure 3.1.

Selecting Directories

The folder icons in the Tree represent directories on the disk. Observe that in Figure 3.1 the root directory, C:\, is highlighted, indicating that it is the current selected directory. If you click a different directory, it becomes selected. You can use the arrow keys to select a different directory. As you select different directories, the Directory changes to show the files in the selected directory. As you move the highlight down below the directory at the bottom of the Tree, the window scrolls up. Figure 3.2 shows the Windows directory selected.

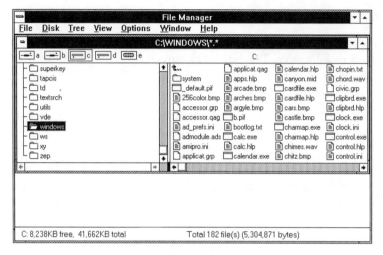

Figure 3.2 *The Windows Directory Selected*

The title bar of the Directory window displays the full DOS path of the current selected directory. This display is convenient when you scroll the window so that the highlighted folder is out of view. You can always determine the selected directory from the window title.

You can open multiple Directory windows by double-clicking the drive icons or selecting a drive icon with the keyboard and pressing Enter. Figure 3.3 shows the File Manager with two Directory windows open.

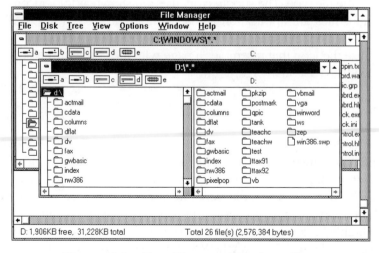

Figure 3.3 *Two Directory Windows Open*

Closing the Directory Window

You cannot close the only open Directory window. If you select its Control menu, you will see that the Close command is not available. If you double click the Control menu box or press Ctrl+F4 in an attempt to close the window, nothing happens. The directory window is an integral part of the File Manager. There is always a current disk drive and always a current directory for that drive, so there is always something for the primary Directory window to display. When you have more than one Directory window open, as in Figure 3.3, you may close one of them.

Displaying Subdirectories

The Tree initially shows only the subdirectories at the first level below the root directory. If a subdirectory itself has subdirectories, you can display them by double-clicking the folder icon or by selecting it and pressing the Plus (+) key (from either the alpha numeric keyboard or the numeric keypad). Figure 3.4 shows the Brief subdirectory expanded to show its subdirectories.

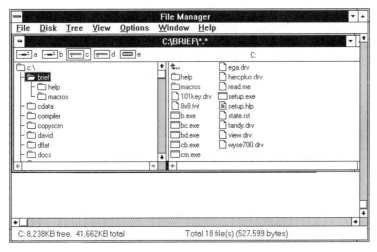

Figure 3.4 *An Expanded Subdirectory*

After you expand a subdirectory you can double-click the folder icon or press the Hyphen key to collapse the subdirectory. If you press the Asterisk key, you will expand the current branch of the tree. If you press Ctrl+Asterisk you will expand every directory and subdirectory in the Tree.

The Tree menu has commands that do these same operations. If you turn on the Indicate Expandable Branches toggle command on the Tree menu, the directories that have subdirectories will be displayed with the + (plus) symbol inside the folder. Directories that have been expanded and can now be collapsed have the – (minus) symbol.

Figure 3.5 shows the Tree fully expanded and maximized to show as much of the tree structure as possible.

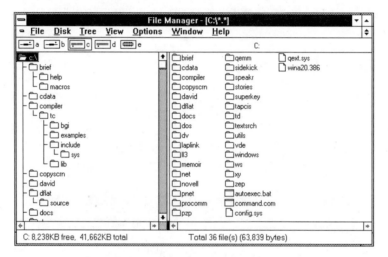

Figure 3.5 *The Tree Fully Expanded*

Maximizing and Minimizing the Directory Window

As you saw in Figure 3.5, if you maximize the Directory window, it fills the File Manager application window's workspace. If you minimize the Directory window, it becomes an icon at the bottom of the File Manager's workspace, as shown in Figure 3.6. Try that now and then restore the Directory window by double-clicking its minimized icon or choosing Restore on its Control menu.

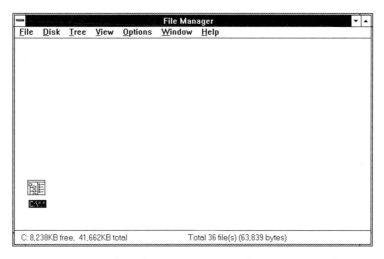

Figure 3.6 *The Directory Window Minimized*

Moving Around the Directory Window

You can move around the Directory window by clicking one of its parts or by pressing Tab. The highlighted area will move between the selected drive icon, the Tree, and the Directory. If you have more than one Directory window open, you can move between them by pressing Ctrl+Tab.

Selecting a File

When the Directory is active, you can move the highlighted file cursor around with the arrow keys or by clicking a selected file. If you press Enter or double-click the selected file to choose the file, one of several things will happen depending on the file type:

Choosing a Subdirectory

If you choose a subdirectory file, indicated by its Folder icon, the File Manager will change to that subdirectory just as if you had selected it on the Tree.

Choosing an Application File

When you choose an application file, indicated by an application icon, Windows executes the application. An application file is one that has the filename extension .EXE, .COM, .BAT, or .PIF. Select the C:\WINDOWS subdirectory. Then choose the file named CALC.EXE. This file is the executable file for the Windows

Calculator accessory program. The Calculator will execute, as shown in Figure 3.7.

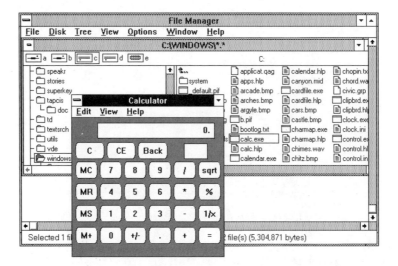

Figure 3.7 *The Calculator Run from the File Manager*

Exit from the Calculator and continue.

Choosing a Document File

A document file is any file that is neither a subdirectory nor an application file. When the document file is represented by the *unruled* document icon, there is nothing that the File Manager can do when you select it. Choose the file named APPLICAT.GRP from the C:\WINDOWS subdirectory. You will see the display shown in Figure 3.8.

Figure 3.8 *Cannot Run Program Dialog Box*

Choosing an Associated Document

Associated document files are files associated with the applications that created them. They are represented by the *ruled* document icon, such as the ARCHES.BMP icon in Figure 3.2. Later you will learn how to make those associations. Some associations are already made when you install Windows. For example, files with the .WRI filename extension associate with Windows Write, files with the .TXT and .INI extensions associate with the Notepad, and files with the .BMP extension associate with Paintbrush. Choose the file named ARCHES.BMP from the C:\WINDOWS subdirectory. Paintbrush executes and you see the window shown in Figure 3.9.

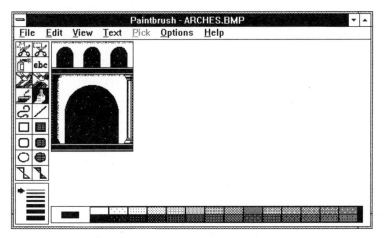

Figure 3.9   *Running an Application from an Associated Document*

Exit from Paintbrush and continue.

Navigating the File Manager

As you have seen, you can move about freely among the Tree, the Directory, and the various drive icons by using the mouse or the keyboard. The File Manager has shortcut keys for most of the movements you can make. Table 3.1 summarizes the shortcut keys that are not also menu commands.

Table 3.1   *File Manager Shortcut Keys*

Key	Move to	Tree	Directory
Home	First entry in the window	x	x
End	Last entry in the window	x	x
Right Arrow	Next lower subdirectory	x	
	File name to the right	x	
Left Arrow	Parent directory	x	
	File name to the left	x	
Up Arrow	Next higher entry	x	x
Down Arrow	Next lower entry	x	x
PgUp	Page backward	x	x
PgDn	Page forward	x	x
A,B,C,...	Entry that begins with...	x	x
Ctrl+UpArrow	Next higher entry, same level	x	
Ctrl+Down Arrow	Next lower entry, same level	x	
Ctrl+A,B,C,...	Select disk drive	x	

Managing File Manager Displays

File Manager can display its information in several ways. These choices appear as menu toggles and commands on the View, Options, and Window menus. You can tell the File Manager to save these settings when you exit so they will be in effect again the next time you execute the File Manager.

View Menu

The File Manager's View menu has commands to control how the File Manager displays data in the directory windows. Figure 3.10 shows the View menu.

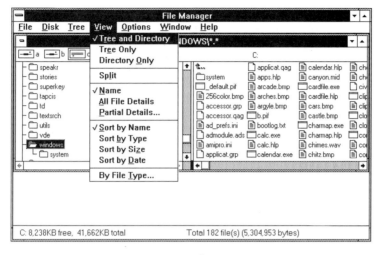

Figure 3.10   *The View Menu*

Tree and/or Directory

The first three commands on the View menu control whether the File Manager will display the Tree only, the Directory only, or both, which is the default. The three commands are mutually exclusive toggle commands. You have already seen the display of both. Figure 3.11 shows the Tree display alone. Figure 3.12 shows the Directory display alone.

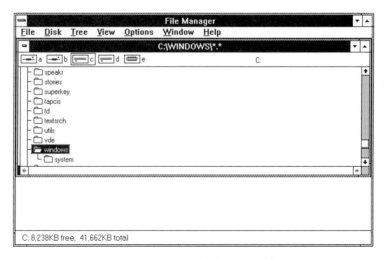

Figure 3.11   *The Tree Display*

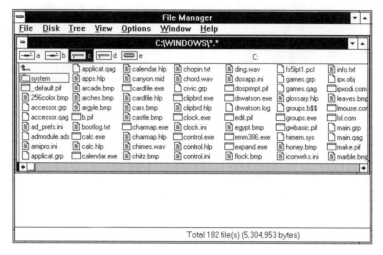

Figure 3.12 *The Directory Display*

Split

The Split command displays a vertical bar between the Tree and the Directory. You move the bar with the mouse or the keyboard. The bar defines where the window will split between the Tree and the Directory. Press Enter or click the left mouse button when the bar is where you want the split to occur. Press Esc to ignore the command.

Name

In its initial configuration the File Manager displays files in the sequence of the filename and with no other data except for the icon. The View menu allows you to modify the settings. The Name command tells File Manager to display the file names only, the default setting. You use the command to return to that display after you have used one of the next two commands.

All File Details

If you choose the All File Details toggle, the File Manager displays not only the files' names but their sizes, the date and time they were last written to, and their DOS file attributes. Figure 3.13 shows the C:\WINDOWS Directory with the All File Details view selected.

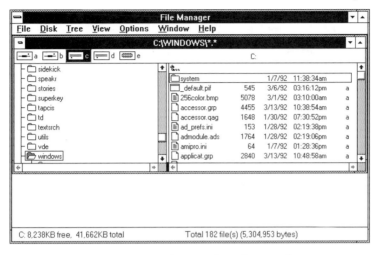

Figure 3.13   *Displaying the File Details View*

Partial Details

If you want to view only a subset of the file details, choose the Partial Details command on the View menu. You will see the Partial Details dialog box shown in Figure 3.14.

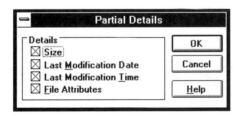

Figure 3.14   *The Partial Details Dialog Box*

Select the check boxes that correspond to the details you want to view. Figure 3.15 shows the Directory with the Size and Last Modification Date details selected.

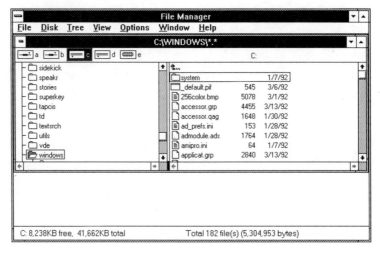

Figure 3.15 *Displaying Selected Details*

Sort By Name, Type, Size or Date

The By Name command tells the File Manager to sort the directory display by the file name, which is the system default, and which is how you are currently viewing it. Use this command to return to the name sort after using one of the next three commands to change the sort sequence. The By Type command sorts the directory display by the file name's three-character extension. Figure 3.16 shows the directory sorted by the file type. You can select from two other sort fields, file size and modification date, to sort the Directory.

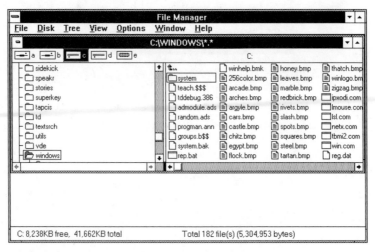

Figure 3.16 *The Directory Sorted by the File Type*

By File Type

Directories can include many different files and file types. The By File Type command allows you to further select which files will display. You can select from the various types to which Windows assigns specific icons and you can specify a DOS file name with wild cards to filter out just the files in which you are interested. Figure 3.17 shows the By File Type dialog box with the specified file name changed to *.INI. Figure 3.18 shows the directory display of .INI files.

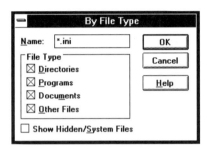

Figure 3.17   *The By File Type Dialog Box*

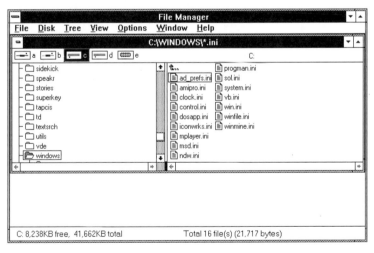

Figure 3.18   *Displaying *.INI File Types*

If you *deselect* any of the File Type check boxes in the By File Type dialog box, the files that correspond will *not* display. Documents are those files that have the ruled document icon, and Other Files are those that have the unruled document icon.

The Show Hidden/System Files check box tells File Manager to display any hidden or system files. DOS hides two system files in the root directory of the boot disk, which is usually C:. Other applications hide files for one reason or another. Figure 3.19 shows the root directory of the C drive with Show Hidden/System Files selected. The IO.SYS and MSDOS.SYS files are the hidden system files that DOS uses. The letters to the right of the file entries are the file's attribute flags. The H means that it is hidden. The S identifies it as a system file. The A is the attribute bit. Another attribute, read-only, would be represented by the letter R. You will learn the meaning of these flags later in this chapter.

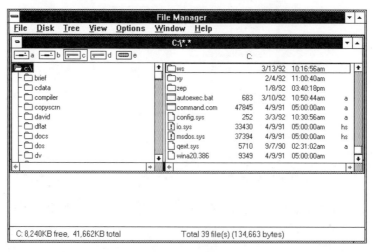

Figure 3.19   *Displaying Hidden and System Files*

Options Menu

Figure 3.20 shows the File Manager's Options menu.

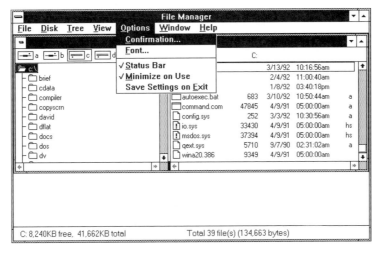

Figure 3.20 *The Options Menu*

Font

The Font command displays the Font dialog box shown in Figure 3.21.

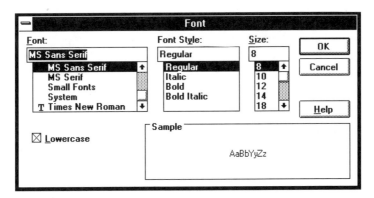

Figure 3.21 *The Font Dialog Box*

You can select the font type, style, and size. The Lowercase check box, which is selected by default, tells the File Manager to display the file information in lower-case. You can deselect the check box so that the displays will be in uppercase.

Status Bar

The Status Bar toggle command on the Options menu will remove the status bar display from the bottom of the Program Manager.

Minimize on Use

The Minimize on Use toggle on the Options menu will cause the Program Manager to minimize itself whenever you run an application from the Directory.

Window Menu

The Window menu has Cascade and Tile commands. These commands work like the corresponding commands in the Program Manager. Figure 3.22 shows the Program Manager with tiled windows.

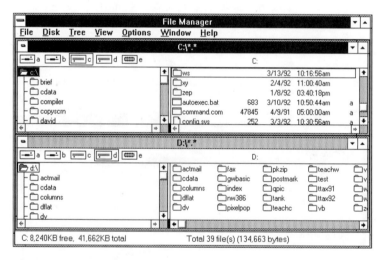

Figure 3.22   *Tiled Windows*

Refresh Command

Under certain circumstances the computer will be working and changing what an active window should be displaying, but the display does not get updated. If you run Windows from a network, you might be looking at the contents of a Directory at the same time another user at another workstation adds or deletes a file.

Your Directory does not change because your copy of Windows does not know that the change took place. The same effect occurs if a program running in the background changes the contents of the directory you are viewing.

The Refresh command on the Window menu refreshes the contents of the current window. Use it whenever you suspect that what you are looking at might not be current.

File Manager Commands

Now that you know how to display and navigate the File Manager, you are ready to move on to the commands that allow you to manage the files on your disk system.

Creating a New Directory

The Create Directory command on the File menu allows you to add directories to one of your disks. The new directory will be subordinate to the selected directory in the Tree.

To add a new directory to the C: drive, highlight the C:\ root directory in the directory tree and then choose the Create Directory command from the File menu. You will see the Create Directory dialog box shown in Figure 3.23.

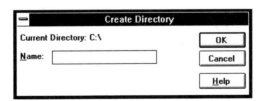

Figure 3.23   *The Create Directory Dialog Box*

Enter the name of the new directory in the Name text box and choose OK. For this exercise enter the name the new directory as Charlie. Figure 3.24 shows that the CHARLIE directory has been added to the C: drive's root directory.

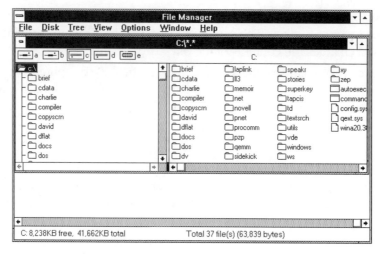

Figure 3.24   *Adding a Subdirectory*

If you specify the name of an existing directory, you will see the File System Error dialog box shown in Figure 3.25.

Figure 3.25   *The Create Directory Error Dialog Box*

To add a subdirectory to an existing directory, select the existing directory in the Tree. Select the CHARLIE directory you just created. Choose Create Directory from the File menu. Enter the name Bobbie and choose OK. You can see in Figure 3.26 that the BOBBIE subdirectory file entry is added to the C:\CHARLIE directory window.

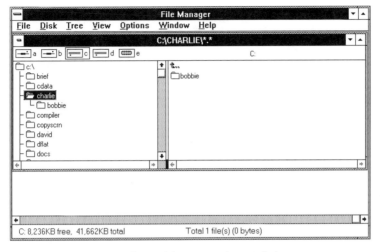

Figure 3.26 *Adding Another Subdirectory*

Moving and Copying

You can move or copy a file from one subdirectory to another and from one drive to another. The procedures differ slightly.

Moving Files on the Same Drive

Open a second Directory window for the C: drive by double-clicking the drive's icon or by selecting it and pressing Enter. Select the C:\DOS directory in one Directory window and the C:\CHARLIE directory in the other. Move the Directory windows around so you have easy access to the workspace of both windows. Figure 3.27 shows how this might display.

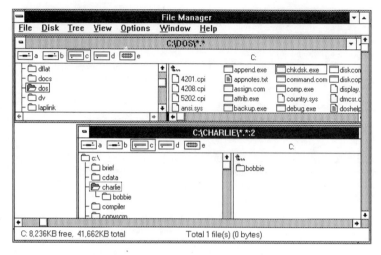

Figure 3.27 *Ready to Move a File*

To move a file with the mouse, click the filename at its origin and drag the icon to the destination Directory window. Do not drag the icon to another icon in the destination Directory window. Drag the icon to an empty part of the window. If the window is filled with file names, drag the icon to the title bar of the destination window.

Move CHKDSK.EXE from the C:\DOS subdirectory to the C:\CHARLIE subdirectory by using the procedure just described. You will see the Confirm Mouse Operation dialog box shown in Figure 3.28. Choose Yes, and the CHKDSK.EXE file moves from the C:\DOS directory to the C:\CHARLIE directory. Note that this is a move operation. The file no longer exists in its original subdirectory.

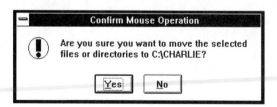

Figure 3.28 *The Confirm Mouse Operation Dialog Box: Confirming a Move*

To move a file using the keyboard, select the file in its original directory window and use the Move command on the File Manager's File menu. Highlight the COMP.EXE file in the C:\DOS directory and choose the Move command. You will see the Move dialog box shown in Figure 3.29.

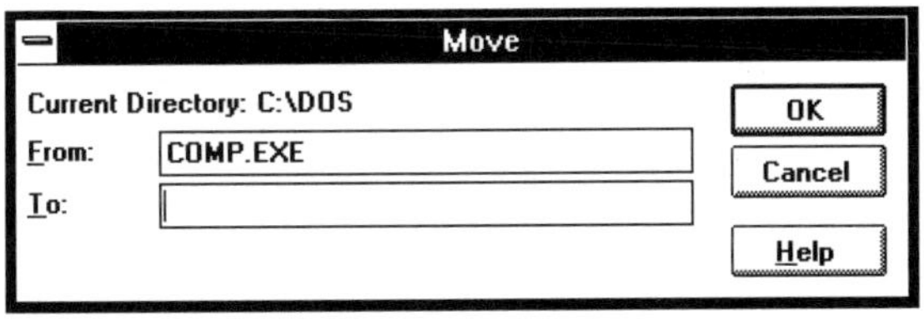

Move

Current Directory: C:\DOS

Erom: COMP.EXE

To:

OK

Cancel

Help

Figure 3.29 *The Move Dialog Box*

You must enter the full DOS path of the directory you want to move the file to. Enter c:\charlie, (it doesn't matter if you enter the name in the upper- or lower-case; Windows reads it as the same thing), and choose OK to complete the move.

Copying Files on the Same Drive

You do not really want to delete the CHKDSK.EXE and COMP.EXE files from the C:\DOS subdirectory, but the Move command did just that. Now you must copy the files from the C:\CHARLIE subdirectory back to their original location. To copy files with the mouse, you use the same drag technique you used to move the files, but with the Ctrl key held down.

Use the Ctrl+mouse technique to copy the CHKDSK.EXE file back into the C:\DOS directory. Hold the Ctrl key down and click on the CHKDSK.EXE file. Drag the icon into the destination C:\DOS directory. Make sure that you drag it to a blank spot and that no file in the destination directory window is outlined by a box as a result of your drag. If the window is filled with file names, drag the icon to the title bar of the destination window.

Release the mouse button and then the Ctrl key. You will see the Confirm Mouse Operation dialog box shown in Figure 3.30. Select Yes to complete the copy.

Figure 3.30 *The Confirm Mouse Operation Dialog Box: Confirming a Copy*

To copy a file with the keyboard you use the same procedure as you did to move a file, but using the Copy command from the File menu instead of the Move command. Use that approach to copy the COMP.COM file from the C:\CHARLIE directory back into the C:\DOS directory.

Moving and Copying to the Tree

You can move or copy a file by dragging it to a directory entry on the Tree as well. When you drag the icon into the Tree, the directory icon that is closest to the file icon you are dragging will be highlighted with a box to indicate that is the potential destination. When you release the mouse button, the move and copy procedures proceed as described above.

Moving and Copying Between Drives

Earlier you learned how to view the Directory windows of two different disk drives. To move or copy files from one drive to another, you must open directory windows for the source and destination drives.

The procedures for moving and copying between drives are the same as those for moving and copying between directories on the same drive, except that they are reversed if you are using the mouse. You hold the Alt key down for moving and hold no key for copying. The idea is that you *move* files on the same disk more frequently than you copy them, and that you *copy* files from one disk to another more frequently than you move them; the less routine operation in both cases requires that you hold down a key.

Select the C:\CHARLIE directory in the Tree, close any other Directory windows that are open, and put a formatted diskette into A:. Next, open a second Directory window for the A: drive, and select its A:\ root directory. Move the Directory windows around so you can see most of both of them. Figure 3.31 shows the File Manager layout with both Directory windows in view.

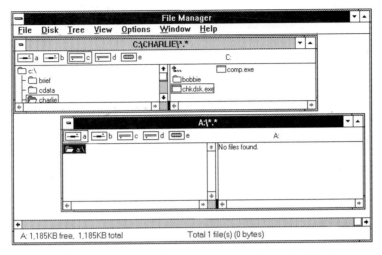

Figure 3.31 *Both Directory Windows in View*

You move and copy between disks with the keyboard the same way you move and copy between directories on the same drive with the keyboard, so this exercise will deal with the mouse only.

To *copy* the CHKDSK.EXE file from the C:\CHARLIE directory to the A:\ directory, click and drag the file from one to the other. Choose the Yes command button on the Confirm Mouse Operation dialog box, and the copy takes place.

To *move* the COMP.EXE file from the C:\CHARLIE directory to the A:\ directory, hold down the Alt key, click and drag the COMP.EXE icon, release the mouse key first, then the Alt key. Choose the Yes command button on the Confirm Mouse Operation dialog box, and the move takes place.

Whenever you move or copy, a dialog box such as the one shown in Figure 3.32 displays. It goes away when the operation is completed. For short copies between fast disk drives, the dialog box is a brief flash; you hardly realize it was there. But the dialog box is useful for long copies, with big files, or wherever floppy diskettes are involved, or for copying of subdirectories or groups of files, which you will learn about soon. If you realize that you made a mistake after the operation begins, you can choose the Cancel button to stop the move or copy.

Figure 3.32 *Moving or Copying*

After you have finished this exercise, the screen looks like Figure 3.33.

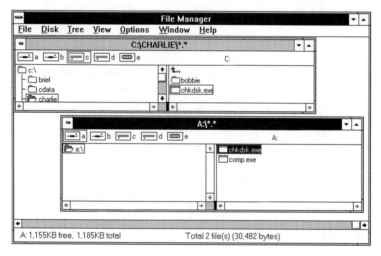

Figure 3.33 *Move Completed*

Copying to an Icon

You can move or copy a file to an icon in the destination Directory. Drag the COMP.EXE file from the A:\ Directory window to the BOBBIE folder icon in the C:\CHARLIE Directory window. Release the mouse button when the BOBBIE folder icon is outlined by a box. The screen will display the usual Confirm Mouse Operation dialog box. Choose Yes to complete the copy. If you now select the BOBBIE subdirectory, you will see that the COMP.EXE file has been copied there.

Moving and Copying Directories

You move and copy directories by using the same procedures as for moving and copying files. When you move or copy a directory, three things happen. First, a new directory with the same name is created at the destination. Second, all the files in the directory are moved or copied. Third, you move or copy any subdirectories below the one you have addressed as well as all their files.

Starting from Figure 3.33, use one of the copy procedures to copy the BOBBIE directory from the C:\CHARLIE Directory window to the A:\ Directory window.

Mark a Group of Files

You can mark groups of files to be moved, copied, or deleted. You will learn about deleting later. The files can be contiguous or scattered, but a group is always contained within the same directory window.

Organize the File Manager application window so that there are Directory windows for the C:\DOS and A:\ directories, moving and sizing them so you can get a good look at both. Figure 3.34 shows how this might look.

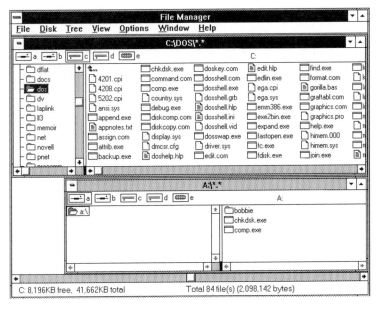

Figure 3.34 *Working with Two Drives*

To mark a group of adjacent files with the mouse, click on the first one, move the mouse to the last one and hold the Shift key down to click the last one. Mark several files in the C:\DOS directory window this way. Observe that you can have only one group of files marked in this manner.

To mark non-adjacent files and groups of files with the mouse, hold the Ctrl key down while you click each one. You can also hold down Shift and Ctrl to mark several non-adjacent groups of adjacent files. Use the C:\DOS Directory window to practice marking groups with the mouse.

To mark a group of adjacent files with the keyboard, use the cursor keys or the first letter of the first file to select the first file in the group. Hold the Shift key down while you move to the last file in the group.

To mark a group of non-adjacent files with the keyboard, move the cursor to the first one and press Shift+F8. A blinking dotted outline will surround the se-lected file. Use the arrow keys to move the blinking outline to the next file you want and press the Spacebar to select it. You can also describe an adjacent group in this mode by moving from the selected first file to the last file in the group while holding the Shift key down. Once again, practice in the C:\DOS directory window.

Figure 3.35 shows a group of non-adjacent files marked in the C:\DOS direc-tory window.

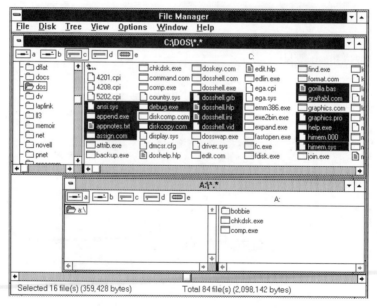

Figure 3.35 *Selecting Non-adjacent Files*

Moving and Copying Groups

You move and copy groups of files by using the same procedures for moving and copying single files. Start the mouse drag from any of the marked file names.

Note that the icon for a group resembles a stack of pages rather than the icon being dragged.

A group can include files and subdirectories. The Moving or Copying dialog boxes that display during moves and copies are similar to the one in Figure 3.32. The file names change as each file in the marked group is moved or copied.

Deleting

You can delete a file, a directory, or a group of files by first marking them and then choosing Delete from the File menu or pressing Del. Mark several files in the A:\ directory and choose Delete. You will see the Delete dialog box shown in Figure 3.36.

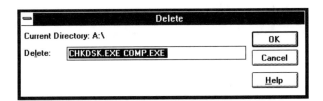

Figure 3.36   *The Delete Dialog Box*

The text in the Delete text box in Figure 3.36 is a list of the files in the group. You can move the cursor to the home position and horizontally scroll the text to read the entire list.

When you choose OK to verify that the list is correct, File Manager displays the dialog box shown in Figure 3.37, once for each file in the list. You may choose the Yes command button to delete the file or the No command to bypass deleting the current file and proceed to the next. If you choose the Cancel command button, the File Manager stops deleting altogether. You can choose the Yes to All command to tell File Manager to delete all the files without asking for further confirmation.

Figure 3.37   *Deleting Each File from a List*

Confirmation

The business of confirming the delete of every file in a list can be annoying and time-consuming, particularly when the list is long or includes a directory or two. You can tell the File Manager not to pester you to confirm every delete if you are sure that you will always know what you are doing. The Confirmation command on the Options menu displays the Confirmation dialog box shown in Figure 3.38.

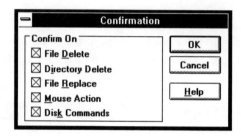

Figure 3.38 *The Confirmation Dialog Box*

The check boxes in the Confirmation dialog box allow you to turn off the confirmation requests for deletes of files, deletes of subdirectories, when a move or copy is going to replace an existing file, the Confirm Mouse Operation dialog boxes for moving and copying, and certain disk operations. Think carefully about eliminating confirmation for when a file is about to be replaced, because unlike the other kinds of file deletion, it can be very hard to predict the conditions under which you might accidently replace a file you wanted to keep.

If you change the settings in the Confirmation dialog box, you can make those changes permanent when you exit from the File Manager by choosing the Save Settings on Exit toggle command on the Options menu.

Renaming

Sometimes you want to change the name of a file, directory or group. The Rename command on the File menu allows you to do these operations.

Renaming Files and Directories

You can rename a file by selecting it and then choosing the Rename command from the File menu. You will see the Rename dialog box shown in Figure 3.39. You enter the new name of the file in the To: field. If you specify the name of an existing file in the same directory, you will see the dialog box shown in Figure 3.40, unless you have turned off the confirmation of file replacements with the Option menu's Confirmation command. Renaming a directory is the same as renaming a file.

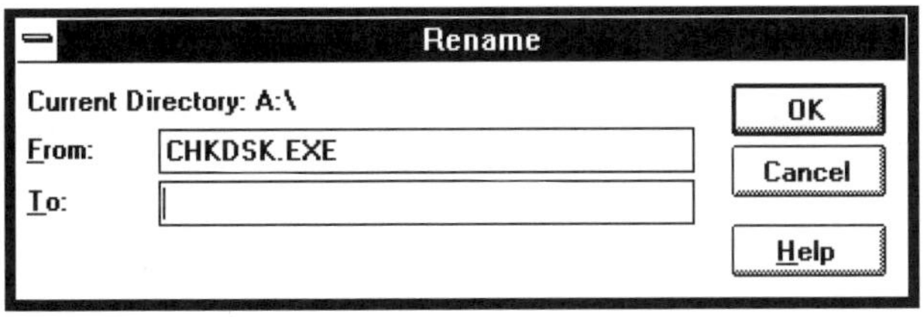

Figure 3.39   *The Rename Dialog Box*

Figure 3.40 *Renaming to an Existing Name*

Renaming Groups

If you mark a group and specify a complete file name in the To: field of the Rename dialog box, the File Manager will not perform the rename operation. There is a proper way to rename groups of files. Suppose you wanted to change the file extensions of several of the files. You can mark the group and enter *.SAV, for example, in the To: field of the Rename dialog box. Figure 3.41 illustrates this operation.

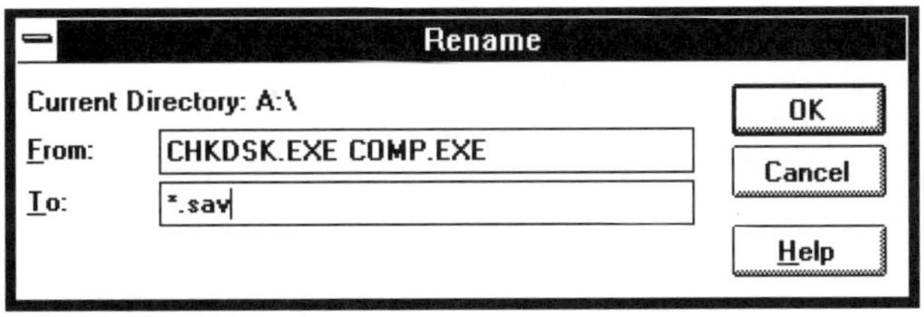

Figure 3.41   *Renaming a Group of Files*

Searching for Files

The File Manager will help you find files on your hard disk. The Search command on the Files menu allows you to search for files that match a file name specification. Suppose you wanted to find all the files that have the extension .TXT. Figure 3.42 shows the Search dialog box where you would specify this information.

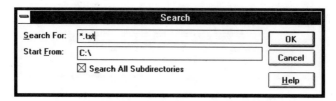

Figure 3.42 *The Search Dialog Box*

You can use DOS file name wild cards in the Search For: field of the Search dialog box. The Search All Subdirectories check box tells the File Manager to search the entire current disk. If you turn the check box off, it searches only the current directory and its subdirectories.

The search operation builds a Search Results window with a list of the files that match the search criteria. Figure 3.43 shows the Search Results window that the *.TXT search created. This window is like the Directory in all respects except one. You cannot move or copy files to it from other directory windows. Other than that, all the commands that work with the Directory work with the Search Results window.

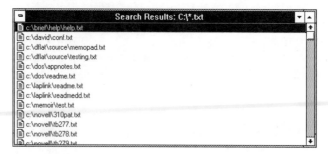

Figure 3.43 *The Search Results Window*

There can be only one Search Results window. If you do a second search without closing a prior Search Results window, the search results reuse the existing window.

Printing Files

The Print command on the File Manager's File menu allows you to print document files that are associated with applications. Recall that you can launch an application from the File Manager by choosing the icon of a document file that is associated with that application. You can likewise print an associated document file by using the Print command on the File menu. When you choose the Print command, the currently selected file name appears in the Print dialog box, as shown in Figure 3.44.

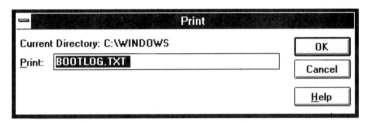

Figure 3.44   *The Print Dialog Box*

You can enter a different file name along with its path if the file named in the Print dialog box is not the one you want. Choose OK. If the file is other than text, you will see the Print dialog box shown in Figure 3.45. Make the changes to the Print dialog box to reflect the way you want the document to be printed and choose OK.

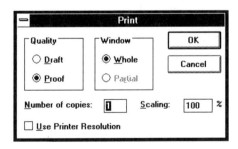

Figure 3.45   *Trying to Print a Non-Text File*

Attributes

Every file has four attributes associated with it—read-only, hidden, system, and archive. They are either on or off. The archive and system attributes are usually maintained by DOS and have no meaning to applications. A file with the system attribute belongs to DOS itself. DOS sets the archive attribute whenever an application writes to a file. This attribute allows backup utility programs, such as DOS's own BACKUP, to determine that a file has changed since the last backup operation. The BACKUP program sets the archive attribute off when it backs up a file. If a file's archive attribute is still off when the next BACKUP executes, the program knows that the file has not changed and that it does not need to back the file up.

The read-only and hidden attributes are usually maintained by applications. When a file has the read-only attribute set to on, you can view the file but you cannot modify or delete it. When a file has the hidden attribute set to on, you do not see the file in a directory window unless you have selected Show Hidden/System Files on the Include dialog box from the View menu.

Changing the Attributes of a File

With a file selected in the Directory, choose the Properties command on the File menu. You will see the Properties dialog box shown in Figure 3.46.

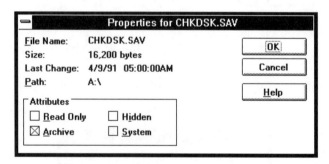

Figure 3.46 *The Properties Dialog Box*

The file attributes are represented by check boxes in the Properties dialog box. The ones that are selected are the attributes that the file currently has. You can change any of these attributes by selecting the corresponding check box. When you choose OK, the attributes take effect. If you select Hidden, for example, the file disappears from the Directory unless you have selected Show Hidden/System Files on the By File Type dialog box in the Options menu.

Changing the Attributes of a Group

Assume that you renamed the group of files to *.SAV in the A:\ directory window as discussed above. Recall the window, choose File Details on the View menu, and mark the .SAV files as a group. Choose the Properties command from the File menu. You will see the display shown in Figure 3.47.

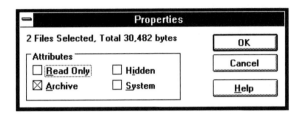

Figure 3.47   *The Properties Dialog Box*

Select the Hidden check box in the Properties dialog box and then choose OK. The A:\ Directory window will appear as shown in Figure 3.48. The file group is no longer visible because you set the hidden attribute bit for all the files in the group.

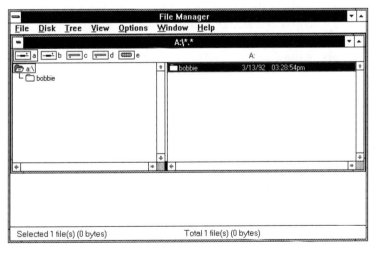

Figure 3.48   *The A:\ Directory Window*

Now select Show Hidden/System Files on the By File Type dialog box from the View menu. The files come into view, as shown in Figure 3.49. Observe that they now have the hidden attribute.

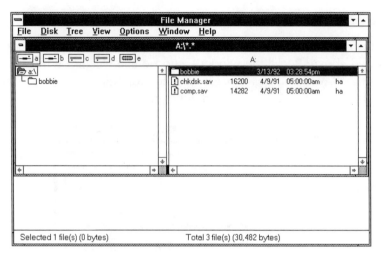

Figure 3.49   *Viewing Hidden Files*

Disk Operations

The File Manager Disk menu provides a number of disk and diskette utility operations. You can copy, label, and format diskettes, and you can build a DOS-bootable system diskette. There are some network disk operations as well, and you will learn about them in Chapter 11.

Copying Diskettes

The Copy Disk command on the Disk menu allows you to copy a diskette. When you choose the command, you see the dialog box shown in Figure 3.50.

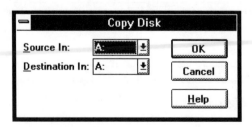

Figure 3.50 *The Copy Disk Dialog Box*

Select the source and destination diskette drives from the two drop-down list boxes. Choose OK. You will see the Confirm Copy Disk dialog box shown in Figure 3.51. Confirm the copy and the Program Manager will perform it.

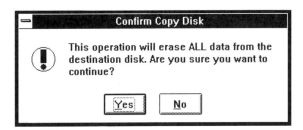

Figure 3.51 *The Confirm Copy Disk Dialog Box*

You can specify that you want to copy to the same disk drive—perhaps you have only one drive of the format you want to copy to. You will be prompted to insert the destination disk when it is needed.

Labeling Disks

Hard disks and floppy diskettes can have names, called *labels* in DOS parlance. You can establish or change the label on the currently selected disk by using the Label Disk command on the Disk menu. You will see the Label Disk dialog box shown in Figure 3.52.

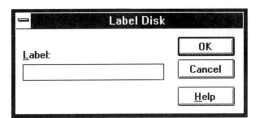

Figure 3.52 *The Label Disk Dialog Box*

If the disk already has a label, the Label field will be filled in. You can fill in a new one, or change the existing one by filling in the Label field yourself. Choose OK to add the label to the disk. The next time you look at the Directory for a disk you've labeled you will see the label to the right of the drive and path just above the Directory display.

Formatting Diskettes

Before you can use a diskette out of the box (unless you bought *preformatted* diskettes) you must format it. The Format Disk command on the File menu is for this purpose. Figure 3.53 is the Format Diskette dialog box that you see when you choose the command.

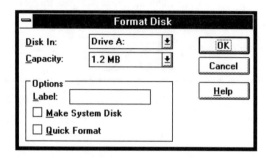

Figure 3.53   *The Format Disk Dialog Box*

Select the drive to format from the Disk In drop-down list box and the diskette format from the Capacity drop-down list box. A high-density 5.25-inch diskette drive can format a 1.2Mb high-density diskette or a 360K (often called double-density) diskette. A high-density 3.5-inch diskette drive can format a 1.44Mb high-density diskette or a 720K (double-density) diskette. If you select High Capacity on the dialog box for the 3.5-inch drive and the diskette is not a 1.44Mb diskette, you will get an error message. If you select High Capacity on the dialog box for the 5.25-inch drive and the diskette is not a 1.2Mb diskette, the format operation will proceed, but at a slow rate with a lot of retries. Usually the format will fail before it completes.

You can enter a label into the Label field, and select the Make System Disk check box to make a DOS-bootable disk (described below), and select the Quick Format check box, which will do a quick format if the diskette has already been formatted once. Choose OK to begin formatting.

Inasmuch as formatting wipes all data from a diskette, the File Manager asks you to verify your intentions with the dialog box shown in Figure 3.54. Choose Yes to continue.

Figure 3.54 *The Confirm Format Disk Dialog Box*

While the format operation is running, the dialog box shown in Figure 3.55 displays. You can choose Cancel at any time to stop the operation.

Figure 3.55 *Formatting a Diskette*

When the format is complete, you will see the Format Complete dialog box shown in Figure 3.56. Choose Yes to format another diskette. Choose No to return to the File Manager.

Figure 3.56 *The Format Complete Dialog Box*

Making System Diskettes

Some diskettes have DOS stored on them and you can use them to boot DOS. This format supports those computers, usually much older ones, that do not boot from a hard disk. Some network workstations use the shared hard disk of the file server to store information, but boot from DOS on a diskette. The Make System Disk command on the Disk menu allows you to copy the necessary DOS files to a diskette to make it into a DOS-bootable diskette. When you choose the command, you see the dialog box shown in Figure 3.57.

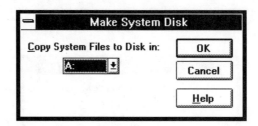

Figure 3.57   *The Make System Disk Dialog Box*

Select the drive you want to make into a system diskette from the drop-down list box on the dialog box and choose OK. The dialog box shown in Figure 3.58 displays while the File Manager copies the DOS system files to the diskette.

Figure 3.58   *Making a System Disk*

Running Applications from the File Manager

In Chapter 2 you learned to use the Program Manager to execute programs from defined groups of applications. The File Manager offers additional ways to run programs. Any file with an application icon is a program that you can execute. The application icon resembles a window with a title bar across it. The File Manager offers several ways to start an application that has this icon.

Some applications are Windows applications and others are not. Windows knows how to execute each one, so the effect of executing from the File Manager is the same as if you had installed the application in a Program Manager group and executed it from there.

There are two reasons for using the File Manager to execute an application. First, you might not use the program often enough to want to keep it in a Program Manager group. Second, you might want to execute the application for a specific type of document file but not always the same document. The File Manager allows you to associate document file types with specific applications.

Choosing Executable Files

You can execute an application just by choosing its file name from the Directory. Open a Directory window for the C:\WINDOWS directory. Double-click the CARDFILE.EXE file or move the highlight cursor to it and press Enter. The Cardfile application executes. Terminate the Cardfile application and continue.

Select one of the .PIF files the same way to execute the application with the parameters listed in the .PIF file. Terminate the application and continue. You will learn how to use the PIF Editor to create and modify PIF files for non-Windows DOS applications in Chapter 11.

You can also execute .COM and .BAT files from the File Manager with this procedure.

The Run Command

The File Manager has a Run command on the File menu. This command works exactly like the Program Manager's Run command detailed in Chapter 2.

Dragging a Document to an Application

You can click on a document file and drag it to an application. This action runs the application with the document file as its input, just as if you had entered the application's name and the document file's name into the Run command.

Open a Directory window to display the C:\ directory and another one displaying the C:\WINDOWS directory. Move the two Directory windows around so that you can see the AUTOEXEC.BAT file in the C:\ directory and the NOTEPAD.EXE file in the C:\WINDOWS directory. Drag the AUTOEXEC.BAT document file's icon to the NOTEPAD.EXE application file. You will see the display shown in Figure 3.59.

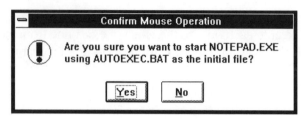

Figure 3.59   *Dragging a Document to an Application*

When you choose Yes, the Notepad executes with AUTOEXEC.BAT as its document file. Terminate the Notepad application and continue.

Associating Applications and Documents

You can tell the File Manager that document files with a particular extension are associated with an application. Then, whenever you choose a file with that extension, the File Manager executes the application with the document file as the input.

Some document file extensions are associated with applications by default when you install the application. Table 3.2 shows those associations.

Table 3.2   *Document to Application Associations*

Document Extension	Application	Application File Name
.BMP	Paintbrush	PBRUSH.EXE.
.CRD	Cardfile	CARDFILE.EXE
.INI	Notepad	NOTEPAD.EXE
.PCX	Paintbrush	PBRUSH.EXE
.REC	Recorder	RECORDER.EXE
.TXT	Notepad	NOTEPAD.EXE
.WRI	Write	WRITE.EXE

You learned earlier in this chapter that when you choose ARCHES.BMP, the Paintbrush application executed with ARCHES.BMP as its document file.

You can make your own associations of documents to applications. For example, the DOS QBasic program (included with DOS 5.0) uses files with the .BAS extension. DOS includes a sample QBasic program called GORILLA.BAS. Many shareware and public domain programs are .BAS files.

Open a Directory window for C:\DOS and select the GORILLA.BAS file. Then choose the Associate command from the File menu. You will see the Associate dialog box, as shown in Figure 3.60.

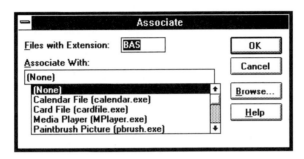

Figure 3.60 *The Associate Dialog Box*

By selecting the GORILLA.BAS program file you told the Associate command what kind of files you want to associate with QBasic: fill in the path and name of the QBasic interpreter (program) file and choose OK, or you can use the Browse command to find it. QBasic is in the C:\DOS subdirectory with a file name of QBASIC.EXE. With the dialog box filled out, choose OK. The GORILLA.BAS file now has an Associated Document icon, which means that when you choose it, you will run an application, in this case, Qbasic. If you double-click the file now, you will run the QBasic application with GORILLA.BAS as the input file.

File Manager as Default Shell

As you learned in Chapters 1 and 2, Windows begins in the Program Manager. Some users find themselves always executing the File Manager as the first thing they do. They would prefer that Windows begins that way. However, you can modify the Windows startup procedure to begin with any program you want, although it should probably begin with some kind of program that allows you to run other programs and look at your files. Such a program is called a *shell* program and the Program Manager and File Manager are both shell programs.

When Windows begins running it reads a file called SYSTEM.INI to load a number of operating parameters. One of those parameters specifies the name of the shell program. SYSTEM.INI is a text file, and you can change it from the Notepad. Figure 3.61 shows the file loaded into the Notepad.

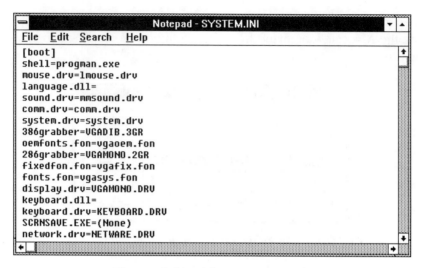

Figure 3.61   *The System.INI File*

Because .INI files are associated with the Notepad all you need to do to get the file is to double-click it. You are interested in the second line of text in Figure 3.61. To cause Windows to load the File Manager as the shell, change the line to read:

```
shell=winfile.exe
```

With the line changed to the new value, save the file by choosing the Save command on the Notepad's File menu. Exit from Windows and reload it. Windows will start running in the File Manager. You can still use the task list, which is not a part of the Program Manager but is an integral part of the Windows multitasking executive.

Summary

With a sound understanding of Program Manager and File Manager, you are ready to learn how Windows supports the exchange of data between applications with the Clipboard. Chapter 4 introduces the Clipboard and teaches you the many ways you can use it with Windows and DOS programs.

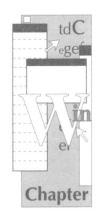

The Clipboard

This chapter is about the Windows clipboard, the method by which you move data between applications. In this chapter you will learn:

- ◆ Cutting and copying text and graphics data into the Clipboard
- ◆ Pasting text and graphics data from the Clipboard into an application
- ◆ Using the Clipboard with non-Windows DOS applications
- ◆ Viewing the contents of the Clipboard
- ◆ Saving into and loading from Clipboard files

The Clipboard is an integral part of the multi-program Windows environment. It is a method by which applications exchange text and graphics data under your control. The Clipboard is a temporary data storage facility. It can contain text or graphics. You can put data from an application into the Clipboard, and you can write data from the Clipboard into an application.

How The Clipboard Works

To transfer data from one program to another, you tell the sending program to write the data to the Clipboard, then you tell the receiving program to read the data from the Clipboard. The Clipboard remembers its contents until you delete them, copy other data to the Clipboard, or exit from Windows.

It helps to examine the circumstances under which you would want to transfer data from one application to another. Consider these examples.

Suppose that you are using the Notepad to write a memo to one of your civic organization's members. You can call up the Cardfile record for that member, copy the member's name and address into the Clipboard, return to the Notepad, and paste the name and address from the Clipboard into the memo.

Or you may want to prepare graphics illustrations in one program, Paintbrush for example, and integrate them into a document created with your word processor. The Clipboard offers a way to do that.

Or you might want to include the rows and columns of a spreadsheet in a report. By using the Clipboard, you can move the required information from the spreadsheet program into your word processor document, even if the two programs use incompatible file formats.

N O T E

Some applications programs use the Clipboard to exchange data without your intervention. You should be aware of this possibility so that you will not be surprised if you find that every now and then the Clipboard contains data other than what you expected.

Sending data to the Clipboard is called *cutting* and *copying*. An application that can cut or copy first marks the block of text or graphics to be cut or copied. *Cutting* implies that the data block is deleted from the sending application when it is transferred to the Clipboard. *Copying* implies that the sending application retains the data block, but transfers a copy of it to the Clipboard.

The Clipboard holds either text or graphics images at any one time. The format depends on the sending application. If the sending application is a graphics application such as Paintbrush, the Clipboard's contents will be a graphics image. If the sending application is a text application such as Notepad, the Clipboard's contents will be text.

Taking data from the Clipboard and putting it into an application is called *pasting*. You paste text data from the Clipboard into a program that processes text, and you paste graphics data from the Clipboard into a program that processes graphics. A text-only application such as the Notepad cannot paste graphics data from the Clipboard. If the Clipboard contains graphics data, it appears to be empty to a text-only application. Likewise a graphics-only application cannot paste text data from the Clipboard.

Some applications can process both text and graphics. Windows Write is such an application. If the Clipboard contains text, Write pastes text into the document. If the Clipboard contains graphics, Write pastes graphics into the document. When cutting or copying from Write, you first mark a block of data—but it must be all text or all graphics. The format of the data that you mark determines the format that the Clipboard receives.

Do not confuse the text you see in some Paintbrush images with the Clipboard's concept of text versus graphics. Text in a graphics-only application is really a graphics representation of the letters and numbers. Even though it appears to be text on the screen, it is internally represented as a graphics image.

N O T E

Non-Windows DOS applications can exchange only text with the Clipboard. If the DOS application runs in a window—386 enhanced mode only—you can transfer selected blocks of text to the Clipboard. If the application runs full-screen, you must transfer the entire screen to the Clipboard. Pasting into a DOS application works only with unformatted text. The paste operation transmits the data as if the Clipboard was typing into the application.

The Clipboard Viewer is a Windows application with an icon in the Main group. With it you can view the Clipboard's contents, save the current Clipboard to a file, and load a previously saved Clipboard file.

For the exercises that follow, you will use some of the applications that you have already seen. Although the details of these applications come later in the book, you will use subsets of their features to learn about the Clipboard. Other exercises will use the Wordstar non-Windows DOS application discussed earlier. If you do not have this program, you can follow along in the book.

Sending Applications Data to the Clipboard

You use the Cut or Copy commands from the File menus of Windows applications to send data to the Clipboard. You use other means to send data from non-Windows DOS applications. The procedures for sending text and graphics are similar.

Sending Text to the Clipboard from a Windows Application

Begin by executing the Notepad from the Accessories Group. Type some text into the Notepad, as shown in Figure 4.1. Type any text you want, not necessarily the text in the figure. You might want to set the Word Wrap toggle command to on in the Notepad's Edit menu.

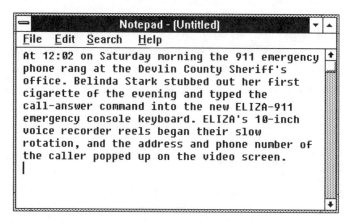

Figure 4.1 *The Notepad with Some Text*

To send text to the Clipboard, you must mark it. To mark text with the mouse, move the cursor to the first character of the block, hold down the left mouse button, and drag the cursor to the last character of the block. As you move the mouse, the text highlights the marked block. Release the mouse button when the text block is marked properly. If you start to mark another block, the first block marking is cleared.

To mark text with the keyboard, move the keyboard cursor to the first character of the block. Hold the Shift key down and move the cursor with the arrow keys. As you move the cursor, the text highlights the marked block. You can release the Shift key and move the cursor to clear the marking of a block. Figure 4.2 shows the Notepad with a marked block.

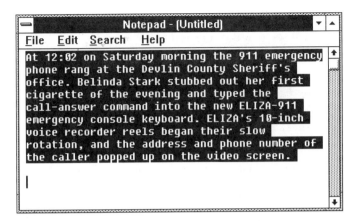

Figure 4.2   *A Marked Block of Text*

To copy the marked block to the Clipboard, choose the Copy command from the Notepad's Edit menu, shown in Figure 4.3.

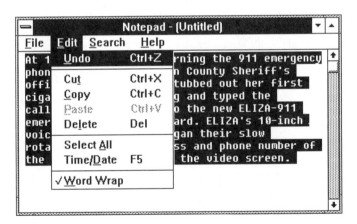

Figure 4.3   *Notepad's Edit Menu*

The Cut command has the same effect as the Copy command except that Cut deletes the marked block from the Notepad when it transfers the text to the Clipboard. The Cut and Copy commands are displayed in a bold font on the menu, indicating that they are available. If no block was marked, the commands would not be available. You can use the Ctrl+C or Ctrl+X accelerator keys to execute the Copy and Cut commands without opening the menu.

If you execute the Clipboard Viewer application from the Program Manager's Main group, you will see that the selected text is now in the Clipboard, as shown in Figure 4.4.

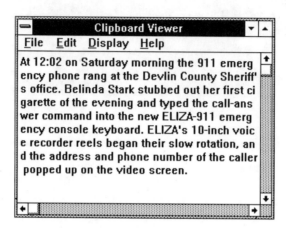

Figure 4.4   *Text in the Clipboard*

Observe that the text is unformatted and words break at the right margin. The Clipboard is a text repository, not a text editor or formatter.

Sending Graphics to the Clipboard from a Windows Application

Begin by executing Paintbrush from the Accessories group. Paintbrush is a graphics application. To send graphics data to the Clipboard, you must have a picture in the Paintbrush's workspace. Use the Open command on the File menu to find a graphics data file. Windows includes a number of .BMP files in the C:\WINDOWS subdirectory that are compatible with Paintbrush. Open the file named WINLOGO.BMP and you will see the display shown in Figure 4.5.

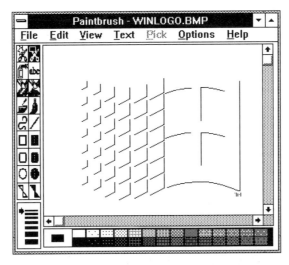

Figure 4.5   *The Paintbrush with Some Graphics*

To transfer graphics data to the Clipboard you must mark a block. To mark a graphics block, click the rightmost scissors icon in the vertical toolbar at the left side of the Paintbrush window. Then move the mouse cursor to one corner of the block and drag the cursor to the opposite corner. The display shows a dotted rectangle to describe the block. When you have the block where you want it, release the mouse button. If you don't like the way the block turned out, click the mouse button outside of the block and start over. Figure 4.6 shows the picture with part of the display marked as a graphics block.

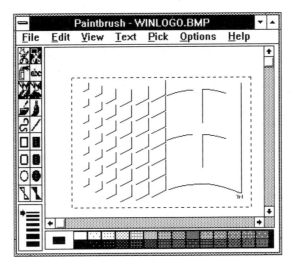

Figure 4.6   *A Graphics Block Marked*

With the graphics block marked, choose Copy from the Edit menu or press Ctrl+C. If you open the Clipboard Viewer application now, you will see that the graphics block is there, as shown in Figure 4.7.

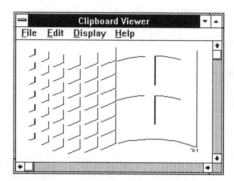

Figure 4.7   *Graphics in the Clipboard*

Sending Text to the Clipboard from a DOS Application Running in a Window

In the examples in Chapter 1, you had a DOS application, WordStar, installed in the Civic group and running in full-screen mode. WordStar is a word processor and you can use it to see how to send text from such an application running in a window to the Clipboard. First you must get it running in a window. Start the WordStar application and press Alt+Enter to switch it into a window. Then start a document by typing some text. Figure 4.8 shows the WordStar application with some text in it.

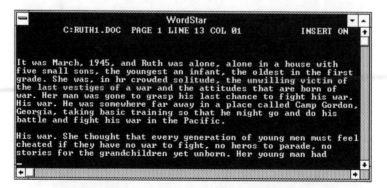

Figure 4.8   *The WordStar Window with Text*

You send text from this application to the Clipboard differently than you did from the Notepad. The Notepad, a Windows application, has its own built-in Cut and Copy commands. DOS applications do not. But a window that runs a DOS application has its own version of the Control menu—with extra commands that support Clipboard operations.

First you must mark a block of text. You can move the mouse cursor to a corner of the block of text and drag the cursor to the opposite corner. The text block will display in reverse video. To turn the block off, press the right mouse button.

To mark a block of text with the keyboard, choose the Edit command from the window's Control menu. You will see the cascaded Edit menu, as shown in Figure 4.9. The Copy command on the Edit menu is not available because no text block is marked yet.

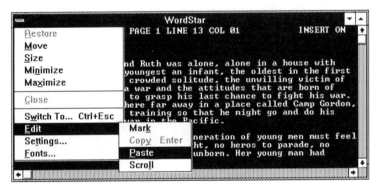

Figure 4.9   *The Control Menu's Edit Menu*

Choose Mark on the Edit menu. The menus disappear, and a blinking block cursor appears in the upper-left corner of the window. Observe that the window title now says "Mark WordStar." Move the blinking cursor to the upper-left corner of the block of text you want to transfer to the Clipboard. Hold down the Shift key and use the arrow keys to move the cursor and describe the block. Figure 4.10 shows the WordStar window with a block of text defined.

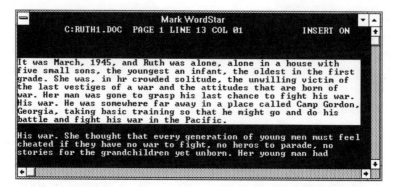

Figure 4.10   *Text Marked in a DOS Application Window*

With the text block marked, choose the Edit menu from the Control menu. Figure 4.11 shows the cascaded Edit menu selected with the text block defined under it. The Copy command is now available, so you may choose it. The Copy command copies the marked block to the Clipboard and unmarks the block. There is no Cut command on the Edit menu because the Program Manager does not know how to tell the application to delete text.

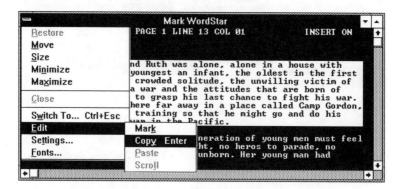

Figure 4.11   *The Edit Menu with Copy Available*

If you run the Clipboard Viewer application now you will see the text copied there, as shown in Figure 4.12. If you are running the WordStar program along with these exercises, you should terminate it before proceeding to the next exercise.

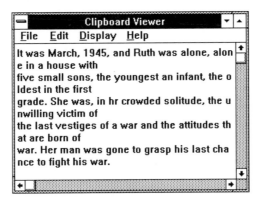

Figure 4.12   *Text in the Clipboard*

Sending Text to the Clipboard from a DOS Application Running Full-Screen

The Wordstar application you added to the Civic group normally runs in full-screen mode. If you are running Windows in standard mode, that is the only option you have for non-Windows DOS applications. When you run the application, it takes over the entire screen. Applications that do that cannot send selected blocks to the Clipboard. They can, however, send the entire text screen.

To send a text screen to the Clipboard from a full-screen DOS application, press the Print Scrn key. When you return to Windows from the DOS application, the Clipboard will have the application's text screen image. You cannot send the screen image of a DOS application that uses graphics displays.

Sending Screen Images to the Clipboard

A useful feature of the Clipboard is its ability to capture window and screen images. This feature is handy for writing procedures for computer users—you can illustrate your documentation with pictures of the screens. The illustrations in this book were prepared with screen and window captures.

Sending the Screen to the Clipboard

To send the full screen to the Clipboard, you press the Prnt Scrn key. Return to the Windows desktop if you have not already done so and press Prnt Scrn. When you execute the Clipboard Viewer application, you will see that the entire desktop has been captured into the Clipboard.

Sending the Current Window to the Clipboard

Often your desktop is cluttered with icons and inactive windows and you want to capture only the current window. To send the current window to the Clipboard, you press Alt+Prnt Scrn. When you execute the Clipboard Viewer application, you will see that the current window only has been captured into the Clipboard.

Pasting Data from the Clipboard

So far all you have done is copy data into the Clipboard. For it to be of any use, you need to be able to get it out of the Clipboard and into another application. Open the Membership Roster Cardfile application from the Civic group. You will need to add a first record to the Cardfile and then save the database in order to use it. Type a name and address on the first card, as shown in Figure 4.13.

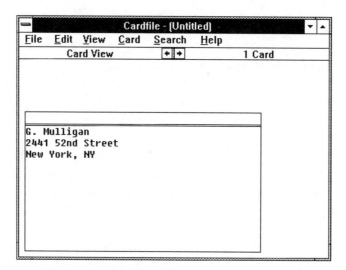

Figure 4.13 *A Cardfile Record with Some Text*

Choose the Save As command from the File menu and type "members" into the Filename field of the File Save As dialog box. Choose OK on the dialog box to build the first record into your membership roster. The Cardfile's window title updates to show the name of the MEMBER database. From now on when you use the Membership Roster, a record will be there.

Pasting Text from the Clipboard to a Windows Application

Now suppose you are using the Notepad to write a memo to the person named on this card. Mark the name and address text the way you learned earlier and choose Copy from the Edit menu. That gets the name and address into the Clipboard. You may exit the Membership Roster Cardfile application now.

Call the Notepad from the Accessories group. As usual, you will see a blank Notepad window. Press Ctrl+V or choose Paste from the Edit menu. The name and address appear on the Notepad as shown in Figure 4.14.

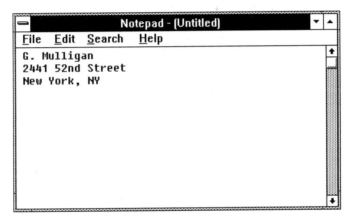

Figure 4.14   *Text Pasted from the Clipboard to the Notepad*

Pasting Graphics from the Clipboard to a Windows Application

Suppose you want to include a picture in the letter you are writing. The Notepad cannot handle graphics, but Windows Write can. Close the Notepad, open the Write application, and choose Paste from the Edit menu to paste the text of the name and address on the screen as shown in Figure 4.15. The text is still in the Clipboard from before. The Clipboard does not erase its contents unless you tell it to do so—or copy something else to the clipboard.

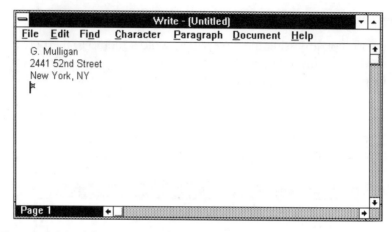

Figure 4.15 *The Name and Address Pasted into a Write Document*

Open Paintbrush and open the WINLOGO.BMP file just as you did in an earlier exercise. Mark the graphic and copy it to the Clipboard. Exit Paintbrush and return to Write. Choose Paste from the Edit menu and watch the picture you saved come into your document, as shown in Figure 4.16.

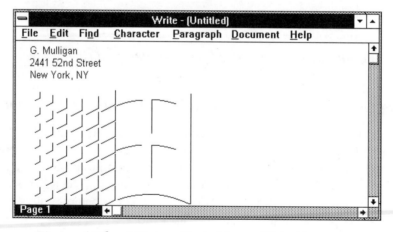

Figure 4.16 *A Picture Pasted into a Write Document*

Pasting from the Clipboard to a DOS Application Running in a Window

Open your Membership Roster Cardfile and copy the name and address into the Clipboard again. Close the Cardfile application.

If you do not have the WordStar application installed or if you are running Windows in standard mode, simply follow along with this exercise in the book. Open the WordStar application from the Civic group. Press Alt+Enter to run WordStar in a window. Start a new document in WordStar (the 'D' command key followed by an arbitrary file name). Choose the Edit command from the Control menu to open the cascaded Edit menu. Choose the Paste command. Observe that the name and address text is pasted from the Clipboard into the WordStar application, as shown in Figure 4.17.

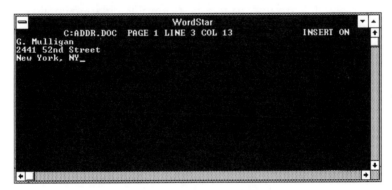

Figure 4.17   *Text Pasted into a non-Windows DOS Application in a Window*

Pasting from the Clipboard to a DOS Application Running Full-Screen

Change WordStar so that it is running in full-screen mode by pressing Alt+Enter. To paste into a non-Windows DOS application that is running full-screen you must first use Alt+Esc to return to Windows. The WordStar application appears as an icon at the bottom of the screen. Open the Control menu for that icon and choose the Paste command from the Edit menu. While the paste operation is underway, the icon's label will change to "Paste WordStar." It changes back to "WordStar" when the paste operation is done. When you return to WordStar, you will see that the Clipboard text is in your WordStar document just as if you had typed it there yourself.

Saving and Reloading Clipboard Files

The Clipboard application's File menu has Open and Save As commands that allow you to save the Clipboard's contents and load a previously saved file into the Clipboard. The commands work just like the same commands on other File menus you have learned about.

Summary

With the Clipboard as one of your tools, you can now freely exchange data between your applications. Your knowledge encompasses the Windows graphical operating environment, the Program Manager, and the File Manager. Chapter 5 moves you one step closer to your mastery of this fascinating operating environment. There you will learn how to use the Control Panel to maintain the operating parameters that let your computer make the most of its hardware and to customize the appearance of Windows to suit your own taste.

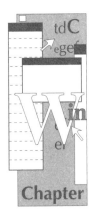

Chapter 5

Managing the System: The Control Panel

This chapter is about the Control Panel, the application with which you control your operating environment. In this chapter you will learn:

- Defining the desktop colors, patterns, wallpaper, and fonts
- Defining communication port parameters
- Setting keyboard and mouse parameters
- Adding printers to your system
- Selecting international display formats
- Setting the system date and time
- Installing sound effects and multimedia software drivers

The Control Panel is an application in the Program Manager's Main group. You use the Control Panel to manage the appearance of your desktop and certain characteristics of the hardware and the operating environment.

Figure 5.1 is the Control Panel application window. It contains an icon for each of the items you manage with the Control Panel. When you choose an icon, you execute a process that controls one of the Control Panel functions.

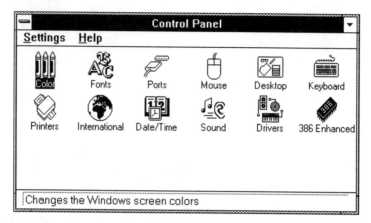

Figure 5.1   *The Control Panel Application Window*

Color

It is difficult to see with black-and-white examples the breadth of color control you have with the Control Panel. You can make dramatic changes in the appearance of your desktop, particularly if you have a color VGA. You can change the color scheme of the desktop components, selecting from a set of defined schemes or building your own scheme by selecting from a color palette. You can even create your own colors. You change colors by choosing the Color icon on the Control Panel. Figure 5.2 is the Color dialog box that you will see.

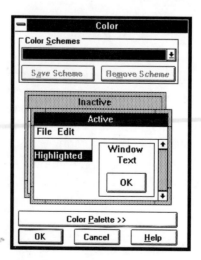

Figure 5.2   *The Color Dialog Box*

Selecting a Color Scheme

The Color Schemes field is a drop-down list box that records the names of the defined color schemes. You can select one from this box, you can use the Remove Schemes control button to delete a scheme from the list, or you can build your own scheme and add it to the list.

The stacked windows in the display represent the components of the desktop. As you try different schemes, the colors in this display change to allow you to view the effects of your changes.

Building a Custom Color Scheme

The Color Palette command button expands the Color dialog box, as shown in Figure 5.3. This dialog box allows you to build custom color schemes.

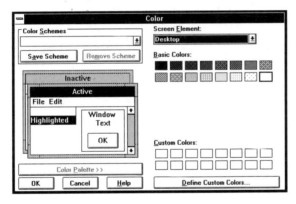

Figure 5.3   *The Color Palette Dialog Box*

The Screen Element field is a drop-down list box that lists the components of the desktop. You select one of these to identify the component for which you will select a color. The Basic Colors field is an array of boxes with color selections in them. You can click one of them to assign that color to the current selected screen element. Or you can tab to the field and use the arrow keys to select one of the boxes. When a dotted outline surrounds the box you want, press the Spacebar to assign that color.

Building a Custom Color

The Custom Colors field is an array of white boxes. You can build a custom color into one of the boxes and assign it to the current selected screen element. To build a custom color, first select the box just as you did one of the Basic Colors boxes. Then choose the Define Custom Colors command button. You will see the Custom Color Selector dialog box shown in Figure 5.4.

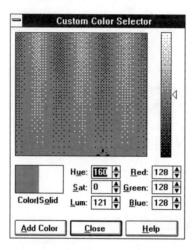

Figure 5.4 *Custom Color Selector Dialog Box*

The Custom Color Selector dialog box shows a window with a two-axis color spectrum and a cross-hair cursor. The cursor controls the hue and saturation of the color. Moving the cursor right or left increases or decreases the hue. Moving the cursor up or down increases or decreases the saturation. You can move the cursor by dragging it with the mouse or by changing the values in the Hue and Sat fields. The vertical bar to the right of the spectrum window controls luminance. You move its pointer up and down with the mouse or by changing the value in the Lum field.

The Color|Solid box shows the effective color and its solid color component. When the color is one you like, choose the Add Color command button to add that color to the selected Custom Colors box. Select another Custom Colors box and build another color. When you have built all the colors you want, choose the Close button on the Custom Color Selector dialog box. The Custom Colors are now available to be used in the same way you use the Basic Colors in building a color scheme.

Saving the Custom Color Scheme

When your customized color scheme is complete, choose the Save Scheme command button. You will see the Save Scheme dialog box shown in Figure 5.5. Enter a name for the color scheme. It will be added to the Color Schemes drop-down list and selected as the current color scheme.

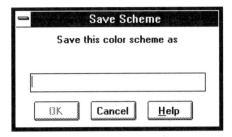

Figure 5.5   *Save Scheme Dialog Box*

Installing the Color Scheme into the Windows Desktop

When you have the scheme you want named at the top of the Color Schemes drop-down list box, choose OK. The new color scheme will be in effect on your desktop.

Fonts

The Control Panel allows you to install and delete screen fonts in the graphical user interface. Fonts are descriptions of typefaces as they relate to printing. Your printer already knows how to print the fonts in its repertoire. Windows, however, needs to know how to display the same fonts on the screen so that your screen documents resemble your printed output.

When you installed your printer during the installation of Windows, the printer installation procedure added the fonts that the printer can print. You can, however, enhance some printers with additional fonts not known to Windows. You can also use a printer that is unknown to the original distribution of Windows. Often the vendors of these printers and fonts will supply screen fonts with their products. These are the fonts that you can add with the Fonts section of the Control Panel.

Viewing Installed Fonts

When you choose the Fonts icon from the Control Panel you see the Fonts dialog box shown in Figure 5.6. The Installed Fonts list box shows the fonts that are currently installed. The Sample text box shows what the font looks like on the screen. If the font is available in several sizes, the sample shows them all. The Sample field changes as you select fonts from the Installed Fonts list box field. Figure 5.6 shows the sample for the Courier font.

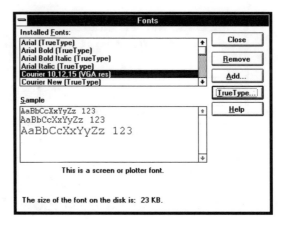

Figure 5.6   *The Fonts Dialog Box*

Adding a Font

The Add command button allows you to add a font. Fonts are distributed as files with the .FON extension. You usually get them on diskettes from their vendors. When you choose the Add command button, you see the Add Fonts dialog box shown in Figure 5.7.

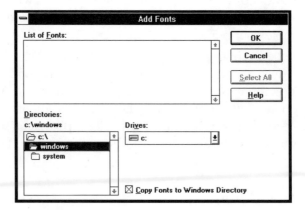

Figure 5.7   *Add Font Files Dialog Box*

You can use the dialog box to select a different drive and directory for the program to look in to find the font files. The List of Fonts list box displays all the font files found on the selected drive and directory. If you are installing more than one font, hold down the Ctrl key as you click each one in the list. You can select the

Select All check box to install all the fonts from the list. Choose OK to add the fonts.

The Copy Fonts to Windows Directory check box causes the fonts to be copied from their source to the C:\WINDOWS\SYSTEM subdirectory. When this option is off, the fonts are installed to be loaded from their original source media. You would do this to conserve space on your hard disk. Font files are usually large.

Removing a Font

If you are not using a font, and it is taking up space you need, you can remove it. You can add it again later if you need it. To remove a font, point to it in the Installed Fonts list and choose the Remove command. You will see the Remove Font dialog box shown in Figure 5.8. Select the Delete Font File from Disk check box to cause the font file to be deleted when you remove the font from the installed list of fonts. Choose Yes to remove the font. You can install it again later.

Figure 5.8   *The Remove Font Dialog Box*

Ports

The Control Panel lets you define the initial values of your communications ports. The communications ports, COM1 through COM4, are the hardware input/output devices that allow you to connect to a modem, to another computer, to printers that have serial rather than parallel interfaces, and to video terminals. Each of these connections requires that certain configuration items be established. The values of these configuration items are usually specified in the documentation that accompanies the hardware device to which you connect the COM port or the software program that uses it.

When you choose the Ports icon on the Control Panel, you see the Ports dialog box shown in Figure 5.9. You can click on one of the port icons or use the Tab key to select the one you want and then choose the Settings command button. You will see the Settings for COM: dialog box shown in Figure 5.10.

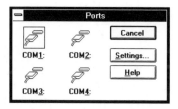

Figure 5.9   *Ports Dialog Box*

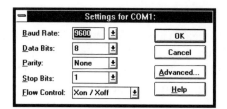

Figure 5.10   *The Settings for COM: Dialog Box*

The five fields on the Settings dialog box are drop-down list boxes that allow you to select from the configuration parameters available to the port. The configuration must match that of the device connected to the port. If you are communicating with a remote computer through a modem, the configuration must match that of the remote computer. The Advanced Settings command button opens another dialog box that allows you to specify the hardware port address and interrupt request line for the selected communications port.

Mouse

You can train your mouse by using the Control Panel's Mouse function. Double click the Mouse icon in the Control Panel. You will see the Mouse dialog box shown in Figure 5.11.

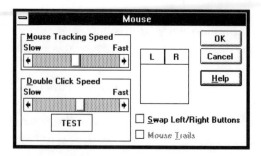

Figure 5.11   *Mouse Dialog Box*

The Mouse Tracking Speed scroll bar is for adjusting the sensitivity of the mouse. In the faster settings, the mouse moves faster, that is, the cursor moves farther across the screen in relation to the distance you move the mouse across your desk. As you change the setting, the mouse changes its behavior. You can test the setting as you change it.

The Double Click Speed scroll bar adjusts the interval of time between clicks that the mouse software uses to distinguish a double click from two independent single clicks. The faster settings shorten the interval. The Test button allows you to test the setting. It changes color when you double-click it.

The L/R boxes are for testing the buttons to make sure they work. When you press a button, the corresponding box changes color, returning to its original color when you release the button. You can use the Swap Left/Right Buttons check box to reverse the meaning of the left and right buttons. This can be useful for left-handed people.

The Mouse Trails check box causes the mouse to leave a slowly disappearing trail as you move it across the screen. On some laptop computers with LCD displays, the mouse cursor is difficult to spot as you move it. It moves faster than the display can refresh its pointer. By using the Mouse Trails option, you will find the cursor easier to locate. The check box is disabled if the image presented by your display adaptor does not benefit by the use of mouse trails.

When the mouse behaves the way you want it to, choose OK. If you want to ignore your changes and return to the mouse's original behavior, choose Cancel.

Desktop

The Desktop icon in the Control Panel allows you to change the pattern that the desktop uses for its background display, the rate that the keyboard cursor blinks, the spacing of icons and windows, the width of a window's border, the style for a screen saver, and other things. When you choose the Desktop icon in the Control Panel window, you see the Desktop dialog window shown in Figure 5.12.

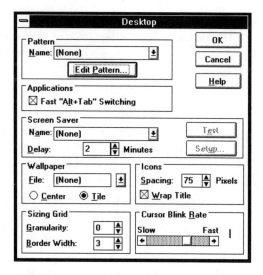

Figure 5.12   *The Desktop Dialog Box*

Desktop Pattern

The Pattern field on the Desktop dialog box specifies one of a number of small patterns that combine to describe the background of the desktop. The field is a drop-down list. Figure 5.13 shows the list dropped down and the Boxes pattern selected.

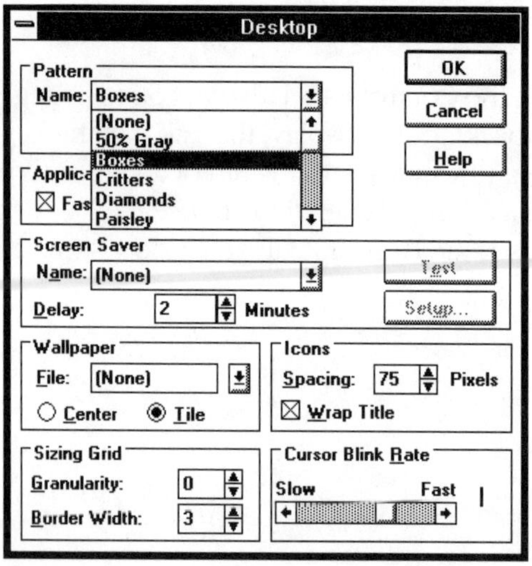

Figure 5.13   *The Pattern Drop-Down List*

If you select the Boxes pattern and then choose OK on the Desktop dialog box, the Boxes pattern will fill the desktop, and the screen will look like that in Figure 5.14.

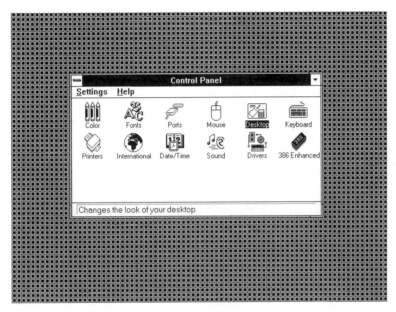

Figure 5.14   *Boxes as a Pattern*

Editing a Pattern

Patterns are made up of small graphics boxes that form side by side and up and down. You can select one of the patterns and edit it by selecting the Edit Pattern command button. You will see the Desktop-Edit Pattern dialog box, as shown in Figure 5.15.

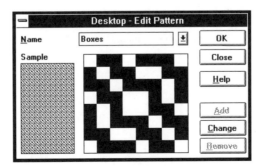

Figure 5.15   *The Desktop-Edit Pattern Dialog Box*

A pattern is an eight-by-eight array of pixels (picture elements). The dialog box includes an exploded copy of the pattern. You can set the pixels on and off by clicking them, forming a new pattern. The Sample window to the left of the pattern shows how the pattern will form into the desktop pattern if you use it. The Name field is a drop-down list that lets you select from the existing patterns. You can change the definition of one of the existing patterns by choosing the Change command button.

Desktop Wallpaper

You can use a .BMP file to form the desktop rather than a pattern. This approach is called using *wallpaper.* Figure 5.16 shows how you can use the Wallpaper File drop-down list to select from the .BMP files available. If you were to choose the cars.bmp file that comes with Windows, your desktop would look like that in Figure 5.17.

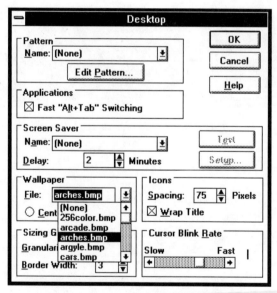

Figure 5.16 *Selecting Wallpaper*

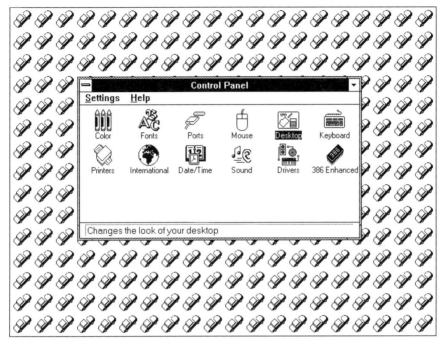

Figure 5.17   *CARS.BMP as the Wallpaper*

Some .BMP files contain bitmaps that do not fill the screen. The Tile option button causes those bitmaps to repeat themselves. The PYRAMID.BMP file that comes with Windows is such a bitmap.

Wallpaper files can come from many sources. A file that you can load into the Paintbrush application can become a wallpaper file. Some users load scanned photographs of their family. Others download wallpaper files from electronic bulletin boards.

Keyboard Cursor Blink Rate

The Desktop dialog window includes a scroll bar that lets you change the rate at which the keyboard cursor blinks. The blinking cursor just below the scroll bar changes its rate to reflect the changes you are making.

Icon Spacing

Sometimes icons collide, particularly if their labels are long. You use the Icon Spacing value to increase or decrease the distance that icons are spaced from one another when they space themselves out. The default spacing is 75.

Grid

When you move windows and icons around, they move smoothly anywhere you drag them as long as the Granularity value is zero. If you change this value, you describe a grid, and the windows and icons tend to snap to coordinates that align with this grid.

Border Width

The Border Width field changes the width of window borders. The default is 3. You can experiment with this value. Figure 5.18 shows the Control Panel application window when the border value is set to 15.

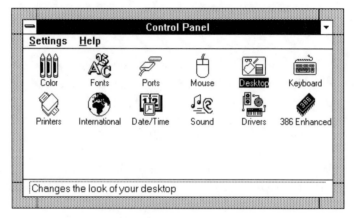

Figure 5.18   *Fat Borders*

Fast Alt+Tab Switching

This check box on the Control Panel enables fast Alt+Tab switching between applications. The default setting is on. When you turn it off, the fast Alt+Tab switching feature is disabled

Screen Saver

You can use the built-in screen saver to tell Windows to blank the screen if a defined number of minutes passes with no keyboard or mouse action. A *screen saver* prevents the screen's phosphors from burning in the patterns of a screen image that does not change over a long period of time. The Name drop-down list box allows you to select from several styles of screen saver, from blanking the screen entirely to using different patterns of moving images. In the Delay field you specify the interval of no action after which the screen saver takes effect. The Test button demonstrates the selected style. The Setup button allows you to change the operating parameters of the various styles.

Keyboard

The Keyboard icon on the Control Panel allows you to modify the keyboard's *typematic rate*, the speed that the keyboard repeats a character when you hold a key down. Figure 5.19 shows the Keyboard Dialog Box.

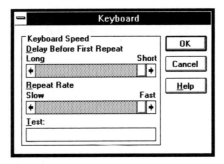

Figure 5.19   *The Keyboard Dialog Box*

To modify the typematic rate, adjust the Delay Before First Repeat and Repeat Rate scroll boxes between their fast and slow settings. Tab to the Test Typematic text box and test the rate by holding a key down. Choose OK when you are satisfied with the new rate or Cancel to ignore any changes and return to the previous rate.

Printers

You can configure and add printers to your system by choosing the Printers icon from the Control Panel. The Printers Dialog Box is shown in Figure 5.20.

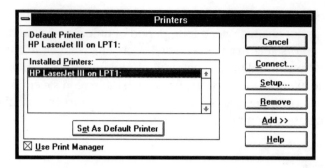

Figure 5.20 *The Printers Dialog Box*

You may have more than one printer device installed, and they may share printer ports or be installed on individual ports. Printers would share ports if you had them connected to the same printer port on your computer through a printer switch, or if you are using network printers. Some applications print to two printers at once. For example, a shipping application could have address labels in one printer and bill of lading forms in another. In such a case, you would install two printers on two printer ports.

The Installed Printers list box lists the printers that you installed either during the installation of Windows or by an earlier use of the Control Panel. The Default Printer field specifies which of the installed printers is automatically used. When you print from an application, the output goes to the default printer unless the application directs print output to a specific printer. You may have several printers installed, but only one of them can be the default printer at any one time.

Installing a Printer

Installing a printer involves adding the printer driver file to Windows and setting the printer's configuration items. The Add command button expands the Printer dialog box, as shown in Figure 5.21.

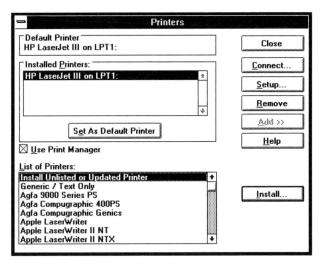

Figure 5.21   *Installing a Printer*

Installing the Printer Driver Software

The List of Printers list box in the Printer dialog box contains all the printer devices known to Windows. The first item in the list allows you to install a printer device not known to Windows or to add an updated printer driver for one of the listed printers. To add the printer driver software, choose the Install command button. You will see the Install Driver dialog box shown in Figure 5.22.

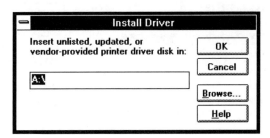

Figure 5.22   *Loading a Printer Driver*

The disk that the Driver dialog box asks for and the driver name that it specifies will vary depending upon the printer you selected to install. Insert the disk and choose OK. The driver file will be installed, and the Installed Printers list on the Printer dialog box will change to reflect the new printer, as shown in Figure 5.23.

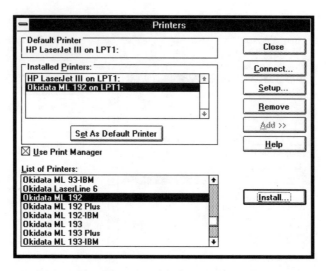

Figure 5.23   *The Printer Added to the Installed Printers List*

Assigning the Printer Port

The printer port for the installed printer defaults to LPT1. You can change this assignment by choosing the Connect command button. You will see the Connect dialog box shown in Figure 5.24.

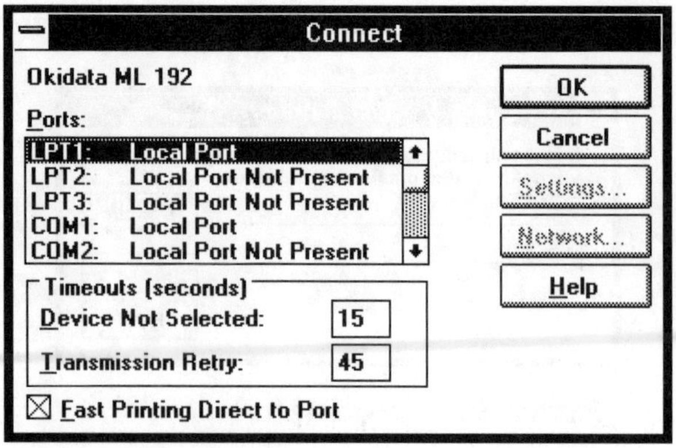

Figure 5.24   *The Connect Dialog Box*

The Ports list box lists the ports to which the printer can be connected. The list indicates whether the port hardware is installed on your computer. You may assign a port that is not installed. This would be appropriate for using network printers, for example. The ports are:

- Three parallel ports: LPT1, 2, and 3
- Four serial ports: COM1, 2, 3, and 4
- EPT, for printers such as the IBM Personal Pageprinter
- FILE, for printing to a file
- LPT1.DOS and LPT2.DOS for running Windows within OS/2.

If you choose FILE, the Print Manager will prompt you for a name to give the file every time an application prints to it. If you assign a COM port, the Settings command button becomes active, allowing you to modify the serial port settings. This command opens the same Settings dialog box you learned about earlier with Figure 5.10, in the discussion on "Ports."

Timeouts

You can specify two timeout values for the printer from the Connect dialog box. The Device Not Selected timeout is the length of time in seconds Windows will wait for the printer to be ready before it displays a Not Ready error message. The Transmission Retry timeout is the number of seconds Windows will wait for the printer to acknowledge a transmission before Windows tries a second time. After a second failure, Windows issues the error message.

When would you change these values? The default values usually work, so you rarely need to modify them. However, if you get a lot of error messages when you know that the printer is functioning properly, you might want to increase the values.

Fast Printing Direct to Port

The Fast Printing Direct to Port check box is selected by default. When deselected, Windows writes to the printer by calling DOS, which results in slower printing. This option allows you to use DOS if you have printer software that intercepts DOS print calls.

When you have selected the printer port for the newly installed printer, choose OK, and the Installed Printers list in the Printers dialog box changes to show the new port assignment.

Setting Up the Printer

Most printer devices have configuration parameters that you can modify. The Setup command button opens a Setup dialog box similar to the one shown in Figure 5.25. The dialog box will be different for each printer, and you can change the settings accordingly. You would use this procedure to routinely configure such items as page orientation and which paper tray to use.

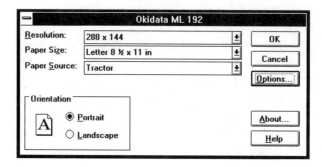

Figure 5.25 *The Printer Setup Dialog Box*

Selecting the Default Printer

You select the default printer by double clicking its entry in the Installed Printers list or by selecting that entry and choosing the Set as Default Printer command button.

Using the Print Manager

The Use Print Manager check box tells windows to use the Print Manager to queue print jobs. Chapter 6 is about the Print Manager. You will usually want to use it because the option allows you to do other work in the same application or to exit from the application while the printer is still printing.

Removing a Printer

You can delete a printer from the Installed Printers list by choosing the Configure command button and then choosing the Remove command button from the

Printers-Configure dialog box, shown in Figure 5.23. You will see the Control Panel dialog box shown in Figure 5.26.

Figure 5.26   *Removing A Printer*

International

The Control Panel's International icon allows you to change the characteristics of your system to match the conventions of different countries. When you choose the International icon, you see the International dialog box shown in Figure 5.27.

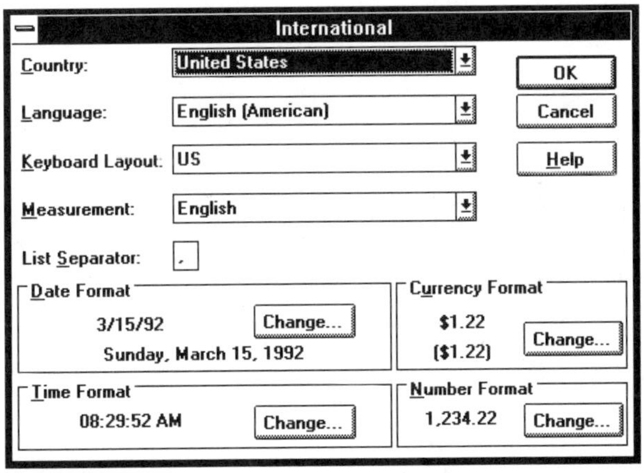

Figure 5.27   *The International Dialog Box*

The Country, Language, Keyboard Layout, and Measurement fields are drop-down list boxes that allow you to select the conventions that match your environment.

You can change the display format of dates, times, currency, and numerical values with the corresponding Change command buttons in the International dialog box. Figures 5.28, 5.29, 5.30, and 5.31 show the dialog boxes that control these displays. The operation of these dialog boxes is typical. You can experiment with them to observe their effects.

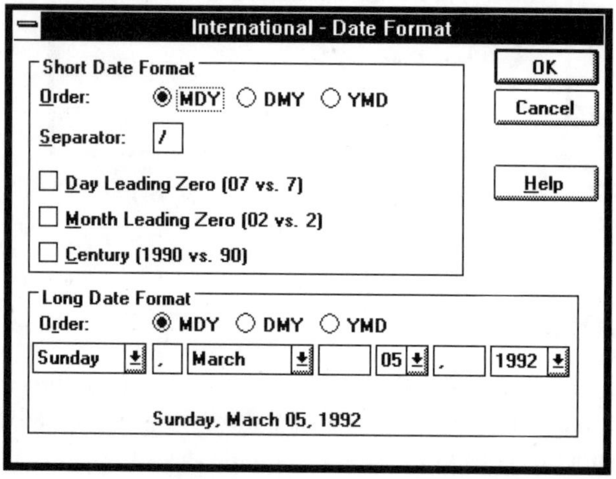

Figure 5.28 *International - Date Format Dialog Box*

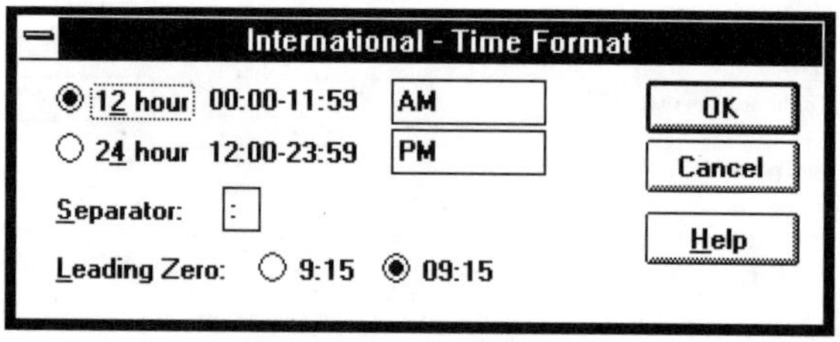

Figure 5.29 *International - Time Format Dialog Box*

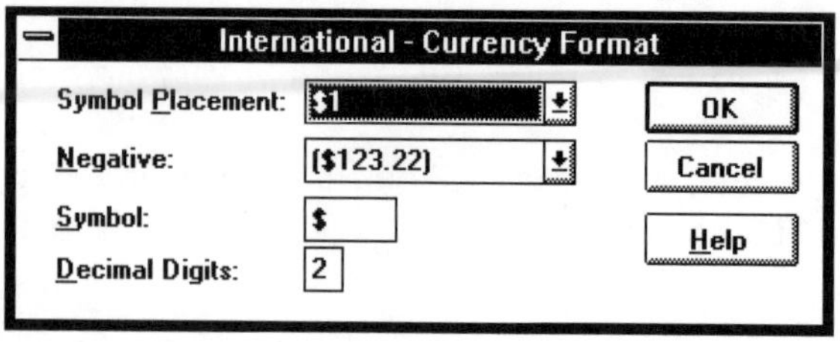

Figure 5.30 *International - Currency Format Dialog Box*

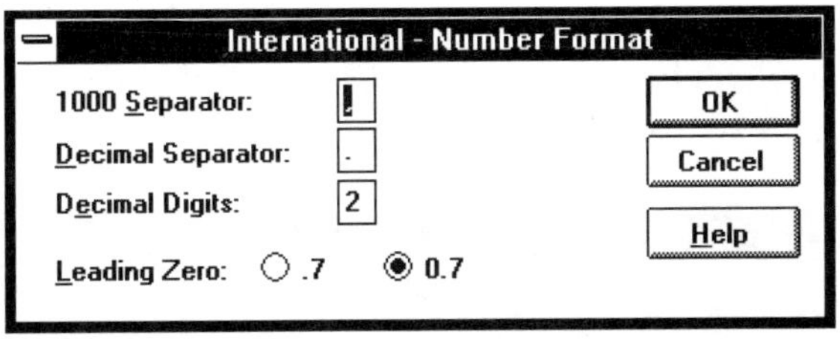

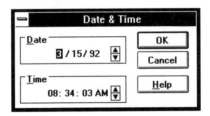

Figure 5.31   *International - Number Format Dialog Box*

Changing the international settings does not guarantee that every application will be automatically translated. Only those applications that include the necessary translation files can conform to the settings you specify.

Date and Time

The Date/Time icon on the Control Panel lets you change the system clock and calendar. Figure 5.32 shows the Date & Time dialog box used to change those settings.

Figure 5.32   *The Date & Time Dialog Box*

You can tab to, or click on, one of the date and time fields and type in the new value, or click the increment/decrement arrows to change the values. Choose OK to record the new date and time or choose Cancel to ignore your changes and retain the original clock and calendar settings.

Sound

Windows uses sound to get your attention for such events as error messages. If you have installed a sound device and its associated driver, Windows can use those devices to create different sound effects for different events. You install sound drivers by choosing the Drivers icon on the Control Panel, described in the next section. When you choose the Sound icon on the Control Panel, you see the Sound dialog box, as shown in Figure 5.33.

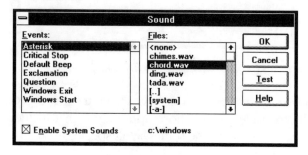

Figure 5.33   *The Sound Dialog Box*

The Events list contains the events for which Windows can generate sound effects. The Files list shows the .WAV files that create the sounds. As you select from the Events list, the dialog box changes the Files selection to show you what .WAV file is associated with the event. You can change the association by selecting a different event. You can test the sound effect by choosing the Test command button. If you deselect the Enable System Sounds check box, you will disable all such sound effects. Choose OK when the dialog box reflects the sound effects that you want to use.

Drivers

The Drivers icon on the Control Panel allows you to install device drivers that control sound effects and other multimedia devices. When you choose the Drivers icon, you see the Drivers dialog box, as shown in Figure 5.34.

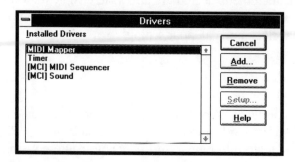

Figure 5.34   *The Drivers Dialog Box*

The Installed Drivers list box on the Drivers dialog box contains the drivers that are already installed. You can add to and remove from that list by choosing the Add command button. Adding and removing drivers follows the same procedure that you learned in the discussion on Printers earlier in this chapter.

Some drivers require setup. The Setup command button on the Drivers dialog box opens the Setup dialog box for the particular driver. Figure 5.35 shows a typical driver Setup dialog box.

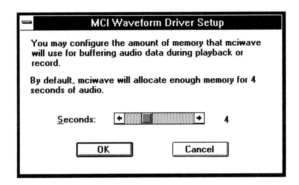

Figure 5.35   *A Driver Setup Dialog Box*

386 Enhanced Mode and Network Icons

If you are running in 386 enhanced mode, you will see the 386 Enhanced icon on the Control Panel. If you are on a network, you will see the Network icon on the Control Panel. These icons allow you to do some advanced operations detailed in Chapter 11.

Summary

You know Windows well by now. You should be able to run most Windows applications without assistance because you understand the Windows common user interface and you know how to manage your applications with the Program Manager, your data files with the File Manager, and your system with the Control Panel. Chapter 6 teaches you the Print Manager, the program that queues and manages your print jobs.

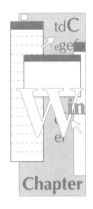

Chapter

6

The Print Manager

This chapter is about the Print Manager, the Windows application that queues and prints reports. In this chapter you will learn:

- ◆ Printing from Windows applications and non-Windows DOS applications
- ◆ Bypassing the Print Manager
- ◆ Controlling the printer
- ◆ Managing the print queue entries

When you print a report or graphic from a Windows application, the Print Manager manages the print job. The Print Manager accepts print jobs, places them in printer-related queues, and prints them from the background while you are doing other work. In addition to intercepting, queuing, and printing the print jobs, the Print Manager provides a Windows interface with which you manage the queues and printers.

205

Printing from a Windows Application

When you print from a Windows application, Windows directs the output to the default printer selected in the Control Panel. While the application is generating the printer output, the dialog box shown in Figure 6.1 is displayed. You can terminate the print job by choosing the Cancel command button from the dialog box, or you can wait until the printing operation completes.

Figure 6.1   *Printing from an Application*

Printing with the Print Manager

If you have checked the Use Print Manager check box in the Control Panel's Printers dialog box, then output an application directs to a printer goes to the Print Manager, which collects the print output into a queue. The dialog box shown in Figure 6.1 is displayed while the Print Manager is receiving output from the application. The application is free to continue after the Print Manager has collected and copied the output to the queue.

You should use the Print Manager to queue printer data when you have long reports or high-density graphics to print and when the length of print data exceeds the buffering capability of your printer. You can usually use the Print Manager at all times with little or no compromise to your productivity.

N O T E

Printing Directly to the Printer

If you have elected not to use the Print Manager from the Use Print Manager check box in the Control Panel's Printers dialog box, then output directed by an application to a printer goes directly to the printer.

When you print directly to the printer, the dialog box shown in Figure 6.1 remains on the screen for as long as it takes to print the output. You cannot return to the application to do other work and you cannot terminate the application. If the printer is slow and the output is long, you will be stuck for a while. You can call a different application and work with it for a while but the current one is dedicated to driving the printer until the output is done.

You should bypass the Print Manager and print directly to the printer only when your printer can accept data faster than the Print Manager can write it to a queue, or if the volume of your print data does not create a bottleneck.

N O T E

Printing from Non-Windows Applications

DOS programs use their own printer management. Some simply print to the DOS standard logical print device, others give you a choice of printer ports, some even use queuing mechanisms similar to those of the Print Manager. However, when you run a DOS application from Windows, that application does not use the Print Manager. Even worse, if the Print Manager is printing for a Windows application, and you begin to print from a DOS application at the same time, your printed output could end up jumbled.

If you are mixing DOS and Windows applications that print, you should tell the Print Manager to Pause all printers until you are certain that the DOS applications are not printing.

Running the Print Manager

The Print Manager is a Windows application. You can execute it from the Program Manager's Main group. If you do not execute the Print Manager yourself, Windows will execute it the first time an application prints through it. When Windows executes the Print Manager, it comes up in its minimized state as an icon at the bottom of the desktop. The Print Manager then terminates itself when the last print job is done. Figure 6.2 shows the Print Manager's icon. When you execute the Print Manager yourself, it continues running until you terminate it.

Figure 6.2   *The Print Manager Icon*

Using the Print Manager Application

Figure 6.3 shows a Print Manager application window. There are two printers installed and each one has print jobs queued. Both printers are paused. A printer can be idle with no jobs queued, paused, or printing. The hand icon to the left of the printer's name and the [Paused] tag to the right tell you the printer is paused. If the printer is printing the icon will be a tiny printer. If the printer is idle, there is no icon.

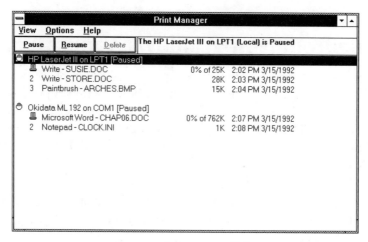

Figure 6.3   *The Print Manager Application Window*

The lists of print jobs are numbered according to their place in the queue. The first entry in the queue has the printer icon instead of a number to indicate that it is the job being printed.

Pausing and Resuming a Printer

You pause a printer by selecting the printer to be paused and choosing the Pause function button. An idle printer will go into pause mode and any subsequent print jobs will wait. A printer that is printing a print job will stop in the middle of that job and wait. There are three indications that a printer is paused. The printer name is preceded by the hand icon, the [Paused] tag follows the printer name, and when you have the highlight cursor on the printer, the information display to the right of the function buttons tells you that the printer is paused.

You resume a paused printer by selecting the printer to be paused and choosing the Resume function button. If there are jobs to be printed, the printer icon and a [Printing] tag surround the printer name, and the information display to the right of the function buttons tells you that the printer is printing. If there are no jobs, there is no icon, the tag says [Idle], and the information display to the right of the function buttons tells you that the printer is idle.

When the Printer is Not Ready

If the Print Manager is printing a job and the printer becomes not ready—perhaps it is out of paper, perhaps you took it off line—you will see the error message in the Print Manager dialog box shown in Figure 6.4.

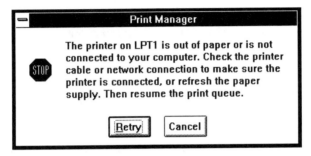

Figure 6.4   *Printer Error*

If you correct the problem and choose Retry on the Print Manager dialog box, the printing resumes. If you choose Retry without correcting the problem, the error message remains. If you choose Cancel, the printer status tag becomes [STALLED] and the Print Manager stops trying to print until you choose Resume again.

Deleting a Print Job

You can delete a print job by selecting the job's queue entry and choosing Delete. You will see the Print Manager dialog box shown in Figure 6.5. Choose OK to delete the job.

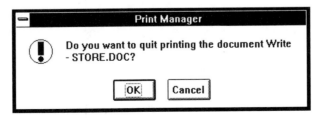

Figure 6.5   *Deleting a Print Job*

If you delete the job at the top of the queue, the one that is printing, you might have to reset your printer, particularly if the print job involves graphics. Some printers cannot recover by themselves from an interrupted stream of graphics data. You might have to power the printer down and up to reset it.

Reordering the Queue

You can change the order of the jobs in the queue by moving any job entry other than the first one to any new location other than the first one. To move a job with the mouse, click on and drag a queue entry to its new location. To move a job with the keyboard, use the arrow keys to move the highlight cursor to the job. Then hold down the Ctrl key and move the dotted outline to the new position. When you release the Ctrl key, the job entry moves.

Assigning Print Manager Priority

The Print Manager Options menu, shown in Figure 6.6, has three commands that allow you to modify the processing priority of the Print Manager. The processing priority controls how the Print Manager shares the computer's processor with the other applications that are running.

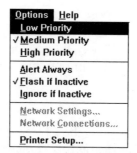

Figure 6.6 *The Print Manager Options Menu*

The three commands are Low Priority, Medium Priority, and High Priority. The commands are mutually exclusive toggles—only one can be in effect. The current priority is indicated by a check mark.

By default the Print Manager runs at medium priority, which means that the Print Manager and other applications share the processor equally. Low priority gives the other programs a larger share, and high priority gives the Print Manager a larger share.

If your jobs are not printing fast enough, give the Print Manager high priority. If your jobs are printing fine, but your other applications are sluggish, try giving the Print Manager a low priority.

Print Manager Alerts

The Print Manager can interrupt whatever you are doing to tell you that the printer needs attention. If the printer is in an error state, the Print Manager will always interrupt you with an error message. But other interruptions are routine. Your printer might be set up to pause between pages, for example. You can control how the Print Manager alerts you to these routine conditions.

The Options menu contains three mutually exclusive toggle commands—Alert Always, Flash if Inactive, and Ignore if Inactive. When you choose Alert Always, the Print Manager displays alert messages regardless of whether the Print Manager application window is active. If you choose one of the other two commands, the Print Manager displays alert messages only if the Print Manager application window is active. If you choose Flash if Inactive, the Print Manager's icon flashes if the Print Manager is minimized. If the Print Manager window is inactive, the title bar of the window flashes. If you choose Ignore if Inactive, you get no notice of the condition until you activate the Print Manager application window.

Controlling the Queue Display

The Print Manager View menu shown in Figure 6.7 has two toggle commands to control the queue display. You can turn off the time and date and file size displays with these commands. The only reason to turn them off is if you want to resize the Print Manager application window to a smaller size.

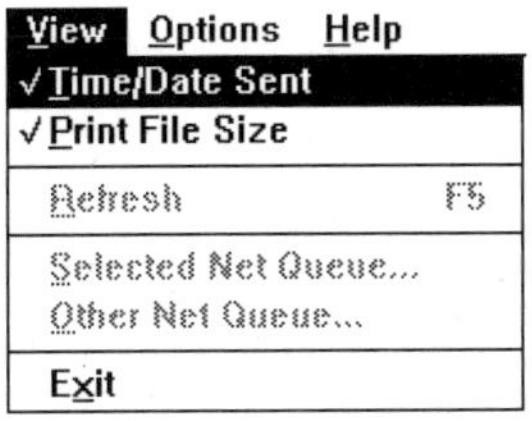

Figure 6.7 *The Printer Manager View Menu*

Printing on a Network

This chapter addressed printing when the printer devices are directly connected to your computer. Chapter 11 discusses printing on a shared network printer.

Summary

This chapter ends your introductory tutorial to Windows. You know how to use it and make it do what you want it to. The next four chapters are about applications and accessory programs that come with Windows. You will learn to use each of them, from the simple Clock to the complex Recorder. You will get into word processing and graphics. Then, in Chapter 11, you will become a power user.

Chapter 7

Windows Write

This chapter is about Windows Write, the accessory word processor that comes with Windows. In this chapter you will learn:

- ◆ Entering text into a document
- ◆ Defining a document's format
- ◆ Modifying the document
- ◆ Putting graphics into a document
- ◆ Printing the document

Windows Write is a word processing application found in the Program Manager's Accessories group. With it you can write memos, letters, documents, and publications that integrate text and graphics. Write is not a high-end word processor like Word for Windows, WordPerfect, and others, and it is not a powerful desktop publisher like PageMaker, but Write is sufficient for the small word processing needs of most homes and offices.

Typing a Document

When you start Write, you see the Write application window shown in Figure 7.1. The small, four-pointed star in the upper-left corner of the Write workspace marks the end of the document. At first that mark is at the beginning of the document because the document has nothing in it. As you enter data into the document, the mark moves forward.

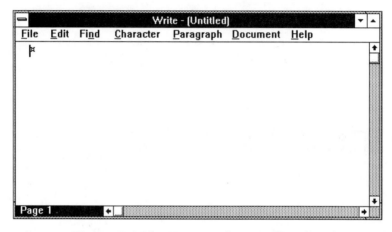

Figure 7.1 *The Write Application Window*

The vertical bar to the immediate left of the star is the keyboard cursor. That is where you will type text or, later, insert graphics. You can move the cursor around the document after you enter some text by using the mouse or the keyboard.

Margins

Type some text into the document. The first thing you might learn is that the lines go well beyond the right margin of the window before a word wraps around. Figure 7.2 shows this condition.

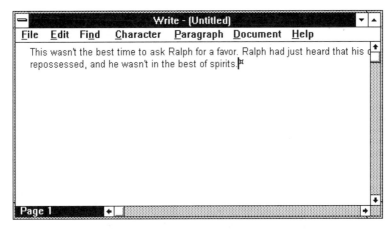

Figure 7.2 *Text Exceeding the Window Width*

Write orients its display to the printed page, trying to show the document on the screen as it will appear on paper. The initial right and left page margins are set to 1.25 inches on 8.5x11 paper, and the size of the default screen font for some printers needs more than a window's width to display what will be six inches of printed text.

Most people prefer to view the entire line when they type. Write's horizontal scrolling refreshes the screen in an uncomfortable way whenever you type on the part of the line that is beyond the right border of the Window. You can resize the Write window so that all the text is visible as shown in Figure 7.3. The width of the window needed to display all the text will depend on which font you are using and the page layout.

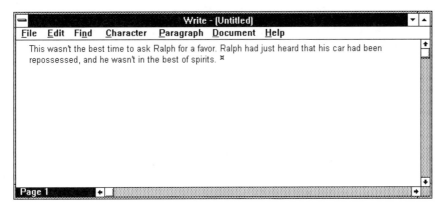

Figure 7.3 *The Write Window Resized*

Moving Around in the Document

After you have some text typed in, try moving the cursor around in the text you have entered. Table 7.1 details the keystrokes that move the cursor.

Table 7.1   *Write Cursor Movement Keystrokes*

Keystroke	Moves the Cursor:
Up, Down, Left, Right	One character position
Ctrl+Right/Left	One word right and left
Keypad 5+Right/Left	One sentence right and left*
Home, End	To the beginning and end of the line
Keypad 5+Up/Down	To the previous and next paragraph
Ctrl+PgUp/PgDn	To the top and bottom of the window
Keypad 5+PgUp/PgDn	To the previous and next page**
Ctrl+Home/End	To the beginning and end of the document

* Keypad 5 is the 5 on the numeric keypad.
** Works only after the Repaginate command, or if you have printed the document.

Marking Text

Many Write commands operate on a marked block of text. You can mark text in the usual ways, as explained in Chapter 4. If you have a mouse, Write provides additional ways to mark text. When you move the mouse cursor to the left margin of the text, the cursor changes to a diagonal arrow that points to the upper-right. When the cursor has this form, you can mark text in several ways. Table 7.2 explains these operations.

Table 7.2   *Marking Text from the Left Margin*

To mark:	Do this:
A line	Click once with the mouse cursor at the line
Adjacent lines	Click the first line and drag the cursor to the last
	Or mark the first line, move to the last line, hold the Shift key down and click
A paragraph	Put the cursor next to any line and double click
The document	Hold the Ctrl key down and click

Moving and Copying Text

You move and copy blocks of text by marking the block and then cutting or copying the text to the Clipboard and pasting it into its new location.

Deleting Text

You can delete a marked block of text by pressing Del. The Undo command on the Edit menu recovers the most recently deleted block of text.

Finding and Replacing Text

Write has commands that let you search the document for a match on a string of text. You can also tell Write to replace instances of a text string with a substitute text string.

Find Text

You can search a document for text by choosing the Find command on the Find menu. A search proceeds through the entire document from the current location to the end, wrapping around to the beginning and back to the current location. If you have a block of text marked, however, the search involves only the marked block. The Find dialog box shown in Figure 7.4 is where you enter the word or phrase you are searching for.

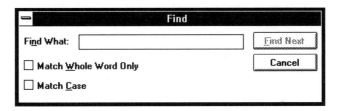

Figure 7.4 *The Find Dialog Box*

The Match Whole Word Only check box specifies that you want matches on whole words only. That way, a search for the word "phone" will not match the word "phonetic," for example. If you select the Match Case check box, the match will occur only if the text matches the Find What text box exactly with respect to upper and lower case.

When you have found the word, you can use the Find Next command button to find subsequent instances of the search text. You can also use the Repeat Last Find command on the Find menu to repeat the find after the dialog box is gone.

The Find dialog box remains in view even when it is no longer the active window. To erase it, choose its Cancel command button or Close on its Control menu.

Replace Text

The Replace command on the Find menu allows you to replace instances of a text string with a different string. Figure 7.5 shows an example of the Replace dialog box for changing "phone" to "telephone." You can choose Find Next to proceed to the next match, Replace to change the current match and then proceed to the next match, and Replace All to change every match in the document.

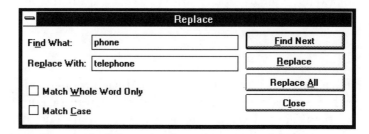

Figure 7.5   *The Replace Dialog Box*

The Replace dialog box remains in view even when it is no longer the active window. To erase it, choose its Cancel command button or Close on its Control menu.

Wild Cards

You can use wild cards characters, white space indicators, and control characters in your search text string as detailed in Table 7.3.

Table 7.3   *Control Characters in a Search String*

Enter	To search for
?	Any character, "b?ck" matches back, beck, etc.
^w	A space.
^t	A tab.
^p	A paragraph mark.
^d	A page break.

Formats and Layouts

Write gives you control over the format and appearance of the document within the abilities of your printer. You can change fonts, justify the text, change spacing and indentation, add headers and footers, use tabs, control page numbers, and set margins.

Characters and Fonts

The Character menu has a number of selections that allow you to control the characters in your document. You can choose from a number of character enhancements, fonts, and sizes. When you make a selection, it affects a marked block of text or, if no block is marked, the typing that follows. Selecting one of these commands has an effect only if your printer supports the effect.

Character Enhancement

The Normal command resets all the other character commands to their default settings. The first group of commands after Normal are Bold, Italic, Underline, Superscript, and Subscript. The last two of these are mutually exclusive.

Common Fonts

The second group of commands allows you to select from the most commonly used fonts on your printer. The names of these commands will be different for different printers.

Font Sizes

The Reduce Font and Enlarge Font commands affect the point size of the font. Fonts are available in different sizes. Not all fonts have all the same sizes, however. The Reduce Font and Enlarge Font commands step through the sizes available to the current font.

Other Fonts

The last command on the Character menu is the Fonts command. It allows you to select from the fonts that the printer has available and to select the size from those available for the selected font. Figure 7.6 shows a typical Fonts dialog box.

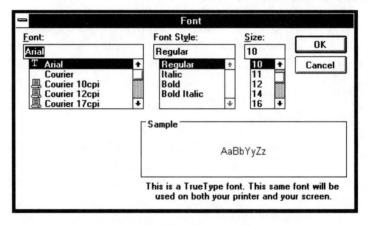

Figure 7.6   *The Fonts Dialog Box*

Paragraphs

The Paragraph menu has commands that effect the format of a selected paragraph or paragraphs. If you want to change a single paragraph, put the keyboard cursor inside that paragraph. If you want to change several paragraphs, mark them as a block.

The Normal command resets all the other commands to their default settings.

Paragraph Alignment

The first group of commands after Normal control the alignment of the paragraph. These commands are mutually exclusive. The Left command aligns the text on the left margin with a jagged right margin, the default setting. The Centered command aligns each line in the center of the page. You might use the Centered command to center a poem, a wedding invitation, or the text of your letterhead, for example. The Right command aligns the text on the right margin with a jagged left margin. Some business stationary stacks the names and titles of the business partners in a right-justified fashion. The Justified command spreads the text out so that it is even at both margins, after the fashion of a newspaper column. Figure 7.7 shows examples of the use of these commands.

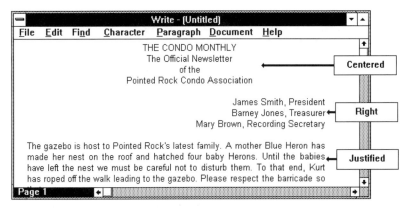

Figure 7.7 *A Document with Different Text Justifications*

Spacing

The spacing commands on the Paragraph menu allow you to use single, one and a half, and double spacing in different parts of the document. If your printer does not support the spacing you choose, Write will not modify the text on the screen.

Indenting

The Indents command on the Paragraph menu allows you to specify automatic indenting. Figure 7.8 shows the Indents dialog box.

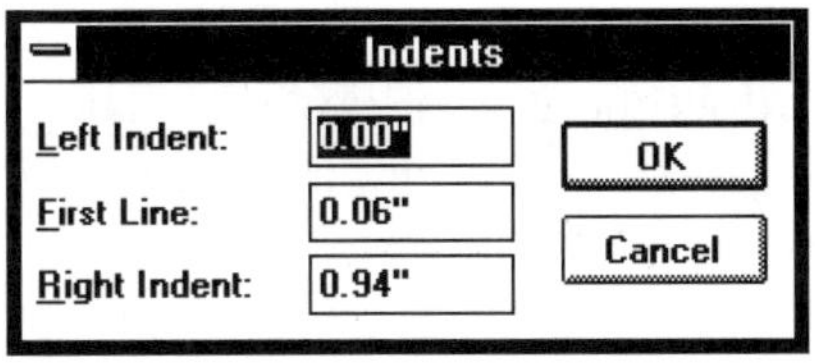

Figure 7.8 *The Indents Dialog Box*

There are three ways to change indenting for the current paragraph. You can tell Write to indent the left side of an entire paragraph a specified distance from the left margin. You can do the same for the right margin. You can also indent the first line of a paragraph a specified distance from the left edge of the rest of the paragraph.

Figure 7.9 shows how you can use an indented paragraph and italics to offset a paragraph. In the example, the center paragraph uses left and right indent values and italics to set itself off from the rest of the document.

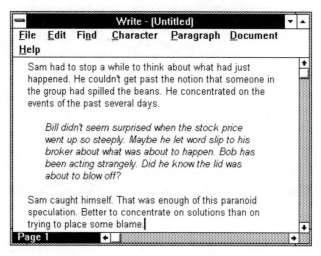

Figure 7.9   *An Indented, Italicized Paragraph*

Headers and Footers

A header is a body of text that prints at the top of every page of the document except, possibly, the first page. A footer is a body of text that prints at the bottom of every page. You can use the Header and Footer commands on the Document menu to describe the content and format of the document's header and footer.

Headers

Figure 7.10 shows the document window and dialog box that allow you to compose a header for your document. The HEADER document window is really a second Write document window. Even when the Page Header dialog box is inactive, it overlaps the HEADER document window. You can use the

Page Header dialog box to specify how far the header begins from the top margin of the page. You can also tell it whether to print on the first page. Many documents use the first page as a title page and do not print the header there. If you choose the Insert Page # command button, the (page) label appears in the header text at the current cursor position, as shown in the figure. This location is where the page number will print in the header on every page.

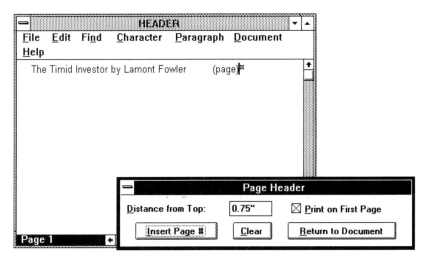

Figure 7.10 *The Document Header*

Choose the Clear command button to clear the header. If you make no other changes, the document will have no header. Choose the Return to Document command button when the header is the way you want it. Do not try to close the HEADER document window unless you want to exit from Write.

Footers

Page footers work just like page headers except that you specify the distance from the bottom margin rather than the top.

Page Layout

You can control the page layout by choosing the Page Layout command on the Document menu. The Page Layout dialog box is shown in Figure 7.11.

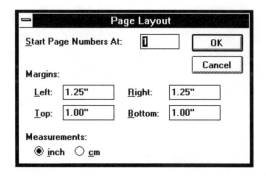

Figure 7.11   *The Page Layout Dialog Box*

The first field allows you to change the first page number of the document. You would use this feature for printing a file that was one of several chapters in a document, for example. You cannot use this feature to generate page numbers that follow the format 1-1 or 1.1. You can, however, achieve the same effect by including the 1- or 1. in the header or footer and following it with the (page) label.

The four margin fields control the margins that Write will print within. Some printers have built-in margin controls, so you might need to set the left and top margins to zero.

You can specify whether the measurements used throughout Write are metric or inches by selecting the Measurements option button.

Tabs

The default for tabs in a Write document is two to the inch. You can set overriding tab positions. There are regular tabs and decimal tabs. A regular tab works like one on a typewriter. A decimal tab is for entering numbers with decimal places. The characters you type go to the left of the decimal point until you type the decimal point itself. Then the characters go to the right of the decimal point.

There are two ways to set tabs. One way uses the Tabs command on the Document menu. The other way uses the Ruler, which has other uses as well. You will learn about the Ruler in the next section. Figure 7.12 shows the Tabs dialog box.

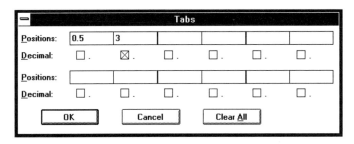

Figure 7.12   *Setting Tabs*

The Tabs dialog box shows a report with tab stops set at half an inch and at three inches. The tab at three inches is a decimal tab. Tabs in Write are not associated with specific paragraphs the way spacing, indenting, and alignment are. The tab setting is for the entire document.

The Ruler

Write displays the Ruler at the top of the window. If you have a mouse you can use the Ruler to change the format. The Ruler supports several of the operations you just learned. Besides letting you view and change the tab and indent settings, the Ruler includes icons that let you click on the spacing and alignment of the document.

Displaying the Ruler

You display the ruler by selecting the Ruler On command on the Document menu. The Ruler On command becomes the Ruler Off command when you are displaying the Ruler. Figure 7.13 shows the Ruler being displayed for a document.

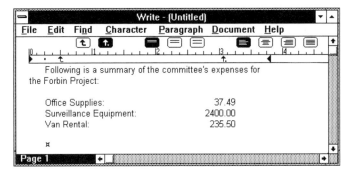

Figure 7.13   *The Ruler*

The ruled line shows measurements in inches or centimeters, depending on which you chose in Page Layout. The ruled line begins at 0, which corresponds to the left margin of the page. Directly below the ruled line is a format line. It shows you where the tabs and indent markers are set.

Indenting with the Ruler

The right-pointing arrowhead at the left end of the format line is the left indent marker. The small dot just to its right is the first line indent marker. If the left indent and first line indent markers occupy the same space, the dot is white inside the black arrowhead. There is a left-pointing arrowhead that marks the right indent, but it is off screen in Figure 7.13. You can move these indent markers by dragging them with the mouse cursor. The first line marker will not go to the left of the left indent marker.

Changing Tabs with the Ruler

The upward-pointing arrow with the curled shaft at the one-half-inch mark is a regular tab. The arrow with the straight shaft and the small dot next to it at the three-inch mark is a decimal tab. You can set either kind of tab by clicking its corresponding icon above the ruled line and then clicking in the format line where you want the tab to appear. You delete a tab by dragging it off the left end of the format line.

Changing Spacing with the Ruler

The three icons in the center of the space just above the ruled line select single, one and a half, and double spacing. Place the keyboard cursor inside the paragraph you want to change and click the spacing you want. As you move the keyboard cursor from paragraph to paragraph, the spacing icon in effect is highlighted.

Changing Paragraph Alignment with the Ruler

The four icons at the right of the space just above the ruled line select left alignment, center alignment, right alignment, and justification. Place the keyboard cursor inside the paragraph you want to change and click the alignment you want. As you move the keyboard cursor from paragraph to paragraph, the alignment icon in effect is highlighted.

Graphics

You can integrate text and graphics into a Write document. Graphics come from the Clipboard—you cannot read a graphics file directly into Write. A picture occupies the entire width of the page regardless of the width of the picture itself, you may not enter text on a line to the right or left of a picture.

Inserting a Picture

Assume that you have a graphics picture that you composed in Paintbrush, and that it looks like the picture in Figure 7.14. You will learn about composing such pictures with Paintbrush in Chapter 8.

Figure 7.14 *A Picture for a Document*

Now suppose that you want to use that picture as the letterhead for your document. To transfer a picture into a Write document you must first get the picture into the Clipboard. Point the mouse at the scissors icon with the dashed rectangle. That icon represents the Paintbrush tool for defining rectangular areas on the screen. Click the mouse to select the tool and move the mouse cursor into the picture area. The mouse cursor will change to a crosshair. Select the part of the picture to send to the Clipboard by starting in the upper-left corner, holding down the left mouse button, dragging the dashed rectangular outline to the lower-right corner, and releasing the button. If the outline does not adequately circumscribe the picture, try again. When the outline surrounds the border in the picture, choose Copy on the Edit menu. The picture is now in the Clipboard.

Start the Write application and begin a new document. Write inserts pictures into a document at the place where the keyboard cursor is positioned. A picture occupies the full width of the page regardless of the picture's actual width, so if the cursor is inside some text, inserting a picture will spit the text.

Inasmuch as the picture is to be the letterhead, you want it at the beginning of the document, so leave the cursor at the beginning of the document and select Paste from the Edit menu. The picture will appear at the beginning of the document, as shown in Figure 7.15.

Figure 7.15   *A Picture Inserted into a Write Document*

Selecting a Picture

The picture that you pasted into the document might be too big to be a letterhead. You can size and move a picture within a document, but first you must select it. To select a picture with the mouse, move the mouse cursor inside the picture and click the left button. To deselect it, click outside of the picture. To select and deselect a picture with the keyboard, use the up and down arrow keys to move in and out of the picture area. A selected picture displays in reverse video, as shown in Figure 7.16.

Figure 7.16   *A Selected Picture*

Sizing a Picture

To size a picture, select it and then select the Size Picture command from the Edit menu. A dotted outline appears around the picture and a square box appears at the center of the picture. The idea is to use the box to modify the shape and size of the outline. When the outline is the size and shape you want, you are done. This procedure is, cantankerous, however, and requires practice and patience.

One method is to place the box at the lower-right corner. Move it with the cursor, but do not click yet. Or move it to the right border with the right arrow key and to the bottom-right corner with the down arrow key. Sometimes this movement will shrink the outline's width too much, and you cannot move the box to the right. You must move the box around and watch the outline change. When the size is where you want it, click the mouse or press Enter.

Sometimes you will find success by stretching or shrinking the outline in one direction and clicking, and then selecting the Size command to stretch or shrink in the other direction.

The outline sometimes snaps out of reach and nothing seems to work. This behavior seems to indicate that Write has only enough memory for certain sizing limits, and the outline will not let you exceed them. You can press Esc to start over.

If you do not maintain the ratio of the dimensions of the original picture, the new size will be distorted. You can select Undo from the Edit menu to return to the original size and start over. The lower-left corner of the Write window will display the values 1.0X/1.0Y. These are the ratios of the width and height of the sized picture compared to the original. As you change the size, these values will change. If you keep the two numbers the same, the relative dimensions of the picture will be close to correct.

Figure 7.17 shows the picture sized smaller for the letterhead. If you are not sure whether the size is correct, print the document to see how it looks on paper.

Figure 7.17 *The Picture Shrunk*

Moving a Picture

You can move a picture horizontally across the page by selecting the picture and then selecting the Move Picture command from the Edit menu. The same dotted outline and box appear as do when you size a picture. Move the outline right and left with the mouse or with the right and left arrow keys. When the outline is where you want the picture to be, click the mouse or press Enter. Figure 7.18 shows the picture moved to the center of the page.

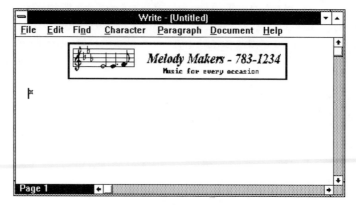

Figure 7.18 *The Picture Moved*

To move a picture vertically within a document, select it, cut it to the Clipboard, move the keyboard cursor to where you want the picture, and paste the picture into its new position.

N O T E

With the letterhead picture at the correct size and in the correct position, you might want to save the document in a file as boilerplate letterhead stationery. That way it will always be available for use in preparing other documents.

Adding Text

Adding text to a Write document is simply a matter of typing. Select a font and then type the body of your letter below the letterhead. Figure 7.19 shows the document with some text added.

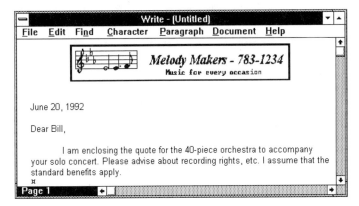

Figure 7.19   *Text Added*

The picture in these examples looks a bit ragged on the screen after you shrink it down. Figure 7.20 shows the letter printed on a laser printer, which has a resolution of 300 dots per inch. You can see that the printed rendition is much better.

Figure 7.20   *The Picture Printed*

Deleting a Picture

You can delete a picture by selecting it and pressing Del. If you decide you didn't want to delete it, you can select Undo on the Edit menu to get it back. Another way to delete is to select and cut the picture to the Clipboard. That way you capture the picture at the same that you delete it.

Pagination

When you print a document, Write will change pages according to the margins in the page layout and the length of the paper as defined in your printer setup. Write will also break pages one line early if the last line on the page would be the first line of a paragraph or if the first line on the next page would be the last line of a paragraph.

Inserting Page Breaks

Sometimes you want to force a page break where one might not otherwise occur. Perhaps every major heading in a document should start on a new page. To insert a page break, put the keyboard cursor where you want the break to occur and press Ctrl+Enter. Write displays a dotted line where the page break will occur.

Repaginating a Document

You can tell Write to indicate where page breaks will occur by using the Repaginate command on the File menu. Figure 7.21 shows the Repaginate Document dialog box. When you choose OK, the page breaks will appear as small >> symbols in the left margin of the document.

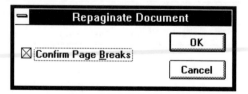

Figure 7.21   *The Repaginate Document Dialog Box*

Confirming Page Breaks

The Confirm Page Breaks check box on the Repaginate Document dialog box specifies that you want to confirm the page breaks as Write assigns them. Figure 7.22 shows the Repaginating Document dialog box used to confirm or change a page break.

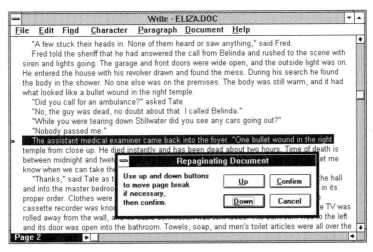

Figure 7.22   *Confirming a Page Break*

You can use the Up and Down command buttons to move the page break among the lines above where Write has decided to place it. When you have it where you want it, select the Confirm command button and the repagination will continue to the next page break. If you select the Cancel command button, repagination stops and you may edit the document.

Printing

Setting Up the Printer

The Printer Setup command on the File menu allows you to select which printer you are going to print to and to change the setup parameters of that printer. The Printer Setup dialog box, which allows you to select from a list of installed printers, also has a Setup command button. It calls a dialog box for specifying the setup parameters for the printer. The setup parameters are the same ones used to control the printer in the Print Manager, and they are different for every printer.

Printing

The Print command on the File menu opens the Print dialog box shown in Figure 7.23. You can select the number of copies and whether you want to print all or just a selected range of pages from the document. If your printer has draft and proof modes, you can select one of them by using the Print Quality drop-down list box. The Print to File check box allows you to print to a file. The Setup command button opens the same Printer Setup dialog box as the Printer Setup command on the File menu.

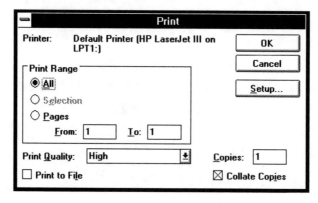

Figure 7.23   *The Print Dialog Box*

Summary

Windows Write is a small but powerful word processor that can support the word processing needs of many users. You learned to integrate graphics from another application into a Write document in this chapter. The Edit menu has a number of commands that support the Windows object linking and embedding feature. You will learn about this feature in Chapter 11.

Chapter 8 is about Windows Paintbrush, a graphics composition program that you can use to prepare graphics pictures.

Chapter

8

Paintbrush

This chapter is about Windows Paintbrush, the graphics accessory program that comes with Windows. In this chapter you will learn:

- ◆ Defining a picture's size and attributes
- ◆ Selecting colors from the palette
- ◆ Using the drawing tools
- ◆ Putting text into a picture
- ◆ Modifying a picture
- ◆ Maintaining picture files
- ◆ Printing pictures

Paintbrush is an application in the Program Manager's Accessories group. It is a graphics composition tool for constructing pictures. You can use Paintbrush to build pictures to integrate into documents, as you learned in Chapter 7. You can use the pictures by themselves, perhaps in presentations.

The artwork for the pictures you create can come from several places. It can come from compatible picture files available commercially. It can come from photographs and illustrations that you load into your computer with a scanning device. It can come from graphic displays captured from other programs. And it can come from original creations you compose by using the Paintbrush design tools.

No book can teach you to be a creative designer. You can learn about the tools and techniques that Paintbrush offers, but how you use them is a function of your own artistic bent. You will see many wonderful and imaginative designs in books and magazine articles that describe Paintbrush and similar programs. Many of those pictures were composed by professional illustrators. Others are the work of talented amateurs. If your first efforts do not measure up to the examples you find in published works, keep trying. With effort you can master the art of interactive graphics design.

If You Have No Mouse

Although all the Paintbrush functions are available to users who use the keyboard and have no mouse, using Paintbrush that way is pure agony. There are keyboard substitutes for mouse actions, but progress is painfully slow. If you intend to use your computer for graphics design, regardless of which program you use, the cost of a mouse is a good investment. Table 8.1 shows the keyboard substitutes for mouse operations.

Table 8.1   *Keyboard Substitutes for Mouse Operations*

Mouse Operation	Keystroke
Click left button	Ins
Click right button	Del
Double-click left button	F9+Ins
Double-click right button	F9+Del

The Paintbrush

Figure 8.1 shows the Paintbrush application window. You build pictures interactively inside the workspace of the window by using the tools and the palette.

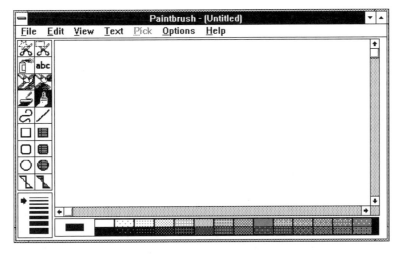

Figure 8.1   *The Paintbrush Application Window*

The boxed icons along the left edge of the window are the *tools.* Each tool selects a drawing function. You select a tool by clicking its icon. The cursor changes shape as you move it around the window. Outside of the workspace, the cursor is the familiar left-slanting pointer. Inside the workspace, the cursor assumes a shape that represents the currently selected tool.

The Line Size Selector in the lower-left corner of the window selects the width of lines that you draw, the size of the eraser's effective sweep, the width of the borders for shapes you draw, and the width of the air brush's pattern.

The Foreground/Background Color Display shows the colors for a picture's foreground—the shapes drawn with the tools—and background. You select colors from the *palette* of colors that appear along the bottom edge of the window.

Picture Size

Paintbrush works with a default picture size that varies depending on what kind of display monitor you use and how much memory you have. You can change this default by choosing the Image Attributes command from the Options menu. You will see the Image Attributes dialog box shown in Figure 8.2.

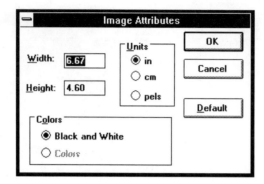

Figure 8.2 *The Image Attributes Dialog box*

The Height and Width text boxes specify the dimensions of the image area. You can specify that the dimensions be expressed in inches, centimeters, or pixels by selecting one of the Units option buttons. If the picture is to be in black and white, you should select the Black and White option button.

The Default command button returns the settings to their original default values.

Picture Attributes

There are several attributes that affect how the various tools operate. When you change an attribute, the tools that it affects will then work differently.

Line Size

The Line Size Selector is the box in the lower-left corner of the Paintbrush application window. It has a stack of horizontal lines of graduated widths. You select a thicker line in the selector to tell Paintbrush to draw and spray thicker lines and erase wider areas. Point the mouse cursor at one of the selector's lines and click and to select it.

Brush Shapes

The Brush Shapes command on the Options menu lets you select the shape of a line drawn by the Brush tool. Figure 8.3 shows the Brush Shapes dialog box.

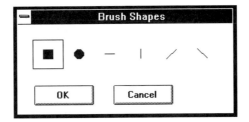

Figure 8.3   *The Brush Shapes Dialog Box*

There are six brush shapes to select from. The default brush shape is a square box. The square outline that surrounds it indicates that it is currently selected. Click on a different shape if you like. The outline will move around your selection. Choose OK when you have the shape selected. Here is a shortcut: double-click the brush tool icon to select the Brush Shapes command. Figure 8.4 shows the effects of the various brush shapes.

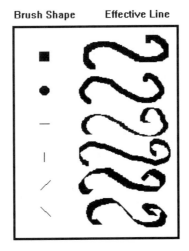

Figure 8.4   *Brush Shapes*

Palette

The *palette* is the row of color boxes along the bottom edge of the Paintbrush application window. When you select one of them by clicking it with the left mouse button, the center box of the Foreground/Background Color Selector changes to the selected color. Subsequent drawing operations use the selected color.

To change the background color, select a color with the right mouse button. This action does not change the background for the current picture, but it does change how some of the tools work. The background color is the border color for filled boxes, circles, and polygons.

When you choose New from the File menu, the current background color becomes the background for the new picture.

Drawing Tools

The *drawing tools* are the icons displayed along the left edge of the Paintbrush application window. Only one of these tools is active at a time. You select a tool by clicking its icon. Figure 8.5 shows the icons and the names of the tools that they represent.

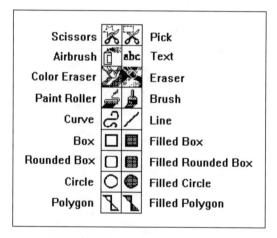

Scissors			Pick
Airbrush			Text
Color Eraser			Eraser
Paint Roller			Brush
Curve			Line
Box			Filled Box
Rounded Box			Filled Rounded Box
Circle			Filled Circle
Polygon			Filled Polygon

Figure 8.5   *Drawing Tool Icons*

Scissors and Pick

You use the scissors and pick tools to outline an area of your picture. This defined area is called a *cutout*. The scissors tool allows you to draw a freehand outline around the cutout. The pick tool allows you to draw a rectangular outline around the cutout.

After you have outlined a cutout, you can do several image manipulation operations on it. Those operations are described in the section titled "Image Manipulation."

When you have a cutout defined, the Clipboard's Cut and Copy commands on the Edit menu are enabled. You use these commands to send the cutout to the Clipboard, as you learned in Chapter 4. If you are not using the Clipboard for data exchange with another program at the time, the Cut command is a convenient way to delete large areas of the picture without having to use the eraser tool.

Airbrush

The airbrush tool emulates a spraypaint can. You select a foreground color and a line size and then move the mouse cursor around holding the left button down to spray a pattern. The subway decoration shown in Figure 8.6 was sprayed with the airbrush.

Figure 8.6 *Airbrush Graffiti*

Text

The text tool allows you to type text of various fonts, styles, and sizes into your picture. The sign on top of the subway shown in Figure 8.6 is an example of text entry. You will learn about text and characters later in this chapter.

Erasers

There are two erasers. The eraser tool erases the area of the picture under the eraser cursor, which is a square box of variable size. You move the mouse cursor across the picture and hold the left button down to erase. The size of the eraser is controlled by the Line Size Selector.

The color eraser tool has two functions. You can drag it across the screen the same way you do the regular eraser. But the color eraser changes a selected color to another color rather than erasing. To specify the color to change, select it as the foreground color. To specify the new color, select it as the background color.

To change all occurrences of the selected foreground color to the background color within the visible part of the drawing area, double-click the color eraser tool.

Paint Roller

The paint roller tool fills an area with the selected foreground color. It spreads the color out, stopping when it hits the edge of a border. The back wall and tiles in the subway picture in figure 8.6 were filled in with the paint roller. If the paint roller finds a break in the border of a form you are trying to fill, it will leak through and fill adjacent forms. Use the Undo command on the Edit menu to undo the fill and try again.

Brush

You use the brush tool to draw freehand. The brush shape and the line size both affect the lines that you draw. Figure 8.7 is a picture of a cowboy that was drawn entirely with the brush.

Figure 8.7 *Drawing with the Brush*

Line

The line tool lets you draw straight lines. You select the line size and foreground color, move the mouse to the starting point of the line, and press and hold the left mouse button. Then you drag the other end of the line to where you want it. Figure 8.8 shows a wire-frame airport drawing made entirely from lines.

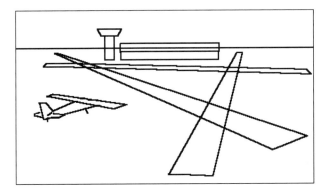

Figure 8.8 *Drawing with Lines*

Curve

The curve tool lets you draw a line in the workspace and then distort it to form a curve. You move the mouse cursor to the beginning of the line and press and hold the left button. Then you drag to the other end. When you release the button, you have drawn a straight line. Now move the mouse cursor elsewhere on the screen and hold the left button down. The line will warp toward the mouse cursor. As long as you hold the button down you can move the mouse to form the curve in different ways and directions. You may release the button, move to a second location and warp some more. When you release the button the second time, you have defined the curve and it becomes a part of the drawing.

Figure 8.9 shows an example of a curve drawn with the curve tool. The advantage of the curve tool is that it draws a much smoother curve than you can draw freehand with the brush. It does, however, take some practice to get used to how it works so that you can draw a curve with a predictable shape.

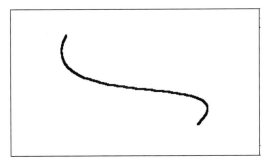

Figure 8.9 *A Curve*

Boxes

You can draw four kinds of boxes. The box and rounded box tools draw a box outline without changing the part of the picture that is inside the box. The outline uses the foreground color. The filled box and filled rounded box tools draw the boxes using the background color as a frame and the foreground color to fill the box. A rounded box has rounded corners. A box has square corners. Figure 8.10 shows a random collection of boxes.

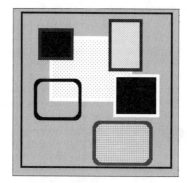

Figure 8.10   *Boxes*

Circles

The circle and filled circle tools allow you to draw circles and ellipses. The filled circle tool draws circles using the background color as a frame and the foreground color to fill the circle. The clown in Figure 8.11 is made entirely from circles and ellipses.

Figure 8.11   *Circles*

Polygons

The polygon and filled polygon tools allow you to draw polygons. After selecting the line size and colors, you select the tool and move the mouse cursor to the start of your polygon. Press the left mouse button and drag the cursor to the end of the first side of the polygon. Release the button. The first side of the polygon displays. Move the mouse cursor to the end of the second side and click. A line displays from the end of the first to where the mouse cursor is. Repeat this step until you are ready to terminate a line at the starting point of the first side. When you release the mouse button this time the polygon displays itself.

The drawing in Figure 8.12 uses polygons to create the pyramids, the pit, the building, and the ship.

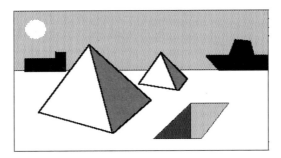

Figure 8.12   *Polygons*

Making New Colors

The palette at the bottom of the Paintbrush application window describes 28 colors. Any of them can be the foreground or background color for your picture. You can modify any or all of the colors, thus defining your own custom palette. You can save that palette definition in a file and retrieve it later.

Changing a Color

Choose the Edit Colors command on the Options menu. You will see the Edit Colors dialog box shown in Figure 8.13. As a shortcut you can double-click any of the color boxes at any time to execute the Edit Colors command.

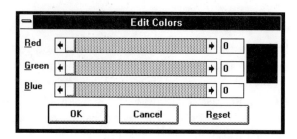

Figure 8.13 *The Edit Colors Dialog Box*

The color represented in the Edit Colors dialog box is the current foreground color. This is the color that you will change, and it will change not only in the Foreground Color display in the lower-left corner of the window but also in the palette box from which you chose it to be the foreground color. You can change a different color in the palette by clicking the color you want to change while the Edit Colors dialog box is still active.

To change the color, move the scroll boxes for the red, green, and blue components of the color. You can drag the boxes, click their scroll buttons, or type new numbers into the text boxes that show the relative value of each color component from 0 to 255.

Some combinations of values give a solid color, while others add texture. When the three values are combinations of 0, 64, 128, 192 or 255, you usually get a solid color, but not always. The default palette for a color system consists of colors with only these values. With other combinations you get a textured color. As you change the values, the sample color in the box at the right end of the dialog box changes so you can see the new color.

If you have selected Black and White in the Image Attributes command on the Options menu, each color in the palette has three components with the same value. When you change the value of one of the components in such a monochrome palette, the values of the other two components change along with it.

When the color is the way you want it, choose OK. To change a color to its original value, choose Reset. Choose Cancel to leave the color the way it was when you executed the Edit Colors command.

You can change any or all of the colors in the palette by using this procedure.

Recording and Retrieving a Palette File

The Save Colors command on the Options menu allows you to save the current palette in a named file with the extension .PAL. Later you can use the Get Colors command to select from among those palettes you have stored.

Text

The "abc" tool icon allows you to enter text into your picture. When you select that icon, you can move the mouse cursor to a location, click to identify the position of the first character, and begin typing. The first character position becomes the left margin of the text you type. If you press Enter, the text cursor moves to the next line at the left margin.

The text is treated as text entry for as long as you type and do not select a different tool icon or move the text cursor with the mouse. When you take one of these actions, the text is anchored into the picture and becomes a part of the graphics picture itself.

Fonts and Styles

There are many character fonts, styles, and sizes you can select from the Fonts command on the Text menu. Figure 8.14 shows the Font dialog box, from which you can select text fonts. Figure 8.15 shows how each of the fonts appears on the screen and the effects of the various character styles.

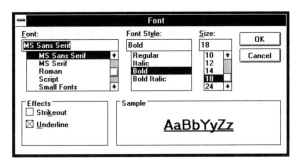

Figure 8.14 *The Font Dialog Box*

Fonts		Styles
Arial	MS Serif	Normal
Courier	Roman	**Bold**
Courier New	*Script*	*Italic*
Fixed Sys	Small Fonts	Underline
Modern	**System**	Outline *
MS Dialog	Terminal	Shadow *
MS Sans Serif	Times New Roman	* Black background, white foreground

Figure 8.15   *Character Styles*

If you change fonts while you are still typing, the entire body of text changes to the new font. Once the text has been anchored, you cannot change its font.

The Text menu has several character styles available. The Normal command turns the other styles off, so you use it to reset everything. The Bold, Italic, and Underline styles are toggle commands. When they are in effect, a check mark appears to the left of the command name in the menu. You can have any combination of the three.

The Outline and Shadow styles are mutually exclusive. The Outline style displays the character as an outline of the background color against the foreground color in the center of each character. For the Outline style to have any effect, you must change the foreground and background colors. The Shadow style displays the characters formed in the foreground color with a shadow made of the background color. As with the Outline style, for the Shadow style to have any effect, you must change the foreground and background colors.

If you change character style while you are still typing, the entire body of text changes to the new style. Once the text has been anchored you cannot change its style.

Image Manipulation

Paintbrush has several operations that allow you to manipulate the graphics picture to achieve certain effects. They all use a cutout defined with the scissors or pick tool.

Moving a Cutout

Move the mouse cursor inside the cutout. Hold the left mouse button down and drag the cutout to its new location. The dashed outline that defines the cutout disappears so that you can see the movement occur.

As you move the picture, you might see some color bleeding between the cutout you are moving and the areas on the screen through which you move it. A lot will depend on the colors. A black on white image will superimpose the cutout over the receiving area without removing any of the detail of the receiving area except where elements of the image intersect. This kind of movement is called *transparent* movement.

You can also move a cutout *opaquely* by using the right mouse button instead of the left. The entire image of the cutout will replace the image covered by the cutout.

Copying a Cutout

To copy a cutout, hold down the Shift key as you drag the mouse away from the original cutout. This action will cause the image inside the cutout to remain in place as you move a copy of it to the new location. You can copy a cutout both transparently and opaquely.

Sweeping a Cutout

If you hold the Ctrl key down while you move a cutout, it sweeps across the screen, repeating copies of itself. The faster you drag it, the further apart the copies will be. You can space them even further apart by tapping the Ctrl key as you drag the cutout. If you sweep with the left mouse button, the swept copies will be transparent. If you sweep with the right mouse button, the copies will be opaque. Figure 8.16 shows examples of both kinds of sweeping.

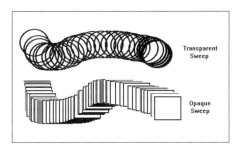

Figure 8.16 *Sweeping*

Sizing

Defining a cutout enables the Pick menu, where you will find commands to flip and size the cutout, tilt it, and change it to inverse video.

The Clear command toggle tells the other commands on the Pick menu to make the change and clear the original copy. Usually that is what you want to do.

The Shrink+Grow command on the Pick menu allows you to change the size of the cutout. First you define the cutout. Then, unless you are retaining the original and making a sized copy, you should choose the Clear command toggle so that it has a check mark next to it on the menu. Then choose Shrink+Grow. You will be back in the Paintbrush workspace with the crosshair cursor and the cutout's outline will be gone. Move the cursor to the upper-left corner of where you want to put the newly sized cutout. Then hold down the left mouse button and drag the cursor to the lower-right corner of the sized cutout. The dotted outline will follow along. When the outline describes the new size, release the button.

You can now move the cursor to another upper-left position and make another resized copy.

If during all this you want to return to the original and start over, choose the Undo command on the Edit menu.

The shape ratio of the sized copies will follow the height and width ratios of the original cutout to the new outline you define with the mouse. If you want to retain the original ratio of dimensions, hold the Shift key down while you describe the new box.

Figure 8.17 shows four cornets. The upper-left cornet is the original. The others are products of the Shrink+Grow command.

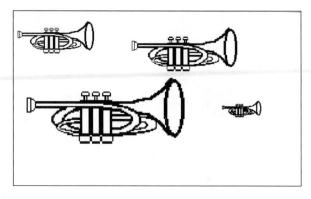

Figure 8.17 *Sizing*

Flipping

The Flip Horizontal and Flip Vertical commands on the Pick menu change the horizontal and vertical orientation of the cutout. The Clear command has no effect on these commands because they take effect in the space occupied by the original cutout. Figure 8.18 shows the effect of flipping.

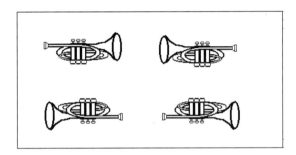

Figure 8.18   *Flipping*

Paintbrush has no rotate command, so there is no way to stand the cornet on end.

Tilting

The Tilt command on the Pick menu allows you to tilt a cutout forward or backward. When you choose the Tilt command, you are returned to the workspace with the crosshair cursor. The cutout outline is gone. Move the cursor to the upper-left corner of the place you want to put the tilted copy and press the left button to display the outline of the tilted cutout. As you move the cursor to the left and right, the base of the tilting cutout outline moves left and right, while its top stays in place. When the outline appears the way you want it, release the mouse button. You can move the mouse to a different upper-left corner and repeat the tilt. You can use the Undo command on the Edit menu to return to your original starting place. Select any tool or menu to lock the tilted cutouts in place.

Figure 8.19 shows a car apparently standing still. Figure 8.20 shows the same car with the illusion of motion added. By tilting forward and adding some horizontal lines, dust, and exhaust, the car appears to be speeding along. Observe how the tilting process modifies the color texture of the auto body and tires.

Figure 8.19 *An Immobile Automobile*

Figure 8.20 *A Speeding Car*

Inverse

The Inverse command on the Pick menu reverses the foreground and background colors of the cutout. Figure 8.21 shows a scanned hand drawing of a piano. Figure 8.22 shows the same drawing after the Inverse command was used.

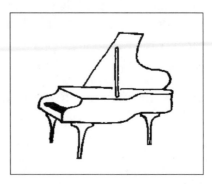

Figure 8.21 *A Scanned Drawing*

Figure 8.22   *An Inverse Drawing*

Views

Viewing the Picture

The View Picture command uses the entire screen to show the picture. This command is useful for looking at pictures that occupy more space than you can see inside the viewing area of the workspace. When you are finished looking at the picture, press a mouse button or a key on the keyboard to return to the Paintbrush display. As a shortcut, double-click the pick tool icon to execute the View Picture command.

Zoom In

The Zoom In command on the View menu allows you to zoom in on the picture and do some detail work. It also serves to zoom the picture back to normal after you have used the Zoom Out command described next.

When you choose the Zoom In command, the cursor becomes a rectangle. You move the cursor to the position that you want to see in more detail, then click. Refer to the airport design in Figure 8.8. Suppose you wanted to remove the intersecting lines on the runways and buildings and add wheels to the airplane. Begin by zooming in on where two of the runways intersect. You will see the display shown in Figure 8.23.

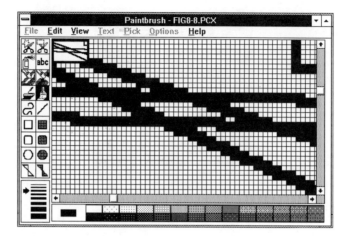

Figure 8.23   *Zoomed In*

The picture in Figure 8.23 is the zoomed-in area magnified several times so that you can see each individual pixel (picture element). The small detail in the upper-left corner of the workspace shows the zoomed-in area as it normally appears.

You edit the image in a zoomed-in area by turning pixels on and off. You turn a pixel on by pointing the mouse cursor at it and clicking the left button. The right button turns a pixel off. You can watch your progress by looking at the detail picture.

You can use the scroll bars to move the zoomed-in area around as you make changes. If you want to undo the changes you made since zooming in, use the Undo command on the Edit menu.

When you are done with your zoomed-in pixel changes, use the Zoom Out command to return to the normal Paintbrush view. Zoom in on another area and make more changes.

Figure 8.24 shows the airport with the changes made.

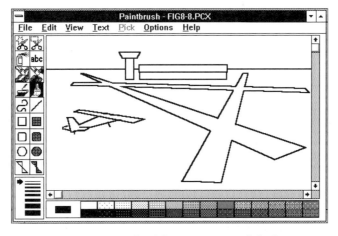

Figure 8.24   *The Airport Modified*

Zoom Out

The Zoom Out command zooms the picture out so that the entire image area is visible within the workspace. Only a few of the Paintbrush actions are enabled when you are zoomed out.

The pick tool is the only tool you can use while you are zoomed out. You can define an outline and the only thing you can do with it is cut or copy it to the Clipboard by using the Cut and Copy commands or copy it to a file by using the Copy To command. Those commands are on the Edit menu. Figure 8.25 shows the airport picture zoomed out with an outline defined and ready to copy or cut.

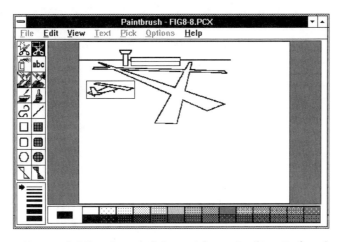

Figure 8.25   *Zoomed Out with an Outline Defined*

If you paste from the clipboard or a file in the normal viewing configuration, the paste operation clips—truncates—any part of the pasted picture that does not fit within the viewed workspace. That means that screen size and window size affect the size of a pasted image. To allow the paste to affect the entire picture area, you must paste while you are zoomed out.

When you are zoomed out and you choose Paste or Paste From on the Edit menu, a crosshatch pattern displays in the upper-left corner of the picture. The pattern is the size of the image that is about to be pasted. In Figure 8.26 you have copied the airplane to the Clipboard, zoomed out, and chosen the Paste command.

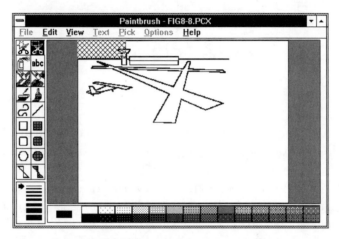

Figure 8.26   *Pasting from the Clipboard*

The crosshatch pattern in the upper-left corner of the workspace indicates where the pasted image will go. You can move it around on the picture by dragging it with the mouse. When you have it where you want it, move the cursor out of the crosshatch and click or choose the Paste command again.

Figure 8.27 shows the new airplane pasted in place.

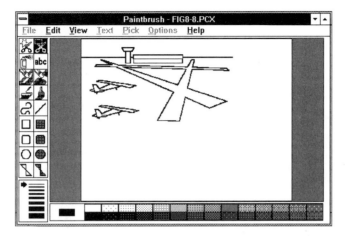

Figure 8.27 *A Second Airplane Pasted In*

Finally, Figure 8.28 shows how, by using several pastes of the airplane and by using the Shrink+Grow command to add perspective, the airport is now populated with a fleet of airplanes.

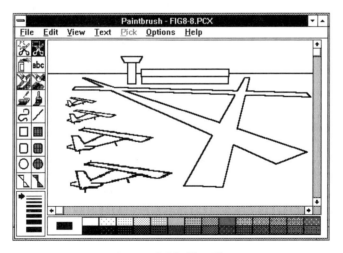

Figure 8.28 *The Fleet*

Suppressing the Tools and Palette

The Tools, Linesize, and Palette toggle commands on the View menu allow you to remove the corresponding components of the Paintbrush screen in order to obtain a larger workspace.

Displaying the Cursor Position

The Cursor Position command on the View menu displays the cursor's X/Y coordinates as two numbers in a small window in the upper-right corner of the Paintbrush application window. The first number is the left-to-right X coordinate, and it ranges from 0 at the left edge of the workspace to 622 at the right. The second number is the top-to-bottom Y coordinate, and it ranges from 0 at the top of the workspace to 424 at the bottom.

Files

You retain your pictures in files, and you might get pictures from other sources that distribute them in files. There are several formats for storing graphics images, and you can read and write all of them. The file extension identifies these formats. The .BMP format is the one used for Windows wallpaper. The other format is the .PCX-type file. You should avoid using .BMP files other than for defining wallpaper files. They require much more disk space than .PCX files, and they take longer to read into memory.

Loading an Existing File

You load an existing picture file into Paintbrush by using the Open command on the File menu. Figure 8.29 shows the File Open dialog box. Use the List Files of Type drop-down list box to select the kind of file you are going to retrieve. The .MSP file type is an older Windows format that Windows 3.1 supports only for compatibility.

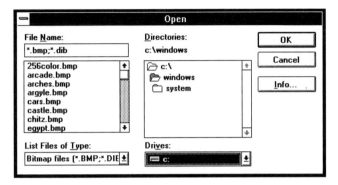

Figure 8.29 *The File Open Dialog Box*

The Info command button will tell you the dimensions of the file in the Picture Information dialog box shown in Figure 8.30.

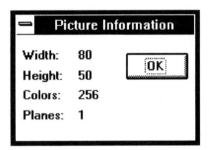

Figure 8.30 *Information Dialog Box*

Saving Your Picture

To save a picture, you use the Save or Save As commands on the File menu. If you read the picture in from an existing file, the Save command writes it to the same file name. If you have generated a new picture and the title bar still says "Paintbrush - (Untitled)," the Save command works just like the Save As command. The Save As command allows you to name the file. It produces the File Save As dialog box shown in Figure 8.31.

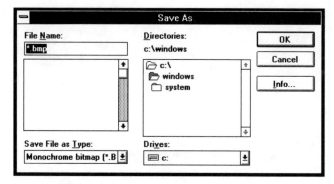

Figure 8.31 *The File Save As Dialog Box*

Starting a New Picture

You start a new picture when you execute Paintbrush, unless you call Paintbrush from the File Manager by selecting a .PCX or .BMP file or from a Program Manager icon that has a file name included among the program's properties. You can change to a new picture after starting or loading a different one by choosing the New command on the File menu. As a shortcut, double-click the eraser tool icon to execute the New command.

Copying to a File

The Copy To command on the Edit menu allows you to copy a cutout to a file rather than to the Clipboard. You will get a Copy To dialog box that looks and works just like the Save To dialog box except that the image copied will have the dimensions of the cutout rather than of the entire picture.

Pasting from Another File

The Paste From command allows you to paste an image into your picture from a file rather than from the Clipboard. The Paste From dialog box looks and works just like the File Open dialog box, except that the image in the file is pasted into the current picture. When you open a file, the image dimensions are that of the file. When you paste from a file you can paste a smaller image into a larger picture or vice versa.

Printing

If you have a printer with graphics capabilities installed, you can print your pictures from within Paintbrush.

Page Setup

Figure 8.32 shows the Page Setup dialog box. You can specify the picture's four margins and brief header and footer text to print with it.

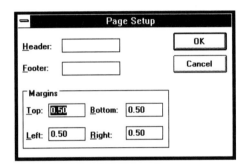

Figure 8.32   *The Page Setup Dialog Box*

Printer Setup

Paintbrush's Print Setup command on the File menu displays the Printer Setup dialog box shown in Figure 8.33. Paintbrush's Print Setup differs from those of other applications, such as Windows Write, in that only installed printers that have graphics capabilities appear in its list box. Paintbrush cannot print to a text-only printer, so it does not allow you to select one.

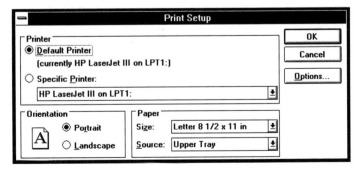

Figure 8.33   *The Printer Setup Dialog Box*

The Setup command button calls the Setup dialog box for the printer you have selected. Each printer uses a different one. You saw the one for your printer when you installed it with the Control Panel. See "Setting Up the Printer" in Chapter 5.

Printing the Picture

When you choose the Print command on the File menu, you see the Print dialog box shown in Figure 8.34. You can select Draft or Proof, but the two options usually produce the same picture. You can print one or more copies by entering the value in the Number of Copies field. Changing the scaling will either enlarge or reduce the picture. A picture with 50% scaling is half the size of one with 100%, which is half the size of one with 200%.

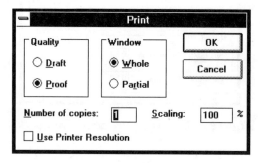

Figure 8.34   *The Print Dialog Box*

The Whole and Partial options indicate that you want to print the entire picture or a cutout portion of it. If you select Partial, you will be allowed to describe a cutout to be printed as the partial picture.

Wallpaper

If you save a picture as a .BMP file, you can use the Control Panel to install it into your desktop as the wallpaper. Chapter 5 explains how to install wallpaper. A unique wallpaper file is the ultimate personal expression. By using high-resolution scanners, the libraries of clip art, custom graphics files that you can download from online services and bulletin boards, and the tools of the Paintbrush, you can decorate your Windows desktop with the wallpaper of your choice. Figure 8.35 shows the wallpaper that greets this author each day.

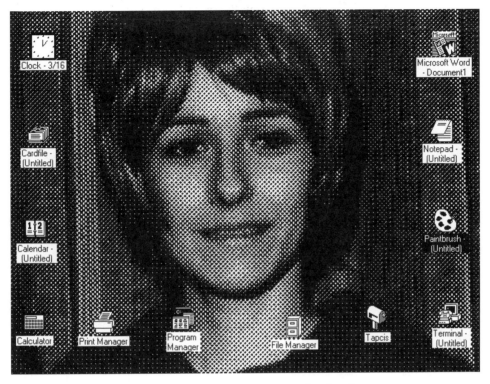

Figure 8.35   *Judy in Windowland*

Summary

In this Chapter you have learned how to make a graphic by using all of the many tools provided with the Windows Paintbrush application.

With the promise of wallpaper you can download from online services and bulletin boards, you might well ask how you go about getting it. The first step is to have a communications program. Chapter 9 is about Windows Terminal, the communications program that comes with Windows.

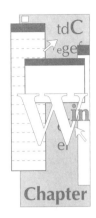

Chapter

9

Terminal

This chapter is about Windows Terminal, the communications accessory program that comes with Windows. In this chapter you will learn:

◆ Setting communications and modem parameters
◆ Defining communications function keys
◆ Calling another computer
◆ Answering a call from another computer
◆ Online dialogues
◆ File transfers

The Windows Terminal program is a small communications program that allows you to connect your computer to online services, electronic bulletin boards, and other computers. You use a modem when you connect to the services and bulletin boards. You can use a modem to connect to other computers, too, or, if the other computer is nearby, you can connect to it directly.

Figure 9.1 illustrates a typical computer-to-computer connection. Both computers have external modems that are connected to the phone line. When one computer dials the phone number of the other, the other computer answers the phone, and the connection is complete.

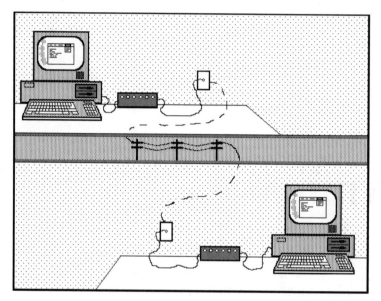

Figure 9.1   *Connecting Two Computers*

The Modem

A modem is a device that translates the data signals that the computer sends to its serial communications port, into tones that telephone lines can carry. This translation is called *modulation*. In the other direction, the modem translates, or *demodulates*, the tones that it receives from a remote modem into data signals that the computer can read through its serial communications port. *Modem* is short for "modulator-demodulator."

Besides translating signals, the modem handles other chores for the computer. It dials and answers the phone, senses the busy signal, and notifies the calling computer when the remote computer's modem has answered.

A modem can be an external device, as shown in Figure 9.1, or it can be installed inside your computer.

Coordinating Connections

Getting one computer to call another, getting the other one to answer the phone, and then getting them to exchange data in a meaningful way requires a good deal of complex, technical coordination. It is the job of a communications program such as Terminal to automate that coordination, but it is your responsibility to provide the parameters that make it possible. Terminal has many parameters for you to set. Do not feel intimidated by the extent of the information you must provide, even if you are a newcomer to computer communications. This chapter will explain the basics and lead you through each step of the process.

Every connection has its own set of parameters, ones that you must define to Terminal in order to successfully make the connection. You might routinely call any of these or similar systems:

- MCI Mail—for electronic mail
- Compuserve—to participate in special-interest discussions
- Numerous bulletin board services—to upload and download free and shareware software
- A friend's personal computer—to chat and exchange files.
- Your employer's computer—to do some work from home.

Each one of these connections has a set of communications parameters and interactive protocols. Fortunately for you, Terminal allows you to record the unique information about each service you call in a file so you do not need to enter the parameters every time you make a connection. This chapter will walk you through some typical sessions.

Regardless of the kind of system you call with Terminal, you are calling a computer. Online services such as Compuserve, Genie, BIX, and Prodigy are distant large computers with banks of modems for handling many subscribers at once. Often you gain access to the service by calling a local time-sharing network such as Tymnet and Telenet, and these, too, are computers. Electronic bulletin boards are typically operated as free services by individuals who dedicate a second phone line to a personal computer that runs public domain bulletin board software.

Running Terminal

Terminal is an application in the Program Manager's Accessories group. When you run it you see the Terminal applications window shown in Figure 9.2.

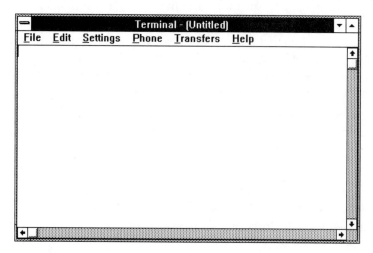

Figure 9.2 *The Terminal Applications Window*

The blinking box cursor in the upper-left corner of the Terminal workspace is the communications cursor. If you start typing now, the characters you type will be sent to the selected communications port. Depending on what device is connected to that port and how the device configures itself when you power up, you might see the characters you type echoed on the screen. Regardless of what you see, when you type you are transmitting the typed characters to the communications port, whether or not anything is connected to it. You will learn what a communications port is later in this chapter.

The Terminal window's workspace is itself a window into a buffer. As you send and receive lines of text, they will appear in the workspace. When you get to the bottom of the workspace, the text at the top will scroll out of sight. The scrolled-off text is not lost. You can use the vertical scroll bar to view it. The buffer holds a maximum number of lines, however. When that number is reached, the text at the top of the buffer is lost. You can control the buffer size with one of the Terminal settings described later in this chapter.

Setting Parameters

In order to call another computer, you must set the values of a number of parameters. These range in complexity from the simple, such as the telephone number, to the arcane, such as the number of stop bits. Although the number and scope of these parameters might dazzle the newcomer, the parameters are industry standards; you should have little trouble finding out what they are for a given setup. Some of them, such as the communications port and the modem commands, are related to your hardware. Others, such as the baud rate, depend on settings required by the computer you are going to call.

You set parameters from the Settings menu, which has commands for several categories of parameter.

Phone Number

The Phone Number command on the Settings menu allows you to define and change the phone number that Terminal is going to call. The command displays the Phone Number dialog box shown in Figure 9.3. Enter the phone number of the computer you are going to call. You can enter punctuation and spaces to make the number more readable, such as:

```
1-(800) 123-4567
```

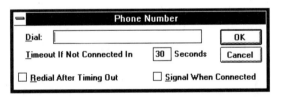

Figure 9.3 *The Phone Number Dialog Box*

If you are dialing from a phone connected to a switchboard, such as you find in offices and hotels, you might need a pause after an initial access digit to gain access to the outside line. You can insert a comma in the phone number to cause the dialing to delay two seconds, such as:

```
9,123-4567
```

The Timeout If Not Connected In field in the Phone Number dialog box allows you to specify the number of seconds to wait for an answer. The Redial After Timing Out check box tells Terminal to try again if there is no answer after the timeout.

The Signal When Connected check box tells Terminal to sound an audible signal when a successful connection is made. Many bulletin board systems are extremely busy, and you get a busy signal every time you call. You can tell Terminal to retry every minute, for example, and to signal you when the call goes through.

Terminal Emulation

When you call a remote computer, you do so to use the software in that computer. Sometimes the software in the other computer expects to be called by a particular kind of terminal device. The remote software will accordingly send particular commands to your computer terminal to tell it to clear the screen, position the cursor, display colors, and so on.

Most bulletin board systems and online services direct their displays to a common denominator, the generic TTY device. They use no special screen-formatting commands so that they can communicate with the largest number of users. But some services, the FIDO network for example, allow a user to specify that he or she uses a particular terminal. FIDO will use the special commands of the ANSI standard terminal if it knows you have one. Other computers you call might simply require a specific terminal. Your communications program must be able to emulate that kind of terminal.

Terminal can provide generic TTY terminal emulation and it can emulate two popular terminal devices used by many online services. The Terminal Emulation command on the Settings menu allows you to tell Terminal which terminal device to emulate. Figure 9.4 shows the Terminal Emulation dialog box. The example sessions in this chapter work with any of the selections.

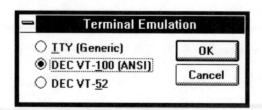

Figure 9.4 *The Terminal Emulation Dialog Box*

Terminal Preferences

There are a number of different ways you can set up Terminal to talk to another computer. The Terminal Preferences command on the Settings menu allows you to set these preferences. Figure 9.5 shows the Terminal Preferences dialog box.

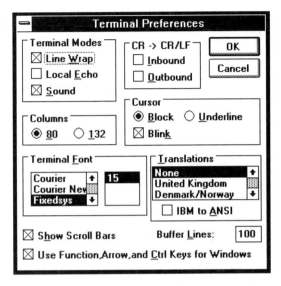

Figure 9.5   *The Terminal Preferences Dialog Box*

Terminal Modes

Line Wrap. Set the Line Wrap check box on so that if the remote computer sends lines that are longer than the number of columns you specify, Terminal will continue the input line on the next line in its workspace instead of truncating the excess characters.

Local Echo. Set Local Echo on if the characters you type to the other computer do not appear on your screen. Here is how it usually works.

When you call another computer and send it a keystroke, the other computer receives it and sends it back to your computer. This returned character is called an "echo." Because Terminal displays every character it receives, the echoed character appears on the screen just after you type it. The relationship between the computers is one of "originator" and "answerer." The answerer echoes the characters of the originator.

Before you call another computer, and if there is a modem connected to your communications port, the keys you type go to the modem. As initially configured by Terminal, a Hayes-compatible modem will echo the command characters it receives back to Terminal and they, too, will appear on the screen. The modem stops echoing when the connection is complete because it assumes that the answering computer will take over.

This echoing behavior of the remote computer is a part of what is called "full duplex" operation. If the remote computer's documentation on its parameters—assuming there is some—specifies that it uses full duplex operation, leave the Local Echo option button off, its default setting. If the documentation specifies "half duplex," set the Local Echo option on.

In the absence of any documentation from the remote computer, begin by assuming that it uses full duplex. Most systems do. If you believe you are properly connected, and you do not see the characters you type being displayed as you type them, try setting the Local Echo option on. On the other hand, you could have Local Echo set on and see each keystroke echoed twice, as in this example:

```
HHeelloo,, DDoollyy
```

In that case, turn the Local Echo option off.

Many online services and bulletin boards require you to enter a password. They intentionally do not echo the password you type to protect you from revealing your password to a passerby who happens to look over your shoulder when you type it. Do not make any decisions about Local Echo based on the behavior of Terminal while you enter a password.

Sound. The remote computer might send you the ASCII BEL character. This character was used in the times of Teletype machines to ring a small brass bell to get the operator's attention. With the Sound check box turned on, Terminal will beep if the remote computer sends the BEL character. If you want to ring the bell of the remote computer once you are connected, type Ctrl+G to send the BEL character.

CR -> CR/LF

The CR -> CR/LF field has Inbound and Outbound check boxes. CR means "carriage return." LF means "line feed." When Terminal receives characters, it displays them on the screen at the current cursor position, advancing the cursor one position for each character received. When Terminal receives a carriage return character—the Enter key—Terminal moves the cursor to the left margin of the current line. When Terminal receives a line feed, Terminal moves the cursor one line down but does not change the column.

The Inbound check box will tell Terminal to add a line feed every time it receives a carriage return. If the remote terminal sends you exactly what its user types, and its user types only the Enter key at the end of every line, each line will overwrite the one that preceded it. In that case you need to add a line feed to the inbound text, so you would select the Inbound check box.

The outbound check box will tell Terminal to add a line feed to the output data stream every time you type the Enter key.

This can get confusing. If you add inbound line feeds and the user at the remote computer adds outbound line feeds, you will get two line feeds for every line and your screen will be double-spaced. The same thing will happen to the other person if you add outbound line feeds and she or he adds inbound line feeds.

What's more, if you do not add outbound line feeds, and the remote user adds inbound line feeds, the remote computer might or might not echo the added line feeds. The remote user would see the lines you type properly, but you would not—your lines would overwrite themselves locally.

What to do? Agree with the party at the other end that you will both add outbound line feeds. Everything should work correctly that way, and you will be compatible with most unattended online services and bulletin boards where the operation of the software is fixed. However, if you begin to see double spacing or line overwriting where you do not expect them, turn the options on or off until things straighten out.

Columns

You can tell Terminal to use 80 or 132 columns as its terminal width. This value determines the width of the workspace and where Terminal should truncate or wrap lines.

Cursor

The Terminal cursor can be a block or an underline, and it can blink or not, depending on your preference. The default is a blinking block.

Translation

The Translation list box in the Terminal Preferences dialog box tells Terminal to translate the characters to the character sets used by other countries. Only change this setting if the remote system recognizes the character set you select.

Show Scroll Bars

You can choose to not show the scroll bars if you do not need to scroll the workspace. You would do this to dedicate more of the screen to the workspace. The Show Scroll Bars check box in the Terminal Preferences dialog box manages this option.

Buffer Lines

The Terminal application buffers the lines it receives, but it keeps only a specified number of lines in the buffer. After you exceed that number, the topmost line is lost when a new line comes in. The default number of buffered lines is 100. You can set the number of lines from 25 to 400 by entering a value in the Buffer Lines field in the Terminal Preferences dialog box.

Terminal Font

Terminal can display the characters you receive in the Courier, System, or Terminal font and in many sizes. This feature is particularly useful to the visually impaired. You select the font and its size with the Terminal Font field in the Terminal Preferences dialog box.

Figure 9.6 shows a typical dialing sequence in the workspace with 24-point Courier font. The font and its size do not affect the size of the Terminal buffer; they affect only the display.

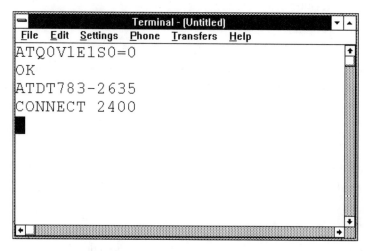

Figure 9.6   *Enlarged Characters*

Function Keys

A typical dialog with an online service or bulletin board will include a number of the routine data entries that you make. For example, many services ask you to enter your name or an identification code. Then they prompt you for a password, which you must enter to gain access to the service.

Depending on how you use the service, there might be commands that you need to enter to navigate throughout the service's menu and command structure. Some services provide a novice command set for newcomers to the service and an expert command set for those who know their way around the menus. You can reduce connect and long distance charges by using the terse expert commands once you know them.

There will be other text and command strings that you enter repeatedly. You might have a personalized salutation or signature for messages you send to other users of the service. The world of online users has its own language of acronyms and symbols with special meanings. IMHO means "in my humble opinion." BTW means "by the way." ROFL means "rolling on the floor laughing." The :-) symbol is a grin. The :-(symbol is a frown. For indifference you use the :-| symbol. If you wear glasses and have a big nose your grin might be the 8^) symbol, and so on.

Assigning Function Keys

You can assign any of these routine text entries to the Terminal function keys by choosing the Function Keys command on the Settings menu. Figure 9.7 is the Function Keys dialog box with some values entered.

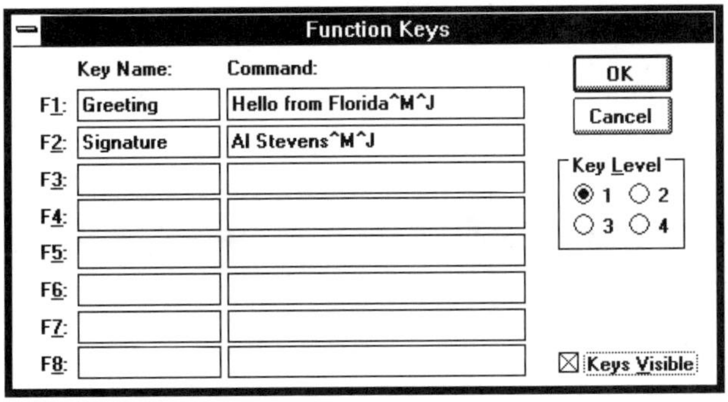

Figure 9.7   *The Function Keys Dialog Box*

There are four levels of eight function keys. Each level is a separate set of eight keys you can assign. You type a name for the function key into the Key Name field and the text value into the Command field. When you choose the function key, Terminal transmits the command text string. A command string can be text for the remote computer or a command to your modem.

Besides text values, you can put control values into the Command field for different effects. A control value is prefixed with the caret (^) character so that Terminal can recognize it. Table 9.1 shows the valid control values.

Table 9.1   *Function Key Command Control Values*

Value	Purpose
^A - ^Z	Sends the associated control byte to the remote computer. ^A = 1, ^B = 2 ... ^Z = 26. These values are the *binary* values 1, 2 ... 26, not the ASCII characters "1", "2" ... "26"
^$Dnn	Causes a delay for *nn* seconds during the transmission of the command
^$C	Dials the phone number
^$H	Hangs up the phone
^$Ln	Changes to Function Key Level *n*, where *n* is a 1, 2, 3 or 4

Two of the most important control-letter values, the ^M and ^J control values you see in Figure 9.7, are the values for the carriage return and line feed. Without them, the text commands leave the cursor just to the right of the text. If you have selected the option in Terminal Preferences to add a line feed after every carriage return, you do not need the ^J control value.

Displaying the Function Keys

If you select the Keys Visible check box, the function keys will display at the bottom of the Terminal applications window, as long as the Show/Hide Function Keys command in the Settings menu is set to Show. Figure 9.8 shows the function keys visible in the Terminal application window.

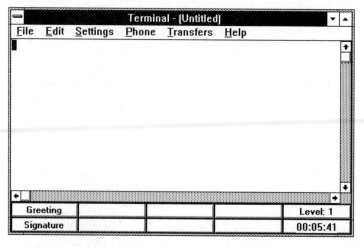

Figure 9.8   *Function Keys in View*

Choosing Function Keys

You can choose a function key by clicking it with the mouse or by pressing Ctrl+Alt+function key associated with the command. Refer to Figure 9.7 to see the keyboard-equivalent function keys. For example, you can choose the Greeting function key in Figure 9.8 by clicking it or by pressing Ctrl+Alt+F1. You can choose the Signature function key by pressing Ctrl+Alt+F2. The keystroke selections work whether you have displayed the function keys in the window or not. Later exercises will use function keys to automate certain aspects of online operations.

Text Transfers

The Text Transfers command on the Settings menu allows you to specify how you wish to send and receive text files between your computer and the remote computer.

Text files are those files with only ASCII text characters in them. A file that you generate with the Notepad is a text file. Write files are not text files because they will have format control values embedded in them, values that are not always ASCII text characters. Files that are not ASCII text are binary files, which you will learn about later.

When a computer sends a text file to another computer, it needs some form of assurance that the file transmits with a minimum of error. Because a text transfer has no error-correcting protocol, you need to establish ways that the two computers can synchronize their exchange of information. It would not do, for example, for the transmitting computer to keep transmitting when the receiving computer needs to stop receiving for a moment, perhaps to write the text to a disk file.

Standard Flow Control

Figure 9.9 shows the Text Transfers dialog box displayed after you have chosen the Standard Flow Control option button.

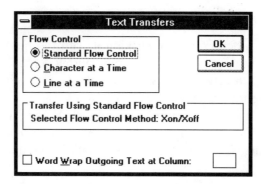

Figure 9.9 *The Standard Flow Control Text Transfers Dialog Box*

The standard flow control will be either Xon/Xoff, Hardware, or None, depending on how you set the Flow Control parameter for the Communications command discussed later. The Standard Flow Control option is the one most often selected for text file transfers.

Character at a Time

Figure 9.10 shows the Text Transfers dialog box displayed when you have selected the Character at a Time option button. If you decide to transmit characters one at a time, you can manage the data flow in one of two ways. First, you can select the Delay Between Characters option button to specify a delay period between characters in tenths of a second. The Terminal transmission will send a character and then wait the specified amount of time before sending another. This method gives the receiver time to do something meaningful with the data stream during the delays between character transmissions.

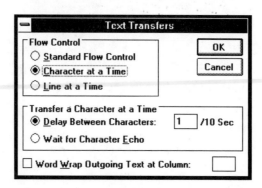

Figure 9.10 *The Character at a Time Text Transfers Dialog Box*

The other way to manage data flow is to select the Wait for Character Echo option button. This option tells Terminal to send a character and then wait for the receiving computer to echo it back before sending another one. This technique assumes that the receiver is in full duplex mode and that when it echoes a character it is telling your computer that it can receive another character. However, some communications programs do not echo the text they receive during a file transfer and so this option would not work with them.

Line at a Time

Figure 9.11 shows the Text Transfers dialog box displayed when you have selected the Line at a Time option button, which allows Terminal to transmit the text file in bursts of one line. A line consists of the characters from the first one in the left margin to the terminating carriage return.

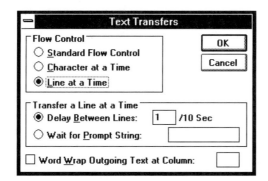

Figure 9.11 *The Line at a Time Text Transfers Dialog Box*

If you decide to transmit text a line at a time, you can manage the data flow in one of two ways. First, you can select the Delay Between Lines option button to specify a delay period between lines in tenths of a second. The Terminal transmission will send a line and then wait the specified amount of time before sending another. This method supposedly gives the receiver time to do something meaningful with the data stream during the delays between line transmissions.

The other way to manage data flow is to select the Wait for Prompt String option button. This option tells Terminal to send a line and then wait for the receiving computer to transmit a specified prompt string before sending another one. This technique assumes that the receiver transmits some kind of prompting string and that when it does it is telling your computer that it can receive another line of text. If the receiver is in full duplex mode you can specify as the prompt string the carriage return that you know the receiver will echo at the end of the line. A ^M in the Wait for Prompt String text box would represent a carriage return. Some communications programs do not echo the text they receive during a file transfer, however, and so this option would not work with them.

Word Wrap

If you select the Word Wrap Outgoing Text at Column check box, you can specify a column number where Terminal will insert a carriage return if the text in a line reaches the column.

Binary Transfers

You learned how to set up the transfer of text files in the discussion just completed. The other kind of file that you will send and receive is a *binary* file. A binary file is any file that is not text. In fact, you can send a text file by using a binary transfer if you wish, and there are times when you will want to do just that.

Any executable program file with the extension .EXE or .COM is a binary file. The .BMP and .PCX files created by Paintbrush are binary files. The data files of database programs, spreadsheets, and word processors are binary files. Any time you need highly reliable error detection and correction during a file transfer, you should use a binary file transfer.

You set up binary file transfers by choosing the Binary Transfers command on the Settings menu. Figure 9.12 shows the Binary Transfers dialog box. The selections in the Binary Files Transfers box are file transfer protocols that your computer and the remote computer can use to exchange binary files. Terminal supports two such protocols.

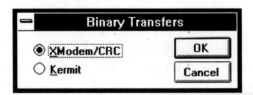

Figure 9.12   *The Binary Transfers Dialog Box*

XModem/CRC

The XModem/CRC protocol can be used when you have eight data bits selected in the Communications parameters dialog box discussed below. You cannot use XModem/CRC if you are using seven or fewer data bits. Some time-sharing networks through which you might gain access to online services require seven-bit data formats.

You also cannot use XModem/CRC if the remote computer's software does not support it. Some implementations of the XModem use the XModem/Checksum protocol, which is usually just called XModem. The Terminal XModem/CRC protocol can sense when the other computer does not use the more advanced CRC version and will adjust itself to the checksum version.

Kermit

Kermit is a file transfer protocol that was named after the frog and that works with either seven- or eight-bit data formats. Kermit is more tolerant than XModem of the time delays that characterize connections through time-share networks during peak hours, so it is often the protocol of choice. As with XModem, you must make sure that the computer at the other end supports Kermit before you can use it.

Communications Parameters

Communication between two computers requires that they use common communication parameters. Proper use of your communications hardware—the serial port and the modem—requires that you configure your hardware properly. You set these parameters by choosing the Communications command on the Settings menu and entering the correct values into the Communications dialog box shown in Figure 9.13. Some of the communications parameter values are common to both computers. Others concern only the hardware of your computer.

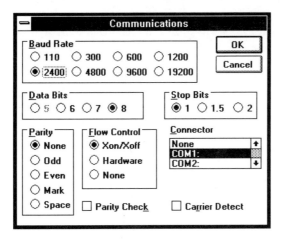

Figure 9.13 *The Communications Dialog Box*

Common Communications Parameters

You set the common communications parameters after determining the compatible values of the other computer. They are not difficult to determine. An online service or a bulletin board must provide information that tells you what these values should be. A typical specification would be 2400,N,8,1, which means 2400 baud, no parity, 8 data bits, 1 stop bit. You will see what these things mean in the discussions that follow.

Baud Rate. The baud rate is the rate at which the computers transmit characters. It is expressed in bits per second. Typical baud rates are 300, 600, 1200, 2400, 4800, 9600, and 19200. The most common ones in use today among personal computer users are 1200 and 2400, although 9600-baud modems are gaining in popularity. A modem can transmit at all the baud rates up to its maximum. If you have a 2400-baud modem, for example, it can usually transmit and receive at 300, 600, 1200, and 2400 baud.

The baud rate is not a function of the modem. The modem accepts commands at whatever baud rate the computer sends them, and it passes data through at the baud rate of the sending computer.

A remote service can usually accept calls from computers at baud rates lower than the published rate. The published rate is the maximum. For example, you can use your 1200-baud modem to call a service that supports 2400 baud. The service senses the caller's baud rate and adjusts its own rate.

Data Bits. The computer sends its data characters through the serial port one bit at a time. The receiving computer receives those bits just as they were sent from the sender. The receiver needs a way to distinguish the characters from what would otherwise appear to be a string of random bits. Therefore the sender frames each character by surrounding its data bits with start and stop bits. There will be seven or eight data bits, depending on the nature of the transmission.

Both computers should agree on the number of data bits. If the online service asks for eight data bits, select the 8 option button in the Data Bits field. If it wants seven, select 7. The Data Bits field allows you to specify five or six data bits. These values are rarely used.

Parity. Immediately following the data bits is the parity bit—if one is required. Usually you will have a parity bit if there are only seven data bits. When you have eight data bits, you usually select the None option button in the Parity field. If there is a parity bit it can be set to Odd, Even, Mark, or Space. If it is Odd, the transmitting system will set its value to one or zero, whichever is required so that there are an odd number of one bits in the bit stream. If the parity bit is to be Even, the transmitting system will set its value to one or zero, whichever is required so that there are an even number of one bits in the bit stream. If the parity bit is set to Mark or Space, the transmitting system will set all parity bits to zero or one irrespective of parity.

Stop Bits. The presence of stop bits allows the receiver to wait for a polarity change to the start bits so it can synchronize itself to the next character in the stream. One stop bit is usually used. Some systems require 1.5 or 2 stop bits, usually at the slower baud rates.

Flow Control. The Flow Control field allows you to specify the method that the receiving computer uses to tell the sending computer to stop sending characters during a text file transfer. The software protocols of the binary file transfers take care of flow control, so you do not need to worry about them for binary file transfers.

When you are transmitting and receiving text through a modem, your flow control will usually be Xon/Xoff. Here is how it works. The transmitting computer begins to transmit characters that the receiving computer collects. There will come a time when the receiving computer must do something with the characters it has collected so far. Usually it will write them to a disk file. This activity will take time away from its ability to continue to read incoming the characters. So the receiver sends the ASCII XOF (Ctrl+S) character to the transmitter to tell it to stop sending. When the transmitter sees the XOF character come into its own input buffer, it stops transmitting and watches for more input. When the receiver is ready to receive text again, it sends the XON (Ctrl+Q) character to the transmitter. When the transmitter receives the XON character, it resumes transmitting data characters.

The Hardware Flow Control option button specifies that the receiver will tell the transmitter to stop transmitting by asserting certain electrical signals at the serial port. A modem can assert these signals, but there is no way for the remote computer to tell the local modem to do so. Therefore, you would use the Hardware Flow Control option only when you are connecting to another computer locally without using a modem—and even then only when both computers have compatible serial ports and software to drive them.

You can select None as the text file transfer flow control method if the computers do not use any. When the receiver has no way to tell the transmitter to stand by, you have a good chance of losing some characters in the stream. The sender will continue to transmit beyond the receiver's ability to deal with the data. You can take this path when the baud rate is slow enough—usually 300 to 1200 baud—so the sender has no way of outrunning the receiver, or when you use one of the time delays in your Text Transfers dialog box.

Local Communications Parameters

These parameters are related to your communications hardware and how you use it and are not necessarily the same as those of the remote computer.

Connector. The Connector field in the Communications dialog box is where you tell Terminal which of the communications ports, COM1, COM2, COM3, or COM4, you are using for modem communications. Most PCs and ATs have one or two communications ports, COM1 and or/COM1 and COM2. More recent machines can have COM3 and COM4 as well.

Communications ports transmit characters in a serial stream with a format and at voltage levels defined by a standard specification called RS-232-C. You will hear these devices referred to by any of these names:

- Communications ports
- RS-232 ports
- RS-232-C ports
- Serial ports
- Auxiliary ports
- AUX devices
- COM1, COM2, etc.

If you have an internal modem it will use one of the communication port assignments. If you have an external modem, you will connect it to one of the ports with a serial cable. If you connect your computer directly to another computer, you will do so with a null modem cable connecting the serial ports of the computers. Null modem cables will be discussed later.

Parity Check. If you are using the Odd or Even parity formats and Terminal sees a parity error in the input, it will display the character as a question mark unless you select the Parity Check check box. Terminal will then display the character as it was received, which might or might not make sense to you, depending on whether the parity error was in the parity bit itself or in one of the data bits.

Carrier Detect. Usually the modem tells Terminal that it has made a successful connection with a remote computer by sending a string that starts with the word "CONNECT." The modem knows that the connection is complete because the remote computer transmits a continuous high-frequency tone to say that it is on line. This tone is called the *carrier signal.*

A certain serial port signal indicates that the modem is detecting the carrier signal. By selecting the Carrier Detect check box you tell Terminal to watch for that signal instead of waiting for the CONNECT message. You would do this if you were using a modem that does not supply the CONNECT message. Older 300-baud acoustic couplers are typical of the modems that require the software to monitor the carrier detect signal.

Modem Commands

The Modem Commands command on the Settings menu displays the Modem Commands dialog box shown in Figure 9.14. Modem commands are strings of text that, when you are not connected to another computer and you send them to the modem, direct the modem to take some action. You will seldom need to change the modem commands.

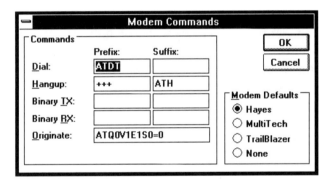

Figure 9.14 *The Modem Commands Dialog Box*

If you do not have touch-tone dialing you will need to change the Dial Prefix from ATDT to ATDP. Other than that, the modem commands provided as defaults should work fine. The user's guide for your modem will define the modem's complete command set. You should refer to it if you want to change the way the modem works.

Saving and Restoring Parameters

Once you have all your parameters set the way you need them for a particular connection, you should save them in a file. You can have separate files for every computer and service you call, each one with its own phone number, terminal settings, communications settings, modem settings, function keys, and file transfer settings.

The File menu has the usual New, Open, Save, and Save As commands. By convention, Terminal settings files have the .TRM extension.

Printing the Online Session

The File menu has a Printer Setup command like the ones you learned about in earlier chapters, but it does not have a Print command. That is because you do not print files or pictures from Terminal; you print online sessions. The Printer Echo toggle command on the Settings causes everything received by Terminal except file transfers to be echoed to the printer.

Timing the Online Session

If you look back at Figure 9.8 you will see that Terminal displays the time of day in the lower-right corner of the screen, among the function keys. You can change that display to an elapsed-time timer by choosing the Timer Mode toggle command on the Settings menu. The timer starts at 00:00:00 when you first select it and proceeds to tick off the seconds. When you make a connection, the timer restarts at zero so you can keep watch on the length of time you have been on line. When you hang up, the timer reverts to the time of day.

Dialing Another Computer

To call another computer, choose the Dial command on the Phone menu. You will see the Terminal dialog box shown in Figure 9.15. If you have not entered a phone number and chosen the Dial command, Terminal displays the Phone Number dialog box shown in Figure 9.3. You must fill it in before Terminal can dial the phone.

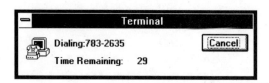

Figure 9.15   *The Terminal Dialog Box*

Observe the displays in the Terminal workspace while the program is dialing. The first line is the command to tell the modem that you are going to originate a call. If you look at the Modem Commands dialog box in Figure 9.14, you will see that the Originate string matches the first line in the workspace. The second line says OK. That is the modem's response to receiving the originate string. The third line is the modem's Dial command. The ATDT prefix appears first, followed by the phone number.

No Answer or Busy

While Terminal is dialing and while it is waiting for an answer, the Time Remaining display in the Terminal dialog box counts down, starting from the value you set in the Phone Number dialog box. If the time remaining reaches zero and you have selected Redial After Timing Out in the Phone Number dialog box, Terminal will reset the count, redial the number and start over. If you have not selected the redial option, the Terminal dialog box goes away, and the Terminal application window looks like that shown in Figure 9.16.

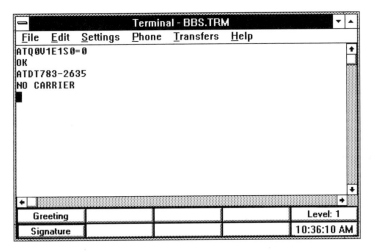

Figure 9.16 *No Answer*

The NO CARRIER message in the workspace is the modem's message that the remote computer did not answer. If the line was busy, you would see BUSY instead of NO CARRIER. If you accidentally call the wrong number and someone answers, some modems will display a VOICE message. You can hear the person talk through the modem's speaker, but you cannot answer. Their phone will be dead, and they will probably hang up.

When the Call Goes Through

If the call is successful, you will see a CONNECT message such as the one shown in Figure 9.17. What follows the CONNECT message will depend on the program that is running in the remote computer. The next thing you might do is enter your name and perhaps a password. The system might display a text menu of choices. You can pick up electronic mail messages that others have left for you, leave messages for them, upload files to the service, and download files that others have contributed. If you are calling the computer of a friend, the two of you might chat and you might exchange files. If you are calling one of the major online services, you might exchange electronic mail with other subscribers, use the service's research facilities, read product reviews, order products, watch the stock market, get weather reports, make airline reservations, or file your own flight plan.

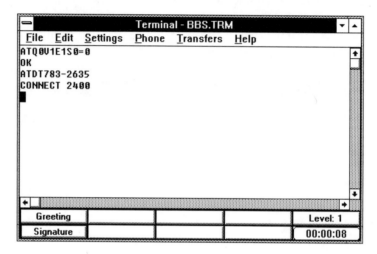

Figure 9.17 *Successful Connection*

When You Are Done

The system you call might have a Goodbye or OFF command that you use to tell it you are signing off. You should wait until it has told you that it is disconnecting and you see the modem's NO CARRIER message. You must choose the Hangup command on the Phone menu or Terminal will not allow you to dial another number.

Calling a Bulletin Board System (BBS)

In the examples that follow a user calls a simulated bulletin board system (BBS). To keep it simple, this "bulletin board" is the host mode of Procomm, a shareware DOS communications program, that is being used by a friend of the user in some other city. Procomm's host mode has some of the features of bulletin board software. You can upload and download files and chat with the user of the Procomm program.

The parameters for communicating with the BBS are mostly the defaults set by Terminal. Of course you need to enter the phone number and the baud rate of your modem. For convenience, the user name and password are function keys. You selected the XModem/CRC file transfer protocol as your default. You saved these few unique settings in a file named BBS.TRM.

Conventional wisdom holds that recording passwords in a system file is an invitation to burglary. You should exercise prudence in this practice. If your system is essentially closed—perhaps it is at home—then you can indulge yourself with the convenience of using function keys to send passwords.

N O T E
That way, if you use a lot of online services and bulletin boards, you do not have to remember all those passwords. It would definitely be imprudent to use the same password for all your accounts.

Here's a hint: Add a Connections applications group in Program Manager. Install copies of Terminal in the group with the names of the various services and BBSs you use in the Program Item Properties Description fields. Put the names of the .TRM files into the Command Line. Then you can simply click onto the particular service you want to call.

In Figure 9.18 you have called and signed onto the BBS.

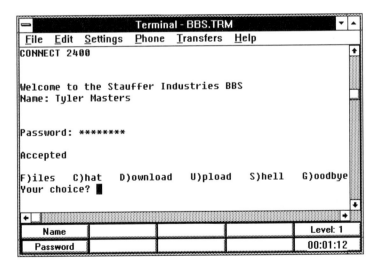

Figure 9.18 *Calling a BBS*

Keep in mind that the dialogs you see in the workspace are those of the remote computer's software, which in this case is the Procomm program, which is not a part of Windows. These examples use Procomm because it is simple and typical.

The lessons to be learned are in the Terminal procedures that allow you to use the facilities of the remote computer.

Chatting with the Other User

Once you are signed on, you can type characters to the remote computer. The Procomm program gives you a menu. To chat with the user at the other end you type C. When the user answers, you can freely exchange text by typing. It is a good idea to size the Terminal applications window to its highest height so that you can view as much of the conversation as possible at one time. Remember that you can use the scroll bars to look at anything in the buffer that might have scrolled off. You can also hide the function keys to gain some additional viewing area.

Figure 9.19 shows the Procomm chat mode. The user at the other end has heard the page and come on line.

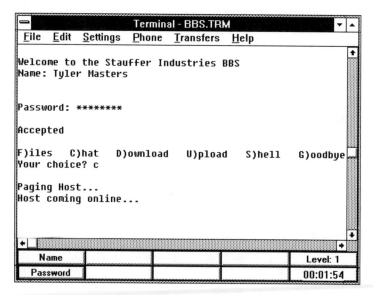

Figure 9.19 *Paging the Host*

In Figure 9.20, the two users are chatting. The shaded areas in the figure show where the local user entered text and whether the text came from typing or a function key. The shading does not actually appear in the Terminal window; it serves to highlight the text in the illustration. The shadowed boxes and arrows are part of the illustration, too. They do not appear on your screen.

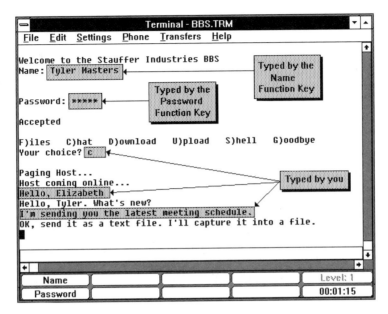

Figure 9.20   *Chatting*

Transferring Files

One of the benefits of calling other computers is that you can easily exchange program and data files with the users of those other computers. If you exchange messages with the other users, you can compose your messages in Notepad while you are off-line and upload them as files once you have made the connection. This approach has two advantages: first, the editors used by online services are usually primitive line editors without many features; second, uploading long messages instead of typing them on line can save connect time and, perhaps, charges. Secondly, you can send and receive text and binary files to and from the remote computer.

Sending Text Files

In the conversation, the user agreed to send a text file, the meeting schedule. The user would have created this file off line, perhaps with the Notepad. Figure 9.21 is the text file, SCHEDULE.TXT, that the user is going to transfer.

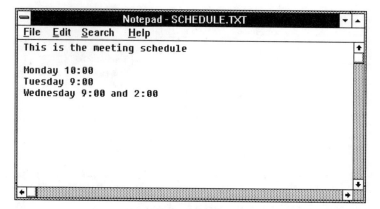

Figure 9.21 *A Text File to Transfer*

To send a text file, choose the Send Text File command on the Transfers menu. You will see the Send Text File dialog box shown in Figure 9.22, in this case with the name of the SCHEDULE.TXT file entered.

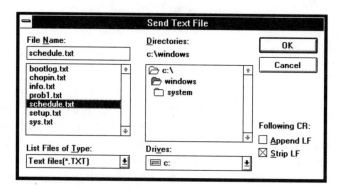

Figure 9.22 *The Send Text File Dialog Box*

When you choose OK in the dialog box, Terminal will send the text file just as if you typed it. The remote computer echoes it, and you see it on the screen, as shown in Figure 9.23.

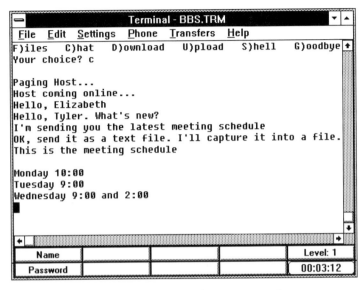

Figure 9.23   *Sending a Text File*

Sending Binary Files

After the local user sends the text file, the remote user exits from the chat mode, and the Procomm menu returns. To send a picture file from Paintbrush you must use a binary transfer. The user in this example tells the remote computer that he or she is uploading the file COMPUTER.PCX by using the XModem protocol. The remote computer says to begin the transfer procedure. You choose the Send Binary File command on the Transfers menu. The command displays the Send Binary File dialog box like that shown in Figure 9.24. The figure shows the COMPUTER.PCX file name selected.

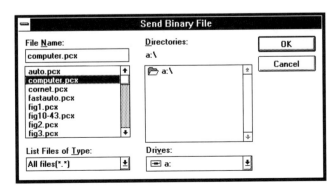

Figure 9.24   *The Send Binary File Dialog Box*

When you choose OK on the dialog box, Terminal begins sending the file. Figure 9.25 shows how the Terminal screen appears while it is sending a binary file.

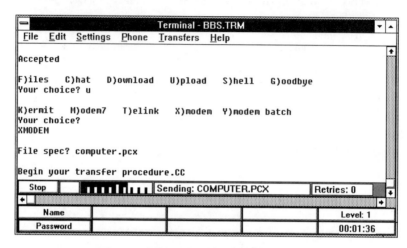

Figure 9.25   Sending a Binary File

The workspace in Figure 9.25 still shows the dialog that used to tell the remote computer a file was coming. The bottom of the window has four new displays. The Stop function button allows you to terminate the transmission in the middle. The ruled scale has a reverse video bar that moves from left to right to indicate the progress of the transmission. The Sending field identifies the file that you are sending. The Retries field shows the number of retries that Terminal has made during the transmission. If this number is high, you might be getting a lot of interference in the phone lines, and you might want to stop the transfer and try it again another time.

Receiving Binary Files

You use the Procomm Files menu option to see what files are in its BBS area. A display similar to that shown in Figure 9.26 will appear. Note that the directory in Figure 9.26 looks just like a DOS directory listing. Procomm is a DOS program that is running in a remote DOS computer, and it uses the DOS DIR command to send you a directory of the files you can see. If the directory is longer and scrolls off your screen before you can read it all, you can use the scroll bars to read the scrolled-off portion.

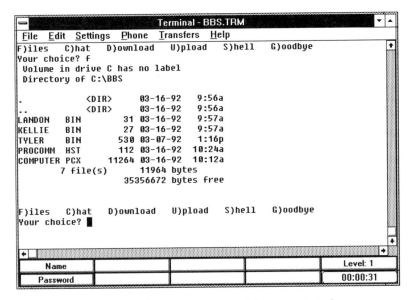

Figure 9.26 *A Directory of the Remote Files*

One of the files in Figure 9.26 is named TYLER.BIN, and, according to a convention agreed to between the remote user and callers to her BBS—a totally fictional setup contrived for the purposes of these exercises—that file is for the local user in this example.

To download a file, you tell the remote computer that you are going to use XModem to download the file. The remote computer tells you to begin your transfer procedure. You choose the Receive Binary File command on the Transfers menu and see the Receive Binary File dialog box shown in Figure 9.27. In the figure the local user has already named the file to be received.

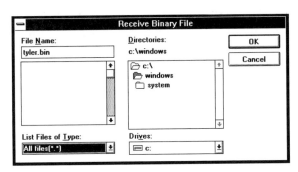

Figure 9.27 *The Receive Binary File Dialog Box*

While the binary file is transferring into your computer, Terminal displays additional information at the bottom of the window, as shown in Figure 9.28. The Stop function button allows you to terminate the reception in midstream. The Bytes count tells you how many bytes have been received so far. The Receiving field names the file that you are receiving, and the Retries field is the number of retries so far.

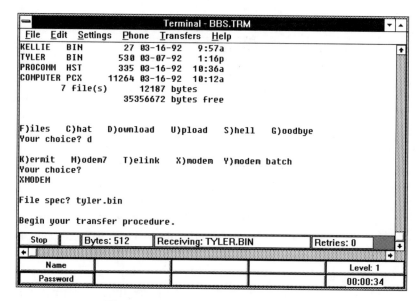

Figure 9.28 *Receiving a Binary File*

Receiving Text Files

Procomm does not have a text option for downloading files to you from its host mode, but other systems you call will. Before the remote computer begins sending a text file, choose Receive Text File on the Transfers menu. Select the appropriate drive and directory and enter the file name in the Receive Text File dialog box shown in Figure 9.29.

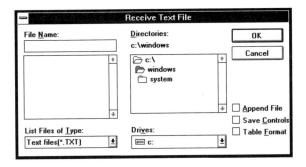

Figure 9.29   *The Receive Text File Dialog Box*

If the file name you enter is that of an existing file, you can append to it or replace it. If you select the Append File check box, the append is automatic. If you do not, Terminal will ask you to verify that you are replacing an existing file.

The Save Controls check box will preserve some non-displayable, non-formatting characters that are in the file. Some text files have more than text in them, depending on the software that generated the files, and this option will preserve most of those control values.

The Table Format check box tells Terminal to replace strings of spaces with Tab characters.

When you are ready to receive, choose OK. You will see the screen shown in Figure 9.30.

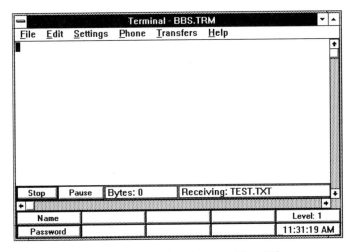

Figure 9.30   *Receiving a Text File*

The remote computer may begin sending the text file now. You can click the Stop function button to terminate the transfer. You can click the Pause button to temporarily pause the transmission. The Pause button will change to a Resume button for when you are ready to resume transmission. The Bytes field displays the number of characters received so far, and the Receiving field identifies the name of the file you are receiving.

During the reception the text will display on the screen. It might display with each line overwriting the previous one, which means that the file has carriage returns without line feeds. In that case, stop the transfer with the Stop button, turn on the CR -> CR/LF Inbound check box in the Terminal Preferences dialog box and transfer the file again.

When the text file has completed transferring, choose the Stop function button at the bottom of the window's workspace.

Viewing Text Files

The Transfers menu has a View Text File command that allows you to select a text file to be viewed on the screen. Figure 9.31 shows the View Text File dialog box.

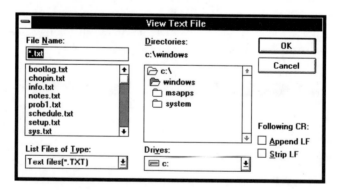

Figure 9.31   *The View Text File Dialog Box*

If you have just downloaded a text file, its name appears in the dialog box's Filename field by default, and any other files with the same extension appear in the Files list box. If you downloaded a text file without line feeds and you wish to view it but do not wish to transfer it again, you can select the Append LF check box.

If you downloaded a file that has line feeds, and you are adding line feeds as well, the file will have an extra blank line for very line in the original. You can use the Strip LF check box to strip the extra line feeds when you display the file.

Viewing a text file writes it into the workspace of the Terminal window just as if you had received it from the remote computer. Figure 9.32 shows how the screen appears while you are viewing the SETUP.TXT file that comes with Windows.

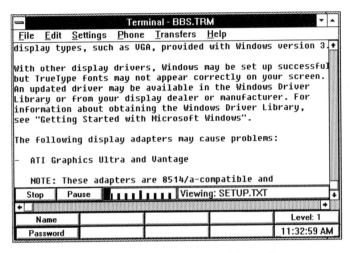

Figure 9.32   *Viewing a Text File*

The ruler bar at the bottom of the screen moves from left to right to track your progress through the file. As it displays, the file will continue to scroll off the top of the window. If you choose the Pause function button at the bottom of the window the display will stop, the Pause function button becomes a Resume function button, and you can use the scroll bars to view upper parts of the file that have scrolled out of sight. Choose the Resume function button to continue viewing the file.

Using Terminal to Answer the Phone

Windows does not provide a way for Terminal be an answering computer. Suppose you and a friend both use Terminal and you want to connect your computers. One of you must call the other, and that means that one of your communications programs must be able to answer the phone. Or perhaps your agreement with a long-distance correspondent is that you take turns calling so that you share the toll charges. That agreement means that your Terminal program must be able to answer the phone.

Echoes and Half-Duplex

Terminal has no option that lets you tell it to work in full or half duplex. Because it always expects to be the calling computer, it expects the remote answering computer to echo the characters that Terminal transmits, but it shares no such reciprocal responsibility. Therefore, you must coordinate a few things with the calling computer.

Because Terminal does not echo the characters it receives, the remote calling computer must echo its own characters as it sends them. Likewise, because you are the answering computer, the remote computer expects to be treated like a terminal and will not echo your characters, so you must echo your own.

Adding Line Feeds

You and the remote user might have to play with this option to see what works best. In Terminal you should set the Outbound option in the Terminal Preferences CR -> CR/LF field to on and leave the Inbound option off. The remote computer should do the same.

Building an Auto-Answer Settings File

Once you have a working configuration defined, you will want to save it for future use. The procedures that follow will work for most connections where Terminal must answer the phone.

Auto-Answer Parameters

In the Terminal Preferences dialog box, set the Local Echo check box to on. Set the Inbound CR -> CR/LF check box to off and the Outbound one to on. Set your file transfer and communications parameters according to your preferences. Those who call your computer must comply or you must agree to change your settings when a caller needs something different.

The Answer Function Key

Assign the name "Answer" to the Key Name field of the F1 function key. Enter this text value into its Command box:

```
ATQ1E0S0=1^M
```

This string is the command that tells the modem to prepare to answer the phone. It is the answer string for Hayes-compatible modems. If you use some other kind of modem, use its answer string. Be sure to follow the Hayes answer string with the ^M sequence to send the carriage return character at the end of the command.

The Reset Function Key

Assign the name "Reset" to the Key Name field of the F2 function key. Enter this text value into its Command box:

```
^$HATQ0E1V1S0=0^M
```

This string tells the modem to hang up and return to originate mode so that it will no longer answer the phone. The command begins with the ^$H sequence to hang up the phone. That sequence is followed by a string taken from the Originate field of the Modem Commands dialog box when the Hayes modem is selected. If you use some other modem, use its originate string. Be sure to follow the command with the ^M sequence to send the carriage return character at the end.

Save the file with the name ANSWER.TRM.

Answering the Phone

Because Terminal was not intended to act as a host, it has no provision for hosting a caller in an unattended session. When someone calls, you must be around to deal with them personally. When you are ready to accept calls, start Terminal with the ANSWER.TRM file loaded. Choose the Answer function key and wait for a call.

Terminal will not tell you that someone has called. If your modem has a loud enough speaker and you are in the same room, you will hear the carrier signal. It will sound until both computers know that the connection is complete. You can tell your caller to send several Ctrl+G keystrokes to get your attention. That will cause Terminal to sound your computer's beep unless you turned the Sound check box off in the Terminal Preferences dialog box.

After you have answered the phone, you and the caller can freely type messages back and forth.

Exchanging Files

To transfer files in the answer mode, you must agree that the receiver prepares to receive the file before the sender starts sending it. Otherwise the receiver's software will treat the incoming data as conversational text to display on the screen. Aside from that consideration, file transfers work just as you have already learned.

Hanging Up

If you want Terminal to answer more calls, choose the Hangup command on the Phone menu. If you want to return your phone line to normal operation, choose the Reset function key that you defined earlier. If you do not choose Reset, the next caller to your line will be greeted by the high-pitched carrier signal, which will continue for a while after they hang up.

Connecting Directly to Another Computer

When you connect your computer directly to another computer, you do so with a cable that connects their serial ports. The cable is called a *null modem* cable because it does the job of the telephone system and both modems, as long as the two computers are relatively close to one another. Two computers connected by a null modem can communicate at speeds much greater than those supported by modems. Terminal allows you to use up to 19200 baud, but other applications have successfully transmitted data through a null modem cable at much greater speeds. You can get a null modem cable at Radio Shack or your computer store.

Assume that you are using Terminal in both computers. You must configure the settings of both computers for compatible communications. You do not need a phone number or any particular terminal emulation. Set Local Echo and Outbound CR -> CR/LF to on in both computers. Set Inbound CR -> CR/LF to off in both computers. You might as well use 19200 baud because that is the fastest rate that Terminal supports. For flow control you can use either Xon/Xoff or, if the null modem cable supports it, the Hardware setting.

When you start Terminal in both computers you should be able to type at one and see the characters on both screens. File transfers will work the same as they do when you connect through a modem, except that they will be faster due to the higher baud rate.

If you are using Terminal to connect your PC to a mainframe or minicomputer, set the Terminal settings to match those of the host computer. When you run Terminal, you should be connected to the host as if you were using an actual terminal device instead of a PC or AT running Windows and Terminal.

As with the other uses, if you regularly use Terminal to connect directly to another computer, you should record a file of the Terminal settings.

Editing and the Clipboard

The Clipboard has special uses in Terminal. You can use it to transfer information that came from the remote computer to another application, and you can use it to send information from another application to the remote computer.

Copying to the Clipboard

You can copy data from the Terminal's buffer to the Clipboard by marking the data and choosing the Copy command on the Edit menu. You mark data with the mouse or keyboard just as you mark it in other applications. You can use the Select All command on the Edit menu to select all the text that is in the Terminal buffer.

With the block marked, choose the Copy command from the Edit menu. The marked text is copied into the Clipboard. You can now call another application and paste the Clipboard text into that application's workspace.

Pasting from the Clipboard

The Paste command on the Edit menu transmits what is in the Clipboard to the remote computer. You can use this feature to transmit data from other applications. Copy the data from the other application into the Clipboard. Then return to Terminal and use the Paste command to transmit the Clipboard data to the remote computer.

Sending Marked Data

You can mark a block of data in the Terminal buffer to send to the remote computer. Mark the block as usual. Then use the Send command on the Edit menu to transmit the marked data to the remote computer. You could use this feature to forward the contents of a communication from one computer to yet another computer. After the first communication is over, call the second remote computer, mark the text of the first communication and use the Send command to forward it.

Clearing the Buffer

The Clear Buffer command on the Edit menu clears the Terminal buffer of all the text in it.

Summary

Inter-computer communications can be reasonably easy once you have the routine procedures in place and recorded into files of Terminal settings. This chapter has covered the basics of using Terminal in the ways that most users will use it. Chapter 10 details the other accessories that Windows provides: Calculator, Notepad, and Cardfile, which you have already seen, Clock, Calendar, and Recorder, which was mentioned in Chapter 7, and Character Map, which displays the character sets of the installed fonts.

Chapter 10

Accessories

This chapter is about some of the accessory programs that come with Windows. You will find them in the Program Manager's Accessories group. You have already learned about the Write, Paintbrush, and Terminal accessories. Each of them had its own chapter earlier in the book. In this chapter you will learn seven more accessories:

- ◆ The Clock
- ◆ The Notepad
- ◆ The Calendar
- ◆ The Cardfile
- ◆ The Recorder
- ◆ The Calculator
- ◆ The Character Map

Chapter 11 describes the remaining accessories, the Media Player, and the Sound Recorder.

Clock

The Clock accessory displays a time-of-day clock on the screen. The Clock runs as an icon. You can choose analog or digital display. Figure 10.1 shows the two icon formats.

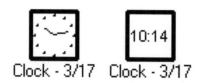

Figure 10.1 *The Clock Icons*

To run the Clock in a window and to choose its display format, double-click the icon or choose the Normal command on its Control menu. Figure 10.2 shows the analog clock window.

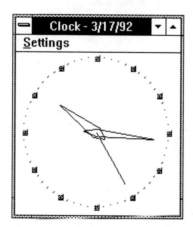

Figure 10.2 *The Analog Clock*

The Settings menu allows you to choose the format for the clock. Figure 10.3 shows the digital display.

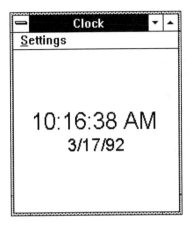

Figure 10.3   *The Digital Clock*

Choosing the Seconds toggle command on the Settings menu turns the sweep second hand display on and off. The Date command toggles the date display in the window title and in the minimized Clock's icon label. If you choose the No Title command, you display the Clock window with no title bar. To get the title bar back, double-click the Clock window.

You do not set the clock's time from the Clock accessory program. You use the Control Panel to set the time.

Notepad

Notepad is a text editor capable of small word processing tasks. Many users find that it contains all the word processing functions they need. Others use it for memos and short letters, preferring to use Write, Word for Windows, or some other more powerful word processor for document preparation. You have used Notepad in some of the exercises in previous chapters, so it is not new to you. Figure 10.4 shows the Notepad application window.

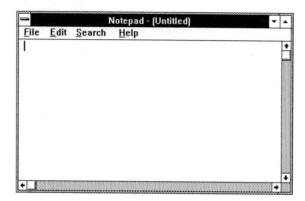

Figure 10.4 *The Notepad Application Window*

Notepad Files

Notepad can support text files of up to about 50,000 characters. The File menu has the usual New, Open, Save, and Save As commands. The default file extension is .TXT, and you can run Notepad from the File Manager by selecting any .TXT file. Notepad will also run if you select an .INI file, which is the extension for Windows' initialization files. .INI files are ASCII text, so Notepad can view and change them. Each .INI file has a corresponding .TXT file that explains the entries in the .INI file.

Entering Text

You enter text by typing. The Word Wrap command toggle on the Edit menu tells Notepad to wrap words at the right window border, keeping all of your text in view. You would want to use that option if you were typing a letter, memo, or document. The paragraphs re-form themselves as you change the size of the window. When Word Wrap is on, the horizontal scroll bar goes away. Word Wrap is off by default when you first run Notepad.

Pressing the Enter key defines the end of a paragraph.

Moving Around in the Text

You can move the cursor to a point in the text file by moving the mouse cursor there and clicking. You can also use the keyboard to move the cursor. Table 10.1 shows the keystrokes that move the cursor in Notepad.

Table 10.1   *Notepad Cursor Movement Keys*

Keystroke	Movement
Up and Down Arrow keys	Up and down one line
Right and Left Arrow keys	Right and left one character
Ctrl+Right/Left Arrow	Right and left one word
Home/End	Beginning and end of the line
PgUp/PgDn	Previous and next screen
Ctrl+Home/End	Beginning and End of the file

Selecting Text

You can select blocks of text for cutting and copying to the Clipboard or for deleting from the file. Click the first character of the block and hold the left button down while you drag the cursor to the end of the block. The highlighted text displays in reverse video. Use the keys in Table 10.1 while you hold down the Shift key to select a block of text with the keyboard.

The Select All command on the Edit menu selects all the text in the file. To deselect a marked block, click the cursor once or press an arrow key.

Deleting Text

When you have selected a block of text, pressing the Del or Backspace key will delete the block. Pressing a character key will delete the block and insert the character. You can use the Undo command on the Edit menu to undo the most recent delete.

When no block is marked, the Del key deletes text one character at a time to the right of the cursor. The Backspace key deletes text one character at a time from under the cursor, which has the effect of deleting text to the left of the cursor.

Cut, Copy, and Paste

The Cut and Copy commands on the Edit menu cut and copy the selected block of text to the Clipboard. The Paste command pastes the current text contents of the Clipboard into the file beginning at the current cursor location.

Searching a Text File

You can search a file for a string value. The Find command on the Search menu opens the Find dialog box shown in Figure 10.5. Enter the text you wish to find in the Find What field. If you want to have the search match your entry exactly on upper- and lowercase letters, select the Match Case check box. The Up and Down option buttons specify the direction you want to search from the current cursor location. Searches proceed forward to the end of the file or backward to the beginning of the file. If Notepad does not find the text, it displays an error message. If it finds the text, it stops searching and marks the found text.

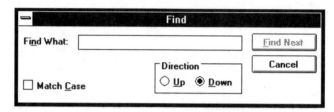

Figure 10.5   *The Find Dialog Box*

The Find Next command on the Search menu continues the search from the point of the last text that was found, continuing in the direction you originally selected.

Date-Stamping a File

The Time/Date command on the Edit menu will insert the current time and date into the text at the current cursor position. If you type in .LOG into a file beginning in the left margin of the first line, Notepad will append the current time and date onto the file and position the cursor on the next line after the date every time you open the file. This feature allows you to define a diary or journal file that always date-stamps your entries.

Figure 10.6 shows the beginning of a personal journal that uses the .LOG convention.

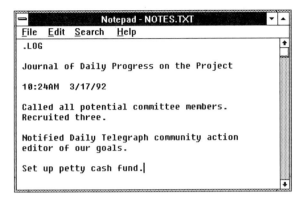

Figure 10.6   *A Personal Journal*

Printing

The File menu has the usual Print and Print Setup commands. You can use the Page Setup command to design the format of the printout of the text file. Figure 10.7 shows the Page Setup dialog box.

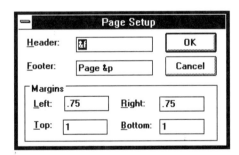

Figure 10.7   *The Page Setup Dialog Box*

You can change the four margin values by entering the new values into the Left, Right, Top, and Bottom Margin fields. You can enter text and certain symbols into the Header and Footer fields. Table 10.2 shows the symbols that insert run-time values into the header and footer.

Table 10.2 *Notepad Header and Footer Symbols*

Symbol	Inserts
&t	Time
&d	Date
&p	Page number
&f	File name
&l	Following text justified left
&r	Following text justified right
&c	Following text centered

Calendar

The Calendar accessory is a personal appointment or scheduling calendar and alarm clock. Figure 10.8 shows the Calendar application window.

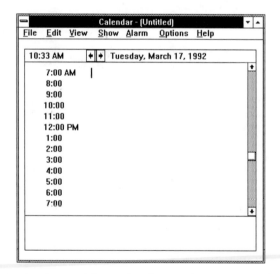

Figure 10.8 *The Calender Application Window*

You might use one copy of the Calendar for your appointments and others to maintain the scheduled use of company resources such as conference rooms, overhead projectors, and company cars. A lawyer or consultant can use Calendar to record time spent on jobs and with clients.

If you are in the business of contracting labor, say, temporary office help, you can use separate copies of the Calendar for the schedules of each of your employees. Your workforce can use the Calendar as time cards. A piano teacher can schedule students; you can record birthdays; a student can schedule classes. You can use Calendar to schedule virtually anything that is based on date and time.

Day Schedule

When you start the Calendar it displays the current day's schedule. The time displayed is the current time, and Calendar keeps it updated. The schedule contains entries for each hour, although you can change that interval. The default display starts with 7:00 a.m. as the first entry. You can scroll to earlier entries and you can change that default.

The bottom of the Calendar is a scratch pad for entering notes about the day's schedule.

You make entries by typing them in. An entry's length can exceed the space given it on its time line in the schedule. It scrolls horizontally. You can move the cursor to new entries or the scratch pad by clicking where you want to type or by using the keyboard. The right and left arrows at the top of the window are mouse function buttons that move to Calender's previous and next days.

Table 10.3 lists the keystrokes that move the cursor.

Table 10.3   *Calendar Keys (Day View)*

Key	Movement
Up/Down Arrow	Up and down the time entries
Enter	Next entry down
Home/End	Beginning/end of the current entry
PgUp/PgDn	Page through the day
Ctrl+Home/End	Start time/start time + 12 hours
Tab	To the scratch pad and back
Ctrl+PgUp/PgDn	To the previous/next day

Figure 10.9 shows a typical day in a Calendar schedule.

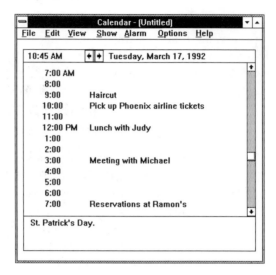

Figure 10.9   *A Typical Day*

Viewing the Month

To view the month, choose the Month command on the View menu. Figure 10.10 shows a month view. You can use the keyboard or the mouse to move around in the month view. Table 10.4 lists the keystrokes for moving around in the month view.

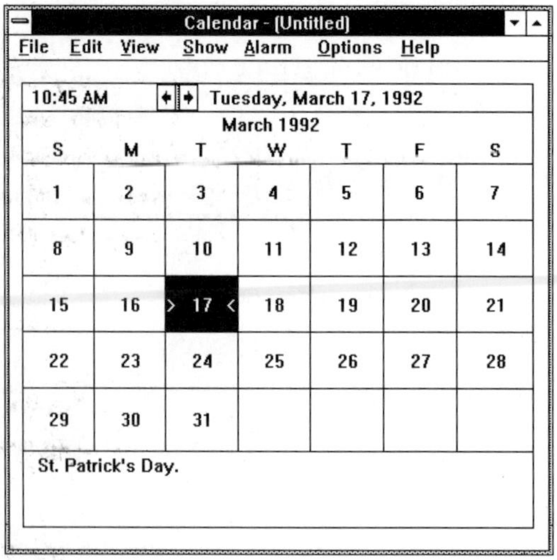

Figure 10.10   *The Month View*

Table 10.4   *Calendar Keys (Month View)*

Key	Movement
Arrow keys	Up and down, right and left, day to day
Enter	Select day view
PgUp/PgDn	Previous/next month
Tab	To the scratch pad and back

If you use the arrow keys to move beyond the first or last day of the month, you will move to the previous or next month. If you double-click a day, you will select the day view for that day.

As you move from day to day, you will see the scratch pad entries for the selected day. The month view and the scratch pad are handy holiday and birthday calendars.

Marking Days

You can mark days in the month days by choosing the Mark command on the Options menu. Figure 10.11 is the Day Markings dialog box. Each check box is a different style of mark for a day. You can choose any or all of them to mark the currently selected day. You might use one symbol for holidays, another for paydays, another for oil changes, and so on. Figure 10.12 shows the Mondays with one symbol each. The first day of the month has all the symbols.

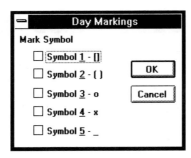

Figure 10.11   *The Day Markings Dialog Box*

```
┌────────────────────────────────────────────────────┐
│ ▬   Calendar - [Untitled]              ▼ ▲          │
│ File  Edit  View   Show  Alarm   Options  Help       │
│ ┌──────────────────────────────────────────────┐    │
│ │ 10:50 AM      │◆│◆│  Tuesday, March 17, 1992  │    │
│ │                    March 1992                  │    │
│ │    S     M     T     W     T     F     S       │    │
│ │  ┌──┐                                          │    │
│ │  [ 1 ]  [ 2 ]  3     4     5     6     7        │    │
│ │                                                │    │
│ │   8    ( 9 )  10    11    12    13    14        │    │
│ │                                                │    │
│ │  15     16   >17<   18    19    20    21        │    │
│ │                                                │    │
│ │  22     23    24    25    26    27    28        │    │
│ │                                                │    │
│ │  29     30    31                               │    │
│ │                                                │    │
│ │ St. Patrick's Day.                             │    │
│ │                                                │    │
│ └──────────────────────────────────────────────┘    │
└────────────────────────────────────────────────────┘
```

Figure 10.12   *Marking Days on the Calender*

Changing the Day View Format

By default the Calendar displays its time entries for a day in one-hour intervals, uses a 12-hour clock, and displays a start time of 7:00 a.m. You can change these settings by choosing the Day Settings command on the Options menu. Figure 10.13 shows the Day Settings dialog box.

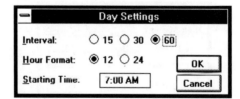

Figure 10.13   *The Day Settings Dialog Box*

Select the Interval option button that represents the time intervals for your daily schedule. Select the 12-or 24-hour time representation. Enter the starting time you want.

Inserting or Deleting a Special Time

The Special Time command on the Options menu allows you to specify a time other than one of the intervals. The command is available only when you are using the Day option on the View menu. This new time interval will appear on the calendar only on the currently selected day. Figure 10.14 shows the Special Time dialog box.

Figure 10.14   *The Special Time Dialog Box*

You can use the Special Time command to delete a special time but you cannot delete one of the normal intervals. If you choose the command while the Calendar cursor is on a special time entry, the dialog box comes up with the special time already entered.

Navigating the Calendar

The Show menu has several commands that allow you to move around in the Calendar. The Today command returns you to the current day from wherever you are. The Previous and Next commands move to the previous and next days. The Date command allows you enter a specific date that you want to view. Figure 10.15 shows the Show Date dialog box. Enter the date in the format shown and choose OK.

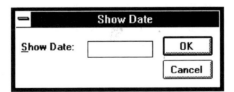

Figure 10.15   *The Show Date Dialog Box*

The Alarm Clock

Calendar, not Clock, is your Windows alarm clock, because it can remind you of an appointment. To set an alarm, move the cursor to the time on the day you want to be alerted, and choose the Set command on the Alarm menu. A small bell icon will appear in the left margin of the selected time entry, as shown in Figure 10.16.

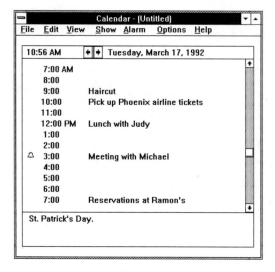

Figure 10.16 *An Alarm is Set*

If the alarm goes off while you are working in the Calendar, an audible beeping alarm sounds and a reminder window displays, as shown in Figure 10.17.

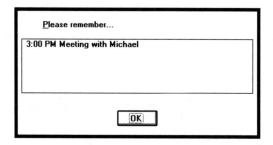

Figure 10.17 *The Alarm Goes Off*

If the alarm goes off when Calendar is minimized to an icon, the audible beeping alarm sounds and the Calendar icon blinks. The audible alarm quits after a time, but the icon continues to blink until you maximize the icon into a window, at which time the reminder window shown in Figure 10.17 displays. If the Calendar is an inactive window, the audible alarm sounds and the Calendar's title bar blinks until you activate the Calendar to view the reminder window.

You can tell Calendar to alert you in advance of the time of the alarm. For example, the appointment that you want to be alerted to might be somewhere else and you need time to get there. The Controls command on the Alarm menu allows you to specify up to 10 minutes advance time for the alarm. Figure 10.18 shows the Alarm Controls dialog box.

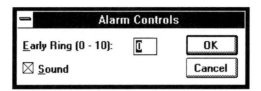

Figure 10.18   *The Alarm Controls Dialog Box*

You can use the Sound check box on the Alarm Controls dialog box to suppress the audible part of the alarm.

To clear an alarm, move to the time entry and choose the Set command again.

Removing Calendar Entries

The Remove command on the Edit menu allows you to delete a range of appointments by specifying the begin and end dates. Figure 10.19 shows the Remove dialog box. Enter the From and To dates and choose OK.

Figure 10.19   *The Remove Dialog Box*

The Calendar and the Clipboard

You can select the text of a Calendar entry and cut or copy it to the Clipboard. You can paste the contents of the Clipboard into an entry. Mark the text with the mouse or keyboard the same way you do in other applications and use the Cut, Copy, and Paste commands on the Edit menu.

Files

The File menu is similar to the Notepad's File menu with New, Open, Save, and Save As commands. You can maintain several calendars by saving each one in its own file. The default file name extension is .CAL, which is associated with the Calendar application in the File Manager; you can execute Calendar by selecting a .CAL file.

Figure 10.20 shows the File Open dialog box. It differs from other File Open dialog boxes in that it has a Read Only check box. If you select this check box, the Calendar will not allow you to make any changes to the file. This option is for convenience rather than for security. You would use it if you are viewing a calendar maintained by someone else.

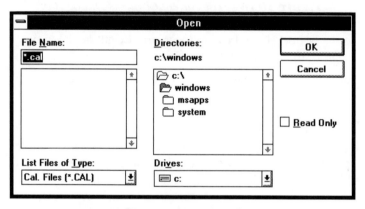

Figure 10.20 *The Calender's File Open Dialog Box*

Printing

The File menu includes Print, Page Setup, and Printer Setup commands. The Print command works differently than the Print commands of other applications, however. It displays the Print dialog box shown in Figure 10.21.

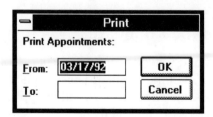

Figure 10.21 *The Print Dialog Box*

Enter the range of dates for the appointments you want to print. If you do not change anything in the From and To fields, the Calendar will print the schedule for the current day.

Cardfile

The Cardfile is an application for storing information in a form that resembles a 3x5 card format. You can store text and pictures, retrieve records by searching, and print card contents. Figure 10.22 shows the Cardfile application window.

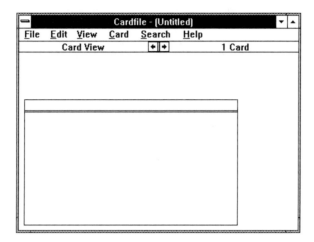

Figure 10.22   *The Cardfile Application Window*

The rectangle that appears in the lower-left corner of the Cardfile workspace is the card itself. The first line of the card is the index line. The rest of the card is the information area. You can type text into the index line, and you can type or paste text and paste pictures into the information area. Although you can change the size of the Cardfile application window, the size of the card does not change.

When you first start Cardfile there are no cards in the file. In Chapter 2, you used the Cardfile to help learn about Program Manager. You built a small database with one card in it. You will go farther than that in this Chapter.

Uses for Cardfile

You can use Cardfile for most applications that require the storage and retrieval of small text entries or pictures. You can store sales prospects, recipes, your Christmas card list, scanned snapshots, and so on.

Building a Cardfile Database

The first card in every Cardfile database is empty. To start a database, you must put something in it. Every card has an index area that contains the text by which the Cardfile sorts the file. In a name and address file, the index would usually be the name. To enter the index for the first blank card, choose the Index command from the Edit menu. You will see the Index dialog box shown in Figure 10.23.

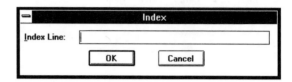

Figure 10.23   *The Index Dialog Box*

Enter a name into the dialog box and choose OK. For a well-ordered name and address file, enter the last name first. The name you enter will appear in the index line of the card, and the cursor will be in the card's information area. Enter the address, phone number, and any other relevant information about the person. If this file is for employees, you might include the social security number and job title, for example. Figure 10.24 shows a card with an index and some information entered. That's all you have to do to build the first card. It is now in the Cardfile database. You have not named or saved the file, but the card is in memory.

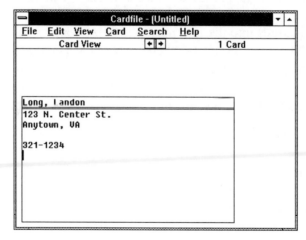

Figure 10.24   *A Filled-Out Card*

To add more cards to the file, choose the Add command on the Card menu. You will see the Add dialog box shown in Figure 10.25. The Add dialog box looks a lot like the Index dialog box. It serves the same purpose when you are adding new cards to an existing file. The Index dialog box's first purpose is to supply the index line for the first card in an empty file. Subsequently you use the Index dialog box when you want to change the index lines for existing cards.

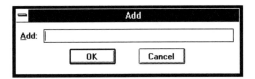

Figure 10.25 *The Add Dialog Box*

Enter a name into the Add dialog box and choose OK. The first card moves back, and the new card takes its place at the front of the stack, ready for an address, as shown in Figure 10.26. Enter an address into the information area of the second card. Add several more cards to the file by using the Add command. The Cardfile application window will look like that shown in Figure 10.27.

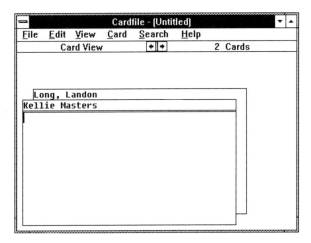

Figure 10.26 *Adding a Card*

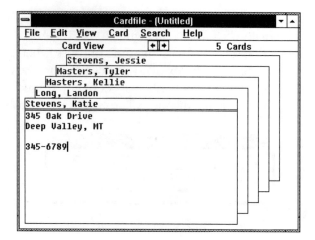

Figure 10.27 *Many Cards in the Data Base*

The file has only five cards in it so far. In actual use, a Cardfile database will grow much larger, and you will not be able to see all the cards in the stack. You can expand the size of the application window to see more of the cards, but most databases will be too big to fit into the window. To view other cards you must move around in the database.

Moving Around in a Cardfile Database

The Cardfile keeps the cards sorted by the index line. The card at the front of the stack is always the current one. You can use the mouse to select a card that is in view by clicking its index line. The card will come to the front of the stack. You can click on the two arrows that are in the line just below the menu bar to move forward or back one card.

Table 10.5 shows the keystrokes for moving around in a Cardfile database.

Table 10.5 *Cardfile Keys*

Key	Movement
PgUp/PgDn	Previous/next card
Ctrl+Home/End	First/last card in the file
Ctrl+letter	Card with index line starting with letter

Later you will learn to search a Cardfile database for cards that match specified text strings.

Editing

You can use most of the standard editing techniques in the Cardfile information area, including copying, cutting, pasting, and deleting text. You mark text by dragging the mouse cursor across it or by holding the Shift key down while you move the keyboard cursor with the arrow keys.

Deleting Text

To delete a marked block of text from the information area, press Del. The Undo command on the Edit menu will undo the most recently deleted block.

Restore

The Restore command on the Edit menu restores any changes you have made to the current card since you moved it to the top of the stack. Restore does not restore changes made prior to the last save of the file, however.

Cutting, Copying, and Pasting Text

The Edit menu's Cut, Copy, and Paste commands work just as they do in other applications. You can cut or copy a marked block of text in the information area to the Clipboard, and you can Paste text from the Clipboard to the information area.

Saving the Database

The File menu has the usual New, Open, Save, and Save As commands. Cardfile databases use the default file name extension .CRD. For these exercises, save the database with the name GIFTLIST.CRD.

List View

The View menu allows you to switch between the card view, the default, and the list view, which lists the cards by their index line. Figure 10.28 shows the Cardfile list view.

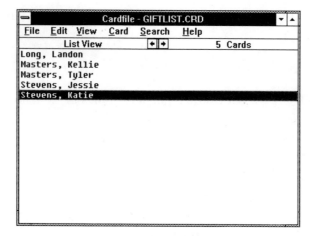

Figure 10.28   *The List View*

The list view allows you to see more of the cards in the stack. It always displays the cards in sequence, with the first card in the file at the top of the list. You can select a card with the arrow keys or by clicking it. If the number of cards exceeds the height of the window's workspace, the window will have a vertical scroll bar. If you double-click an entry, Cardfile opens the Index dialog box for you to change the index value. You saw the Index dialog box in Figure 10.23.

If you select an entry in the list and change to the card view, the card for the highlighted entry will be at the top of the stack.

Searching

If you are in the card view, you can search the Cardfile database for a match on a text string by using the Find command on the Search menu. Figure 10.29 shows the Find dialog box.

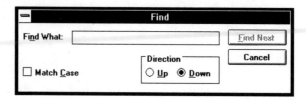

Figure 10.29   *The Find Dialog Box*

Enter the text you want to search for in the Find field, select the proper Direction option button, set the Match Case check box to its appropriate setting, and choose OK. When the Cardfile finds a match on the text, it brings the matching card to the top of the stack and highlights the matching text. The search matches a string regardless of upper- or lowercase differences. The index line is not included in the search.

You can use the Find Next command on the Search menu to continue the search to the next matching card.

To search for matches on the index line, use the Go To command on the Search menu. The Go To command works in both card and list view. Figure 10.30 shows the Go To dialog box.

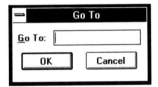

Figure 10.30   *The Go To Dialog Box*

Enter some text into the Go To field to match against the index lines in the cards. The search string will match anywhere inside the index line, not just at the beginning.

The Find Next command does not continue Go To searches.

Pictures

Cards in a Cardfile database can contain graphics as well as text, and the two can be mixed on the same card. The Picture toggle command on the Edit menu allows you to paste pictures from the Clipboard to the database cards.

Pasting Pictures

You might use Cardfile to store clip art that you design with Paintbrush, scan into a Windows graphics application with a scanner device, or acquire as .PCX files from other sources. Each item of clip art can be on its own card. When you want to use one in a design, you copy the picture from the Cardfile database to the Clipboard and paste it into your artwork.

To paste a picture into a card, choose the Picture toggle command on the Edit menu. The cursor will change to a small rectangle to indicate that Cardfile is in picture mode. Paste the picture into the card and use the mouse or the arrow keys to move it where you want it. Figure 10.31 shows a card with a Paintbrush clipart picture pasted onto it.

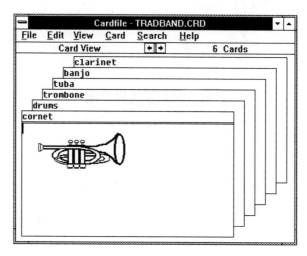

Figure 10.31 *A Picture Card*

Mixing Text and Graphics

You can mix text and graphics in a Cardfile card. After you have pasted the picture onto the card, move the picture to a part of the card where you will not be entering text. Put the card back into text mode by choosing the Text command on the Edit menu. You can now type any text you like. If you type over the picture, the text and picture intermingle, but they do not interfere with one another. Figure 10.32 shows some text added to the card that already has a clipart picture.

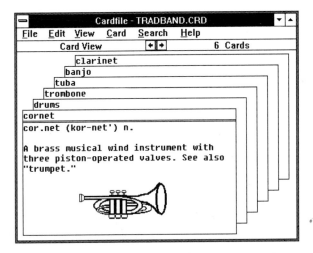

Figure 10.32   *Text and Picture Mixed*

Cutting and Copying Pictures

As long as a card is in picture mode, you can cut or copy its picture to the Clipboard. To put the card into picture mode, choose the Picture command on the Edit menu.

Picture Sizes

A card can record a picture that is much bigger than the visible area of the card. From picture mode you can drag the picture around inside the card as well as copy it to the Clipboard.

Deleting a Card

To delete a card, bring it to the top of the stack and choose the Delete command on the Card menu.

Duplicating a Card

To duplicate a card, bring it to the top of the stack and choose the Duplicate command on the Card menu. Cardfile will create a copy of the card on the top of the stack. You can edit the index line and information area to give the new card its own identity.

Dialing

If you have phone numbers in the cards in your Cardfile database, The Cardfile will dial them for you. You need a Hayes-compatible modem installed and a telephone connected to the telephone line the modem is connected to.

Bring the card to the top of the stack and mark the phone number. If the phone number is the first field on the card that starts with digits, you do not need to mark it. Choose the Autodial command from the Card menu. You will see the Autodial dialog box shown in Figure 10.33.

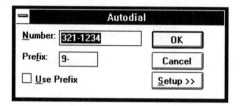

Figure 10.33 *The Autodial Dialog Box*

You can enter a dialing prefix if your telephone requires one. For the Cardfile to dial the prefix, you must select the Use Prefix check box. Choose the Setup >> command button to see the Setup part of the Autodial dialog box shown in Figure 10.34.

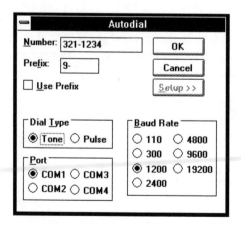

Figure 10.34 *The Autodial Dialog Box with Setup*

These settings should correspond to your Control Panel setup for the communications port. Select the Pulse option button if you do not have touch-tone dialing.

When you are ready to dial, choose OK. The Cardfile will dial the number and display the message shown in Figure 10.35. Pick up the phone and choose OK to be ready when the person you call answers.

Figure 10.35 *Pick Up Message*

Merging Cardfile Databases

You can merge the contents of another Cardfile database into the current one by choosing the Merge command on the File menu. You will see the File Merge dialog box shown in Figure 10.36.

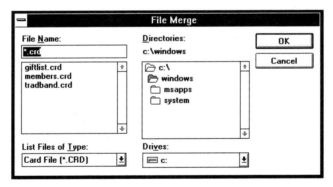

Figure 10.36 *The File Merge Dialog Box*

Select a file to merge from the list of files in the File Merge dialog box. Observe that the dialog box lists the current file along with the others. You are permitted to merge a file into itself this way.

Printing

The Cardfile has the usual Print, Page Setup, and Printer Setup commands on the File menu. The Print command prints the card at the top of the stack. To print the entire file of cards, choose the Print All command on the File menu.

Recorder

Recorder is a program that records user input macros. If you have ever used a DOS keyboard macro program such as Superkey you will understand immediately what Recorder can do for you. If not, some introduction is necessary.

Recorder records macros. A *macro* is a sequence of keystrokes and mouse actions stored for later use. When you want those same keys or mouse movements, you execute the macro by pressing a key.

For example, suppose you are writing a report with Windows Write that repeats the phrase "Ackermann Scholarship Fund" many times. Rather than type the phrase every time it occurs, you can record it into a macro, assigning the Ctrl+A shortcut key to it. Then, whenever you want to type the phrase, "Ackermann Scholarship Fund," you press Ctrl+A, and Recorder types the phrase for you.

Recorder can record macros that repeat themselves. You can build running demonstrations or tutorials by recording macros inside macros.

Recorder is not an interactive macro language—able to wait for user responses—such as you will find in some spreadsheet and database programs. Recorder macros are simple playbacks of actions you make while Recorder is recording.

Recording a Macro

You will begin by recording a simple keyboard substitution to use in Notepad. You can build similar macros for other Windows word processing applications such as Write and Word for Windows.

First you prepare to record the macro. You must be at the place in an application where you are going to use the macro. If you want Recorder to type the name of your company, for example, you must be where you can type it in order to record it.

Run Notepad and have it active and waiting for keystrokes. Set the Word Wrap toggle command in Notepad's Edit menu to on.

Running Recorder

You run Recorder to record a macro, to load a macro file, and to play back macros. Once your macros are recorded and ready to run, Recorder can run as a minimized icon to keep it out of the way of your other applications. Initially, however, you must start it up to begin recording. Figure 10.37 shows the Recorder application window.

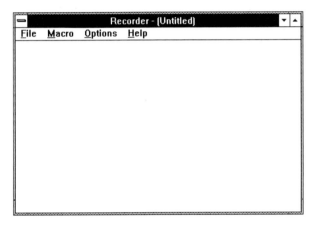

Figure 10.37   *The Recorder Application Window*

To set up the macro, choose Record on the Macro menu. You will see the Record Macro dialog box shown in Figure 10.38. For now, you will use the default settings for most of the fields. You should give the macro a name, so enter the value "Company Name" into the Record Macro Name field. You need a shortcut key to execute the macro from within the application. For the company name, you will use Ctrl+C. Enter the single letter C into the Shortcut Key field. Observe that, of the Ctrl, Shift, and Alt check boxes, only the Ctrl check box is selected. Leave them the way they are for now. You can enter a lengthy description of the macro in the Description text box if you wish. After you have a lot of macros recorded you might want to use this field to keep notes about the macro's purpose, author, or origins.

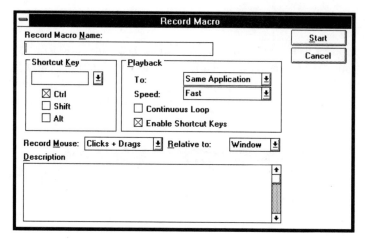

Figure 10.38 *The Record Macro Dialog Box*

To begin recording the macro, choose the Start command button. The Record Macro dialog box closes, Recorder minimizes itself to an icon, and you are back in Notepad ready to type. Observe that the Recorder icon is flashing. This tells you that you are recording a macro. Every keystroke and mouse click you enter into your application will be recorded for playback later.

Enter your company's name. For this example you will type Beiderbecke Brassworks. When you are done, press Ctrl+Break, or click on the blinking Recorder icon. You will see the Recorder dialog box shown in Figure 10.39.

Figure 10.39 *The Recorder Dialog Box*

Select the Save Macro option button and then choose OK. The macro is now recorded in Recorder, and you are back in Notepad. To see that the macro is recorded, activate Recorder. Its workspace now contains one macro, as shown in

Figure 10.40. The macro description in the Recorder workspace does not describe the keystrokes of the macro, only its shortcut key and name.

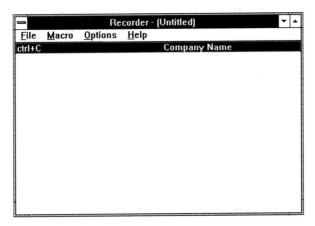

Figure 10.40   *One Macro Recorded*

Minimize Recorder to an icon again. To test your new macro, press the Ctrl+C shortcut key to see "Beiderbecke Brassworks" typed for you. After you are confident that the macro is working correctly, delete the test text from the Notepad workspace and type a memo that uses the macro.

Nested Macros

You can call an existing macro while you are recording another. To enable this feature, you must turn on the Enable Shortcut Keys check box in the Playback field of the Record Macro dialog box. This check box is usually on by default.

Another keyboard sequence you might use frequently is the name and address of your company. Using the procedure you just learned, start with an empty Notepad file and begin recording a macro named "Company Name and Address" with Ctrl+A as the shortcut key. When Recorder returns to Notepad and begins recording, press Ctrl+C as the first key. Then press the Enter key and type the rest of the address. Figure 10.41 shows the Notepad with the text typed on the first line by Recorder when you pressed Ctrl+C and the text that you added on the second two lines for the new macro.

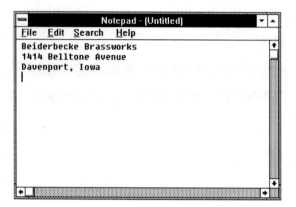

Figure 10.41 *Recording a Nested Macro*

After you have the address typed in, save the macro. If you activate the Recorder window again, you will see that the new macro is added to the list. Return to Notepad, clear the workspace, and press Ctrl+A to see your nested macro execute.

Building Document Templates with Recorder

Suppose you send a lot of memos in your work, and they all have the same format. You would like to automate the preparation of that format. You can use Recorder to build a memo, that part of the format that is common to all your memos.

To build a template for interoffice memoranda, start with an empty Notepad and begin recording a macro named "Memo." Use Ctrl+M for the shortcut key. For the first keystroke in the macro, press the F5 key, Notepad's shortcut for its Time/Date command on the Notepad Edit menu. The time/Date command inserts the current date into the memo template. Press the Enter key twice to go down two lines, then press Ctrl+A to insert your company's name and address. Type Interoffice Memorandum followed by the Enter key twice. Type From: and your name. Press Enter and type To:. Press Enter and type Re:. Use the up arrow key to move the cursor up to the To: line and space over just under your name. Click the Recorder icon or press Ctrl+Break to interrupt recording, then save the macro. Figure 10.42 shows the entire macro as displayed in Notepad.

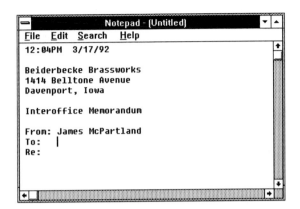

Figure 10.42 *Recording a Document Template*

Whenever you need to send a memo, press Ctrl+M to display the memo template described by this macro. It will write the current date at the top, insert your name and the rest of your memo format, and leave the cursor at the point where you would begin typing the name of the addressee.

If this were an extremely complicated macro, you might substitute another macro for anything else user-specific (in this case, your name). Then you could share the macro with other Windows users, who would use your general macro, but write a short subordinate macro of their own to insert all its user-specific components.

Command Macros

Besides recording text keystrokes, Recorder can record commands. Notepad does not have a single keystroke command to delete a word. To delete a word, you must use the keyboard or mouse to mark a word you want to delete and then press the Del key or choose the Delete command on the Edit menu. The procedure requires multiple keystrokes and mouse actions to do a common, routine task. You can replace this laborious process with a macro. Begin with the Notepad memo shown in Figure 10.43.

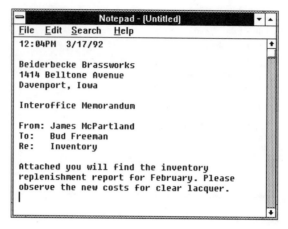

Figure 10.43 *A Memo Built from a Macro Template*

Recording a Delete Word Macro

Position the keyboard cursor on a word and begin to record a macro called "De-lete Word" that uses the Alt+Del shortcut key. The differences here are that you are using Alt instead of Ctrl and the Del key instead of a letter. Figure 10.44 shows the Record Macro dialog box with the Shortcut Key drop-down list box selected. This list has all keys that you can select as shortcut keys. The Alt check box, hid-den now by the drop-down list, is selected, and the Ctrl and Shift check boxes are not. Choose the Start command button. Recorder returns you to the memo in Notepad and begins recording.

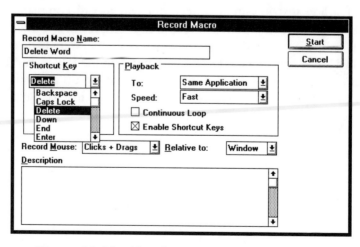

Figure 10.44 *The Shortcut Key Drop-Down Box*

To delete the word that the keyboard cursor is on, you must first mark it. Press Ctrl+right arrow followed by Ctrl+left arrow to move the cursor to the beginning of the word. Hold down the Shift key and press Ctrl+right arrow to move the cursor to the beginning of the next word, marking everything in between. Now press Del to delete the word. All of these keystrokes are being recorded into your Delete Word macro.

To end the macro, use Ctrl+Break to stop recording, or choose the Recorder icon and save the macro. Subsequently, when you want to delete a single word, put the cursor anywhere on the word and press Alt+Del.

Other Possible Macros

You can use these techniques to add new commands to virtually any application, combining many of the application's existing commands into one. For example, to move a marked block from one location to another in Notepad or Write, you cut it to the Clipboard and paste it to where the cursor is positioned. That operation could be a Move Block macro. The same could be done for copying a block.

Many word processors use document layout templates that describe the formats of different documents or sections within a document. You can write Recorder macros to set up such templates within Write by adjusting margins and indents to defined settings at the touch of a key.

The possibilities for macros that enhance the use of applications is limited only by your imagination.

Online Help

With all these macros in place, what about online help for the user? How does one remember all the keystrokes? Recorder is itself your online help facility for recorded macros. Choose the Recorder icon and you get a list of all the macros' shortcut keys and names in the Recorder application window. What's more, the list acts as a menu. Double-click an entry and the macro runs.

Saving Macro Files

With this much work invested, you will want to save the macros in a file for later retrieval. The Recorder's File menu has the usual New, Open, Save, and Save As commands. The default file name extension for Recorder macro files is .REC.

Merging Macros

You can merge the set of macros that are currently in memory into an already-existing .REC file. For example, perhaps you want macros you have built for deleting words and lines to be available for Windows Write as well. You might have several Write .REC files, one for each of the different kinds of documents you use. You can merge your Notepad's macros into all of those Write macro files.

You merge macros by choosing the Merge command on the File menu. The File Merge dialog box is similar to the one you learned about for Cardfile. If you merge macros with shortcut keys that conflict with those that are already in memory, Recorder will display a warning message. You will need to modify the properties of the new macros to assign new shortcut keys to them.

Modifying a Macro's Properties

The Properties command on the Recorder's Macro menu displays the Macro Properties dialog box shown in Figure 10.45. The Macro Properties dialog box displays the properties of the macro that is highlighted in the Recorder workspace. It has most of the same information as the Record Macro dialog box. You can modify the properties of a macro, such as its name and shortcut key, but you cannot modify the keystrokes or mouse actions that the macro records. To modify a macro's keystrokes and mouse actions you must delete the macro and record it again from the beginning.

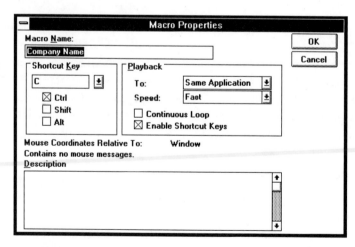

Figure 10.45 *The Macro Properties Dialog Box*

Deleting a Macro

The Delete command on the Recorder's Macro menu deletes the macro that is highlighted in the Recorder workspace after prompting you to confirm the action.

The Macro and the Mouse

Recorder will record mouse actions into a macro, but it does not work well. The Record Macro dialog box allows you to specify Clicks + Drags, Everything, or Ignore Mouse in the Record Mouse field.

When you record clicks and drags, Recorder records the position where the click occurred and the position of the drag, if any, that follows. Those positions are relative to the window or the screen, depending on how you set the Relative To field. Mouse actions in the macro reflect the window and screen as configured when you record the macro. For a correct playback, the window and screen must be configured the same as when you recorded the macro. That is expecting a lot in a dynamic, user-controlled environment such as Windows.

You might have observed a certain random pattern to the way Windows decides to open application windows or place icons, for example. This apparent arbitrary behavior means that you cannot predict with accuracy the size or position on the screen of an application window when Program Manager first opens it. Therefore, any macros that use mouse actions should certainly be oriented to the window only, and the application should probably run in a maximized window. In fact, you should probably make Alt+Spacebar and X the first two keystrokes of any macro, to automatically maximize the window the macro is being used in. This is particularly important if a mouse action in a macro is going to interact with one of an application's dialog boxes. Dialog boxes tend to open in a fixed screen location regardless of the size and position of the application window.

When you select Everything in the Record Mouse field of the Record Macro dialog box, every movement of the mouse goes into the macro. If you use this option, do not try to end the recording session by clicking the Recorder icon. The mouse movement and click that you use to end the session would become part of the session. Use the Ctrl-Break key instead.

If a macro has mouse actions, the Macro Properties dialog box displays the resolution of the video screen where you recorded the macro. Instead of saying, "Contains no mouse messages," the line just above the dialog box's Description field will say something like, "Recorded on (compatible) 640 by 480 display." A macro that uses the mouse does not work properly if you run it on a system with a screen resolution that is different from the one where you recorded the macro.

In normal practice using the mouse in a macro is replete with problems. As a result, it is usually not worth the bother, and in any case it is seldom necessary. Anything you can do with the mouse you can do with the keyboard. Even if you prefer using the mouse in your routine operations, you can use the keyboard equivalent operations when you are recording macros.

One application for using the mouse in macros is in the preparation of demonstrations or computer-assisted presentations. In such uses, the video effects are essential to the message and the operating environment is tightly controlled, so it is worth working around the inherent mouse-in-macro problems to gain the advantages of the visual effects.

Global Vs. Application-Specific Macros

The To: drop-down list box in the Playback field of the Record Macro and Macro Properties dialog boxes allows you to choose between Same Application and Any Application. If you choose Same Application, the macro will run only when the application in which you recorded it is active. If you choose Any Application, the macro will run at any time.

Real Time Vs. Fast Macros

The Speed drop-down list box in the Playback field of the Record Macro and Macro Properties dialog boxes allows you to choose between Fast and Recorded Speed. The Fast setting plays the macro back as fast as it can. The Recorded Speed setting plays the macro back at the same speed as you recorded it. If you are a slow typist, the macro will be slow if you have Recorded Speed set to on. This option is useful when you are developing macros that demonstrate things.

Continuous-Loop Macros

If you select the Continuous Loop check box in the Record Macro and Macro Properties dialog boxes, the macro repeats itself indefinitely after you have started it. It will repeat until you press the Ctrl-Break key. This feature is useful for running non-stop demonstrations.

Ctrl+Break Interruption

You can stop a running macro by pressing the Ctrl+Break key. This feature allows you to stop a continuous-loop macro or to terminate a particularly long-running macro after you realize that you did not mean to execute it.

You can suppress the Ctrl-Break interruption of the macro by turning off the Control+Break Checking toggle command on the Options menu. With Control+Break toggled off, the only way to interrupt a long-running macro is to reset the computer. Setting Control+Break off prevents someone from stopping an ongoing demonstration.

Suppressing Shortcut Keys

Turning off the Shortcut Keys toggle command on the Recorder Options menu allows you to prevent the shortcut keys from running the macros. You would turn this option off when you have global macros and you are running an application that uses some of the same shortcut keys for itself. By default, the command toggle is on.

When shortcut keys are suppressed, you can still run the macros from the Recorder application itself.

Running a Macro from Recorder

You can activate the Recorder application window and run any macro by double-clicking its entry in the workspace list or by moving the highlight bar to it and choosing the Run command on the Macro menu. Recorder will deactivate itself, return to the current application, and run the macro.

Minimize on Use

The Minimize on Use command toggle on the Options menu is normally on. It tells Recorder to minimize itself to an icon when you begin recording a macro and when you run a macro from within Recorder itself. You can turn this toggle off to tell Recorder to become an inactive window rather than an icon. This feature allows you to keep Recorder more readily handy while you are recording and testing macros.

Setting Defaults

Recorder maintains a number of defaults with respect to how it records macros. You can change the values of these defaults by choosing the Preferences command on the Options menu. You will see the Default Preferences dialog box shown in Figure 10.46.

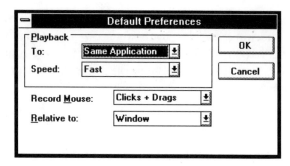

Figure 10.46 *The Default Preferences Dialog Box*

You can change the default values for running macros in the same or all applications, running them fast or at recorded speed, whether you will record mouse actions and if so which ones, and whether a macro runs relative to the window or the screen.

Calculator

Calculator is a small accessory application. You can run it, minimize it as an icon, and have it nearby on your desktop for whenever you need it. There are two calculators built into the application, the Standard Calculator and the Scientific Calculator.

The Standard Calculator

Figure 10.47 shows the standard calculator. It resembles the typical pocket calculator with the usual four functions, a square root function, a percent function, a reciprocal function, and memory.

Figure 10.47 *The Standard Calculator*

Entering Numbers

You enter numbers into the Calculator by clicking its digit command buttons or by typing the numbers in on your keyboard. Turn on Num Lock on your keyboard and use the numeric keypad for the most familiar way to enter numbers.

Use the . (period) function button or key to begin entering digits to the right of the decimal place. The Back command button and the keyboard's backspace key will remove the last digit you entered. The CE (Clear Entry) command button and the keyboard's Del key will clear the current entry from the Calculator's display without modifying the current calculation. The C (Clear) command button and the keyboard's Esc key will zero out the Calculator completely.

Calculating

The +, −, *, and / arithmetic operators and the = operator work just as on any standard calculator. The Enter key and the = key on the keyboard will both do what the = command button does.

The Sqrt command button and the @ key compute the square root of the number in the display. The 1/x command button and the R key compute the reciprocal of the number in the display. The +/− command button and the F9 key change the sign of the number in the display.

Memory

The Calculator has a one-value memory. When the memory is other than zero, the box immediately above the / and Sqrt function buttons displays an M.

The MC command button and the Ctrl+C key reset memory to zero. The MR command button and the Ctrl+R key display the value in memory. The MS command button and the Ctrl+M key store the displayed value into memory. The M+ command button and the Ctrl+P key add the displayed value to the value in memory.

The Scientific Calculator

Change to the Scientific Calculator by choosing Scientific on the View menu. Figure 10.48 shows the Scientific Calculator.

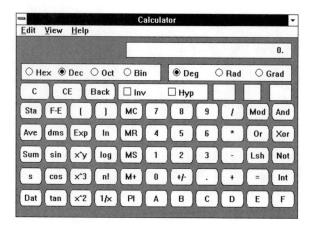

Figure 10.48 *The Scientific Calculator*

Number systems

You can set Calculator to work in the hexadecimal, decimal, octal, and binary number systems by selecting the appropriate Hex, Dec, Oct, and Bin option button. The keyboard keys to select these systems are F5, F6, F7, and F8, respectively. By default Calculator operates in the decimal number system.

Calculator does not allow you to enter digits that do not work with the number system you select. Binary accepts 1 and 0; octal accepts 0 to 7; decimal accepts 0 to 9; hexadecimal accepts 0 to 9, A to F.

When you have a number already displayed, changing number systems converts the displayed value to its representation in the new number system.

When you have selected Hex, Oct, or Bin, the box to the right of the number system option buttons changes to show three option buttons labeled Dword, Word, and Byte. Dword causes the display to show the full value of the word. Word displays the value represented by only the lower 16 bits. Byte displays the value represented by the lower 8 bits. Word and Byte affect the display only; they do not change the value.

Statistical Functions

The Scientific Calculator supports statistical functions. Choose the Sta command button or press the Ctrl+S key. You will see the Statistics Box shown in Figure 10.49. Observe that while the Statistics Box is present, the Calculator box that appears just above the 9 and / keys contains the value "stat."

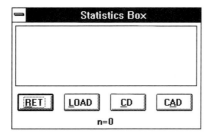

Figure 10.49 *The Statistics Box*

You might need to move the Statistics Box around so you can see more of the Calculator. Choose the RET button in the Statistics Box to return to the Calculator. Enter a value, and choose the Dat command button or press the Ins key. The value appears in the Statistics Box. Enter more values the same way.

Mean. If you want to take the mean of the numbers, choose the Ave command button or press the Ctrl+A key. If the Inv check box in the Calculator is selected, this command computes the mean of the squares.

Sum. To take the sum of the numbers, choose the Sum command button or press the Ctrl+T key. If the Inv check box in the Calculator is selected, this command computes the sum of the squares.

Standard Deviation. To take the standard deviation of the numbers, choose the S command button or press the Ctrl+D key. If the Inv check box in the Calculator is selected, this command computes the standard deviation with the population parameter set to the number of entries in the list of numbers. If the Inv check box in the Calculator is not selected, this command computes the standard deviation with the population parameter set to the number of entries in the list of numbers minus 1. The number of entries is shown in the Statistics Box as the value n at the bottom of the box.

When you compute the value with one of the commands just described, the computed value appears in the Calculator's display.

The Statistics box has four command buttons. The RET button returns you to the Calculator. The LOAD button loads the Statistics Box's currently highlighted value into the Calculator's display. You can do the same thing by double-clicking the entry. The CD button deletes the currently highlighted value from the Statistics Box. The CAD button deletes all values from the Statistics Box.

Logical Operations

Calculator has the Boolean operators And, Or, Not, and Xor. They are command buttons on the right side of the Calculator. The corresponding keyboard keys for these operators are: &, |, ~, and ^.

The Lsh command button and the < key perform a left shift on the value in the display. If the Inv check box is selected, Lsh performs a right shift.

Other Operators

The Mod command button and the % key calculate the modulus of two numbers, which is the remainder derived when the second number is divided into the first. The Int command button and the ; key deliver the integer portion of a number. If the Inv check box is selected, Int delivers the fractional portion of the number.

Calculating Expressions

You can use the (and) command buttons to establish precedence as you enter values and operators into a calculation. The box just above the And key displays the current depth of parentheses. For example, (=3 means there are currently three unterminated left parens.

Trigonometric Input

When you are in the decimal number system, the box just below the display has the Deg, Rad, and Grad option buttons available for setting the trigonometric input to degrees, radians, or gradients. The keyboard keys for these three functions are F2, F3, and F4, respectively.

Notation

When you are in the decimal number system, the F-E command button and the V key switch the display between scientific and normal notation.

Math Functions

Table 10.6 lists the Calculator's math functions, describing their action when the Inv and Hyp check boxes are both off, both selected, or either one selected.

Table 10.6 *Math Functions.*

Command Button	Keyboard Key	Inv	Hyp	Description
cos	o			Cosine
		+		Arc cosine
			+	Hyperbolic cosine
		+	+	Arc hyperbolic cosine
dms	m			Degrees-minutes-seconds
		+		Degrees
Exp	x			Permits scientific notation input
ln	n			Natural (base e) logarithm
		+		e ∧ displayed number
log	l			Common (base 10) logarithm
		+		10 ∧ displayed number
n!	!			Factorial
PI	p			3.14159265359
		+		6.28318530718
sin	s			Sine
		+		Arc sine
		+	+	Arc hyperbolic sine
tan	t			Tangent
		+		Arc tangent
			+	Hyperbolic tangent
		+	+	Arc hyperbolic tangent
x∧y	y			x ∧ y
		+		yth root of x
x∧2	@			Square
			+	Square root
x∧3	#			Cube
			=	Cube root

Clipboard

The Calculator's Edit menu has Copy and Paste commands. You can copy the value currently displayed by the Calculator to the Clipboard to use in another application. You can paste a value from the Clipboard into the Calculator.

If the text in the Clipboard contains certain values, and they are pasted into the calculator, they will execute functions on the Calculator. Table 10.7 shows the corresponding values.

Table 10.7 *Clipboard to Calculator Function Values.*

In Clipboard	Calculator Function or Operation
c	MC
e	Switches to scientific notation
e+	Same as e, indicates positive exponent
e-	Same as e, indicates negative exponent
m	MS
p	M+
r	MR
: letter	Ctrl+letter
: number	Function key (:3 = F3)
\	Dat

Summary

This chapter has described a number of Windows accessories. It marks the last of the chapters that teach Windows to the new user. Chapter 11—the last chapter in the book—addresses the Windows power user by describing some of the advanced uses you can make of the Windows graphical operating environment.

Chapter 11

The Windows Power User

This chapter is about the advanced tools of the Windows power user—the user who has gone beyond the basics. In this chapter you will learn:

- ◆ The Windows Standard and 386 enhanced modes
- ◆ Managing virtual memory
- ◆ Changing your configuration with Setup
- ◆ Using the PIF Editor to define non-Windows DOS applications
- ◆ Running Windows in a network
- ◆ Object Linking and Embedding (OLE)
- ◆ Multimedia extensions to Windows

This chapter contains some Windows knowledge and procedures that you can use to modify the way Windows operates. It also discusses the advanced object linking and embedding feature of Windows 3.1. Finally, the chapter addresses the multimedia support provided by Windows 3.1.

Some of these procedures require a deeper understanding of PC/AT architecture than do previous chapters. Therefore, brief introductions to aspects of PC/AT architecture are in order.

PC/AT Memory

There are three kinds of random-access memory (RAM) that PC/AT-class computers, those using 286, 386, or 486 processors, can have: conventional, extended, and expanded. Depending on your computer and what hardware and software are installed on it, Windows uses all three.

Conventional Memory

All PC/AT computers have *conventional* memory, of which there is a maximum of 640K. They can address up to 1Mb, but the space from 640K up is used by other devices, such as video cards, network cards, and the BIOS read-only-memory (ROM).

Expanded Memory

Expanded memory is a technique whereby a PC/AT computer has extra memory that it cannot normally address. Programs can use it however, by having small segments of it temporarily mapped into holes—address ranges not used by devices—in the conventional address space above 640K. Any PC/AT can have expanded memory. There is a standard method for implementing expanded memory called the LIM 4.0 specification, commonly abbreviated as EMS.

For Windows-compatible EMS to exist in a computer, the memory hardware must be installed and a software driver that conforms to the LIM 4.0 specification must be loaded. Drivers that implement versions of LIM earlier than 4.0 will not work with Windows. Windows will not attempt to use the EMS, but it will still be available to applications. Windows includes an EMS driver that works with 386 systems. When you install Windows, it installs that driver.

Extended Memory

AT class computers with 80286, 80386, and 80486 microprocessors can have extended memory. These processors have an operating mode called the "protected" mode where they can address memory above the 1Mb range. DOS does not run in protected mode. It runs in "real" mode, which can address only the first

1MB of memory. DOS runs this way because the 8086 and 8088 microprocessors do not have the equivalent of protected mode, and DOS must work with all PC machines regardless of the processor they use. The 80286, 386, and 486 microprocessors can switch between real and protected modes. When they run DOS, they stay in real mode. When they run Windows, they run in protected mode.

The standard definition of how extended memory is used by programs is referred to as the XMS specification.

The High Memory Area

A characteristic of the 286, 386, and 486 processors is that they can address the first 64K of extended memory without switching into protected mode. This extra memory is called the high memory area (HMA). Many memory-resident programs, such as network shell programs, use the HMA if it is available. DOS 5.0 will load into the HMA if you want it to. Programs load themselves into the HMA to minimize the amount of conventional memory they occupy.

Operating Modes

Windows operates in the 386 enhanced or standard modes. If you do not specify the mode when you run Windows, Windows will examine your hardware and select the mode.

386 Enhanced Mode

Windows runs in 386 enhanced mode if your computer has a 386 or 486 processor and at least 2Mb of memory. In this mode, Windows uses conventional and extended memory to load and execute multiple tasks. The tasks run concurrently. You can multitask DOS applications along with Windows applications, and Windows can run the DOS applications in a Windows applications window or it can run them in full-screen mode. Windows does not use expanded memory in 386 enhanced mode.

Standard Mode

Windows runs in standard mode if your computer has a 286 processor and at least 1Mb of memory. You can have a mix of Windows and DOS applications loaded at one time. Windows uses conventional and extended memory to load tasks. Windows can multitask Windows applications, but DOS applications are suspended—stop functioning until you return to them—while you are inside the Windows graphical operating environment. Likewise, while you are running a DOS application, all Windows tasks are suspended, and the DOS application takes over the screen. Windows does not use expanded memory in standard mode.

Specifying a Mode

You can use a command line parameter (often called a *switch*) to tell Windows to run in a mode other than the one it would normally select. Your hardware must be compatible with the mode you select.

Specifying 386 Enhanced Mode

If your computer has a 386 processor with less than 2Mb, you can use the /3 command line switch when you run Windows to specify that it should run in 386 enhanced mode.

Specifying Standard Mode

The /S command line switch tells Windows to run in standard mode. You can use this mode if your computer has a 386 processor with between 2Mb and 3Mb and you will not be running any non-Windows DOS applications. Windows will run faster in standard mode under these conditions.

The Control Panel's 386 Enhanced Process

The Control Panel, which you learned about in Chapter 5, has the 386 Enhanced icon if you are running in 386 enhanced mode. When you select it you see the 386 Enhanced dialog box shown in Figure 11.1.

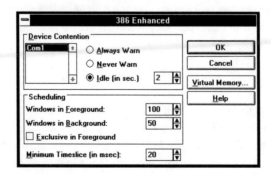

Figure 11.1   *The 386 Enhanced Dialog Box*

You can use this dialog box to adjust the details of the 386 enhanced mode multitasking.

Device Contention

When an application contends for a device while another application is using it, the strategy that you define here prevails.

When two applications attempt to use the same COM port, Windows intercepts their requests and attempts to arbitrate. You can tell Windows what to do by selecting the Always Warn, Never Warn, or Idle option buttons.

The Always Warn option alerts you with a warning dialog box that two applications are contending for the same device. You must determine which one is granted the access.

The Never Warn option tells DOS to grant access to any application that tries to use it. This option could result in output being mixed from two applications. It assumes that you will never run applications that will contend for the same device at the same time.

The Idle option includes the warning dialog box but adds a period of time after a device becomes available in which the warning will still be given. This allows you to set up a condition in which two applications can use a device, one after the other, while preventing a third application from getting the device between the time the first one is done with it and the second one takes it over.

Task Scheduling

A *timeslice* is the length of time a task runs before Windows switches to another task. The Minimum Timeslice field specifies the number of milliseconds in that timeslice. Every non-Windows DOS application gets one timeslice, and the Windows operating environment gets one timeslice, sharing it among all the Windows applications that are running. This value does not control the priority of tasks or the amount of time allocated to a task in one cycle of the task schedule. *Priority* is a function of the proportion of total timeslices in the task-switching cycle that Windows gives to a task.

The Windows in Foreground field specifies the time in relative terms that Windows applications share when a Windows application is in the foreground. This number, which ranges from 1 to 10,000, is added to the Background Priority values of all the non-Windows DOS applications. That total represents the total processing time to be shared among all tasks. The ratio of the Windows in

Foreground field to that total determines the number of timeslices that Windows gives to the Windows applications when one of them is in the foreground.

The Windows in Background field specifies the time that Windows applications share when a non-Windows DOS application is in the foreground. This number, which ranges from 1 to 10,000, is added to the Foreground Priority value of the foreground application and the Background Priority values of all the non-Windows DOS applications. That total represents the total processing time to be shared among all tasks. The ratio of the Windows in Background field to that total determines the number of timeslices that Windows gives to the Windows applications when a non-Windows DOS application is in the foreground.

The Exclusive in Foreground check box specifies that when a Windows application is in the foreground, non-Windows DOS applications are effectively suspended.

Virtual Memory

The Virtual Memory command button allows you to specify the location and type of the Windows swap files. *Swap files* are where Windows puts the images of concurrent applications during multitasking when the available memory will not hold them all. When you choose the Virtual Memory command, you see the Virtual Memory dialog box shown in Figure 11.2.

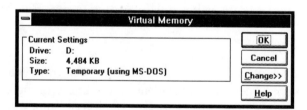

Figure 11.2   *The Virtual Memory Dialog Box*

The Virtual Memory dialog box shows you the drive and size where Windows has its swap file. To change the settings, choose the Change command. The Virtual Memory dialog box will expand, as shown in Figure 11.3.

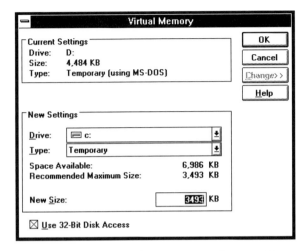

Figure 11.3   *The Virtual Memory Dialog Box Expanded*

You may change the drive, type, and size of the swap file. The type can be temporary or permanent. When the type is temporary, the size shown is the Recommended Maximum Size. When the type is permanent, the dialog box shows Maximum Size and the Recommended Size.

Setup

The Setup application in the Program Manager's Main group allows you to change certain hardware devices in your Windows installation. You would use this program to change your display monitor, your keyboard, or your mouse, to configure Windows to run on a network, and to install applications into the Windows environment.

When you run setup from the Program Manager, or as the program file SETUP.EXE from the File Manager, you see the Setup applications window shown in Figure 11.4.

Windows Setup	
Options Help	
Display:	VGA with Monochrome display
Keyboard:	Enhanced 101 or 102 key US and Non US
Mouse:	Logitech
Network:	Novell NetWare (shell versions 3.26 and

Figure 11.4   *The Setup Application Window*

Changing System Settings

The Setup window lists the current configuration. To change one or more of the settings, choose Change System Settings on the Options menu. You will see the Change System Settings dialog box shown in Figure 11.5.

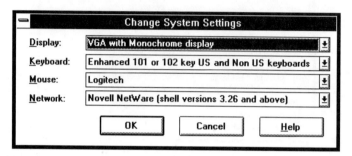

Figure 11.5   *The Change System Settings Dialog Box*

Each of the fields on the Change System Settings dialog box is a drop-down list that lists the possible devices for the field. Select the devices from the lists that match your new configuration and choose OK.

Because you have changed an integral part of the Windows setup, Windows can no longer run without being reloaded. You will be given the opportunity to restart Windows or return to DOS. There are no other choices.

If you have made a change in Setup that is not compatible with your hardware, Windows might not operate correctly. When this happens, you can run the Setup program from the DOS command line. Reboot your computer and remain in DOS. Change to the C:\WINDOWS subdirectory where you installed Windows and run the SETUP.EXE program. Setup will sense that it is in DOS and will use the DOS text mode to display your options. The format will be the same as it was when you first installed Windows.

Setting Up Applications

You can use Setup to install new applications from your hard disk(s) into your Windows environment. Choose the Set Up Applications command from the Options window. You will see the Setup Applications dialog box shown in Figure 11.6.

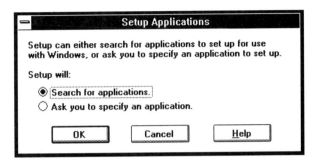

Figure 11.6   *The Setup Applications Dialog Box*

You can tell Setup to search your disks for applications or you can specify an application to install. Select the either option on the dialog box and choose OK. Figure 11.7 is the Setup Applications dialog box where you specify an application to install. You can look around your hard disk with the Browse command, or you can type the path and name of a known .EXE or .COM file for Setup to install. Select the Program Manager group where you want to install the application and choose OK. Setup tries to identify the application from among those that it knows about based on a table of known executable application file names. If it is unsure of the application's name, Setup will display the Setup Applications dialog box shown in Figure 11.8.

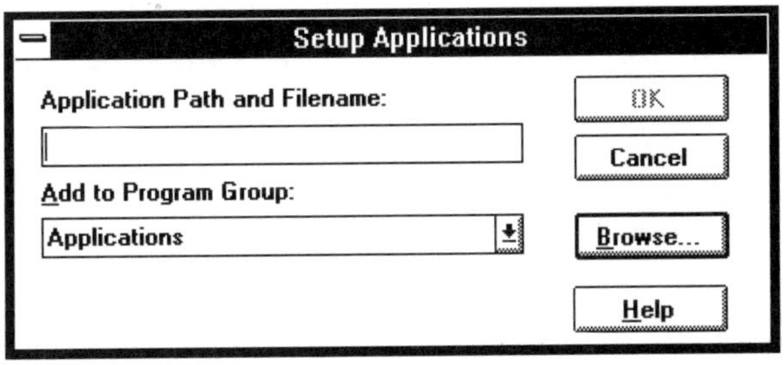

Figure 11.7   *Specifying an Application to Install*

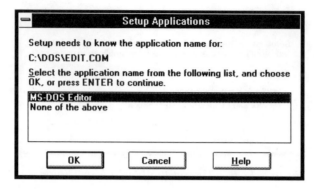

Figure 11.8 *Specifying a Name for a Found Application*

You select the correct name from the list and choose OK. If Windows already has a .PIF file for the application, you will see the Setup Applications dialog box shown in Figure 11.9. Choose the correct action to define a .PIF file for the application and Setup will install the program into the group you selected.

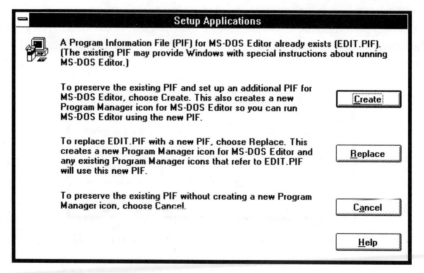

Figure 11.9 *Selecting a PIF Option*

When you tell Setup to search your hard disks for applications, you see the Setup Applications dialog box shown in Figure 11.10. Specify the drives you want searched by highlighting them on the list. You can select multiple items from this list by clicking them on and off with the mouse or by moving the dotted outline to them with the up and down arrow keys and pressing Spacebar.

Setup Applications

Setup can search your hard disk(s) for applications and then
set them up to run with Windows. Select the place(s) you
want Setup to search. Then choose Search Now or press
ENTER.

Setup will search:

Path
C: (Local Drive)
D: (Local Drive)
E: (Local Drive)
Z: FS1/SYS:
Y: FS1/SYS:

Search Now

Cancel

Help

Figure 11.10 *Specifying Drives to Search for Applications*

When you have the drives selected, choose the Search Now command. Setup will
search for applications. When it finds ones that it recognizes, it will either display
the dialog box in Figure 11.8 so that you can select a name, or it will simply col-
lect the application. You can ignore an application by choosing Cancel; Setup will
bypass it and continue the search. When the search is done, you will see the list in
the Set Up Applications dialog box shown in Figure 11.11.

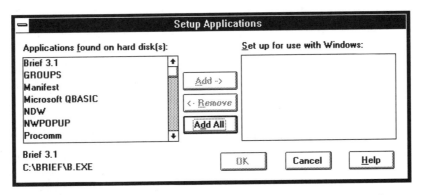

Setup Applications

Applications found on hard disk(s):   Set up for use with Windows:

Brief 3.1
GROUPS
Manifest
Microsoft QBASIC
NDW
NWPOPUP
Procomm

Add ->
<- Remove
Add All

Brief 3.1
C:\BRIEF\B.EXE

OK   Cancel   Help

Figure 11.11 *Selecting the Found Applications to Install*

Select the Applications Found list, press the down arrow key, and a dotted outline will surround the entry. Move the outline box up and down with the arrow
keys. Select applications to add by clicking them or pressing Enter. Selected applications will highlight.

Use the Add command button to move selected entries from the list of found
applications to the list of applications to install. Select applications from the right-
hand list and use the Remove command button to move an application from the
list of those to be set up back to the other list.

When you have the lists set up the way you want them, choose OK. Setup will add the applications to the Program Manager Applications group.

PIF Editor

In Chapter 2 you learned how to use the DOS Prompt icon from the Program Manager to run non-Windows DOS programs. You also learned how to execute programs by using the Run command and by installing the programs into a group with command line execution instructions.

The applications that you ran in those ways used default system settings to acquire system resources to run. They ran in full-screen mode, requiring a predetermined amount of memory, using the video system in a common way, and using default values for how they used the keyboard, command line parameters, and opening disk directories.

Not all DOS programs fit the default settings, and others will work with fewer resources than the defaults reserve, freeing the excess for other applications. For this reason Windows provides a way to tell it about DOS programs, in a file called the Program Information File (PIF). If an executable DOS program file has a matching PIF, Windows will load that file and use its settings instead of the default values.

In Chapter 2 you saw examples of non-Windows DOS applications that ran in full-screen mode and others that ran in windows in the Windows graphical operating environment. Applications run full-screen when Windows is in standard mode. They may run in windows when Windows is in 386 enhanced mode. The option to run a DOS application in a window is one of the things you can specify in a PIF.

The PIF Editor is an application in the Program Manager's Main group that you can use to create and modify PIFs for non-Windows DOS applications. You can run it from the File Manager as well by selecting the executable file PIFEDIT.EXE. You cannot run it by selecting one of its .PIF document files, because selecting a .PIF file from within the File Manager is one way to run the non-Windows DOS program that goes along with the file.

PIF Editor in Standard Mode

When you run the PIF editor in standard mode, you will see the PIF Editor application window shown in Figure 11.12. The fields in the application window are empty. The File menu has the usual New, Open, Save, and Save As commands for creating, saving, and reloading a PIF. The convention is that a PIF will have the same name as the program executable file that it describes. Therefore, a PIF for the TWRP.EXE program would be named TWRP.PIF. When you save a file, the PIF Editor suggests a file name that matches the program.

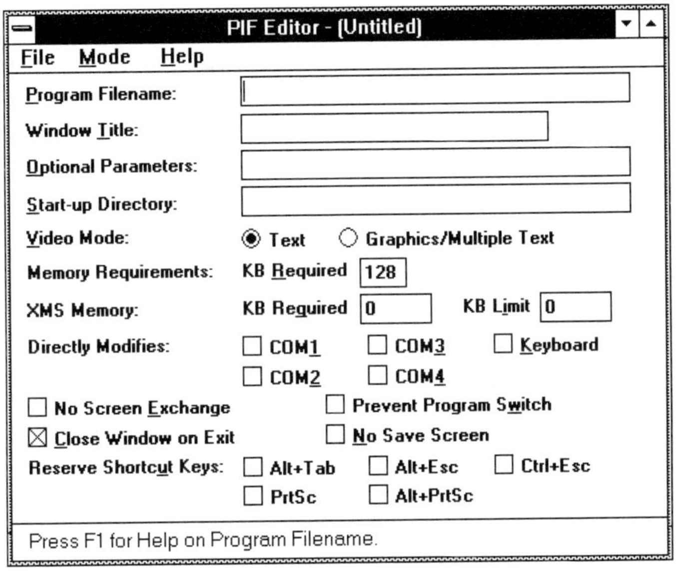

```
┌─────────────────────────────────────────────────────────────┐
│ ▬            PIF Editor - [Untitled]                  ▼ ▲    │
│  File   Mode   Help                                          │
│  Program Filename:    [I                              ]       │
│  Window Title:        [                               ]       │
│  Optional Parameters: [                               ]       │
│  Start-up Directory:  [                               ]       │
│  Video Mode:          ◉ Text    ○ Graphics/Multiple Text     │
│  Memory Requirements: KB Required [128]                      │
│  XMS Memory:          KB Required [0]      KB Limit [0]      │
│  Directly Modifies:   ☐ COM1    ☐ COM3    ☐ Keyboard        │
│                       ☐ COM2    ☐ COM4                       │
│  ☐ No Screen Exchange          ☐ Prevent Program Switch     │
│  ☒ Close Window on Exit        ☐ No Save Screen             │
│  Reserve Shortcut Keys: ☐ Alt+Tab  ☐ Alt+Esc   ☐ Ctrl+Esc   │
│                         ☐ PrtSc    ☐ Alt+PrtSc              │
│ ─────────────────────────────────────────────────────────── │
│  Press F1 for Help on Program Filename.                      │
└─────────────────────────────────────────────────────────────┘
```

Figure 11.12   *The PIF Editor Application Window - Standard Mode*

The Mode menu allows you to switch to the PIF Editor for 386 enhanced mode in case you want to edit a PIF for that environment.

Program Filename

Enter the full path to the executable program file, for example:

```
d:\twrp\twrp.exe
```

Window Title

This entry will become the label under the application's icon.

Optional Parameters

Enter any command line parameters that you use when you run the program from the DOS command line.

Start-up Directory

This entry will specify the DOS drive and directory that Windows will make current when the application runs.

Video Mode

Select the Text option button if the application does not use graphics and uses only one page of text video memory. Otherwise, select the Graphics/Multiple Text option button.

If you choose the Text option and find that you cannot switch from the application to Windows without quitting the application, modify the PIF to use the Graphics/Multiple Text option.

Memory Requirements

Leave this value at 128K unless you know that the application needs more memory. This number tells Windows not to run the application unless there is at least this much memory available. Windows gives all available conventional memory to the application when it runs, regardless of this value.

XMS Memory

These fields tell Windows how much extended memory under the XMS standard must be available to run the application, and the maximum XMS to give to the application. Few DOS applications use XMS.

Directly Modifies

If the application reads and writes to the communications ports by making direct hardware accesses (by passing DOS), you should select the corresponding COM check box. Windows will not allow the application to run if it knows that another application is using the same device.

If the application reads the keyboard directly, select the Keyboard check box. Windows will not attempt to process any keys while the application is running. You must exit from the application to return to Windows.

No Screen Exchange

If you never intend to copy the application's screen to the Clipboard, select this check box to save memory.

Prevent Program Switch

This check box prevents you from switching back to Windows from the application until you exit from it. The option saves memory.

Close Window on Exit

With this check box selected, you will return immediately to Windows when the application exits. Otherwise, you will be able to view the screen that follows the application's termination and press any key to return to Windows. This feature is necessary when applications write messages to the screen and exit immediately. If you did not use this option, the screen would be given up to Windows before you had a chance to read the application's output.

No Save Screen

This check box tells Windows that the application is able to repaint its own screen. Some applications have this capability, so Windows does not need to reserve memory to save the application's screen when other applications are running.

Reserve Shortcut Keys

Windows normally uses certain shortcut keys to manage its multitasking environment. If the application needs some of these keys for its own use, you can reserve them by selecting the appropriate check box.

PIF Editor in 386 Enhanced Mode

When you run the PIF Editor in 386 enhanced mode, you see the PIF application window for 386 enhanced mode, as shown in Figure 11.13. The Mode menu allows you to switch to the PIF Editor for standard mode in case you want to edit a PIF for that environment.

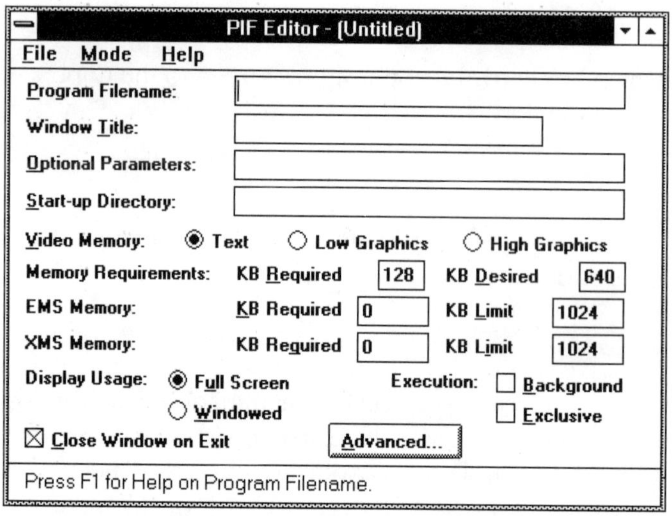

Figure 11.13 *The PIF Editor Application Window - 386 Enhanced Mode*

The Program Filename, Window Title, Optional Parameters, Start-up Directory, XMS Memory, Close Window on Exit fields, and the Reserve Shortcut field on the Advanced Options dialog box, act the same as for the standard mode PIF editor. Following are discussions of the unique fields.

Memory Requirements

The KB Required field has the amount of memory that must be available for Windows to run the application. The KB Desired field is the amount that Windows will give the application if it is available. 640K is the highest amount an application can get. Set the number lower to leave more memory available for other applications if you know that the program can run properly and efficiently with the lower amount.

EMS Memory

These fields work the same as the XMS Memory fields except that they operate on EMS memory instead of XMS memory.

Display Usage

You can run the application full-screen or windowed by selecting the appropriate option button.

Execution

The Background check box allows the application to continue to run while it is in the background. The Exclusive check box prevents other programs from running while the application is in the foreground.

Advanced

The Advanced command button opens the Advanced Options dialog box shown in Figure 11.14.

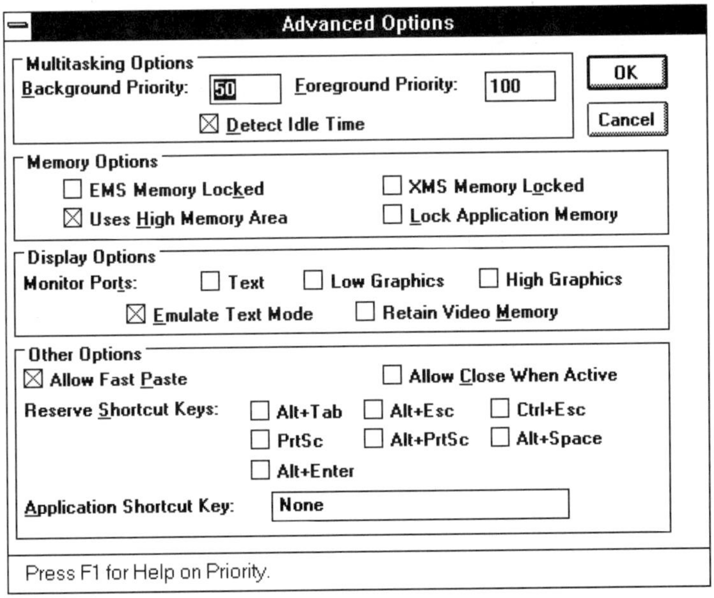

Figure 11.14 *The Advanced Options Dialog Box*

Background Priority. Enter a value from 0 to 10,000. This value is summed with the background and foreground values of other applications that are running. The ratio of the Background Priority value to that sum determines the portion of the total number of timeslices the application gets while it is in the background.

Foreground Priority. Enter a value from 0 to 10,000. This value is summed with the background and foreground values of other applications that are running. The ratio of the Foreground Priority value to that sum determines the portion of the total number of timeslices that the application gets while it is in the foreground.

Detect Idle Time. When this check box is selected, Windows gives the application's resources to other programs while the application is idle, that is, waiting for user input.

EMS Memory Locked. If you select the EMS Memory Locked check box, Windows will not swap the application's EMS contents to its virtual swap file.

XMS Memory Locked. If you select the XMS Memory Locked check box, Windows will not swap the application's XMS contents to its virtual swap file.

Uses High Memory Area. When this check box is set, the application may use the High Memory Area.

Lock Application Memory. This check box tells Windows not to swap the application's RAM contents to disk.

Monitor Ports. These check boxes tell Windows that the application will write directly to the video ports. Windows will monitor the application's use of these ports so that when you go in and out of the application, Windows can properly restore the video screen.

Emulate Text Mode. This option speeds up the application's video displays. Turn it off only if the application's text displays seem incorrect.

Retain Video Memory. This option tells Windows to retain all the application's video memory as long as the application runs. Some applications switch video modes, and if Windows gives the video memory to another application, the memory might not be available when you try to return to the application.

Allow Fast Paste. Some applications cannot keep up with the speed at which the Clipboard pastes characters. Turn off this check box if the application loses pasted characters.

Allow Close When Active. If this check box is selected, you can close down the application from within Windows without returning to the application to exit from it. Depending on what the application does, you could lose data. If the application retains unwritten data in memory pending an orderly exit, those records would be lost if you closed the application from Windows. Select this option only when you know what the application does to shut down.

Application Shortcut Key. The Application Shortcut Key is a key combination you assign to activate the application while it is minimized and you are in the Windows graphical operating environment. To assign a shortcut key, select the field and press the key combination you want to use. It must include the Alt or Ctrl key and must not be one of the key combinations that Windows uses for itself. Windows will tell you if you try to use a shortcut key that is invalid or already in use.

Windows in a Network

A network is a group of computers connected together. In a typical network configuration, one of the computers is the file server and the others are workstations. The file server is unattended and the users work at the workstations. The file server allows users to share disk files and printers on the network. A workstation in a network can have its own disks and printer, and it can share the network disks and printers with the other workstations.

Many network installations have more than one file server. A two-server network, for example, is usually two independent networks that are bridged together. The users of both networks have access to the shared files and printers of both servers.

Workstations run DOS programs just as if the workstations were stand-alone DOS computers. The program files and the data files that are on the file server appear to the DOS programs to be stored on additional DOS disk drives. A network shell program runs inside the workstation. It translates program requests for network disk file accesses into communications with the file server through the cable system that connects each workstation to the file server.

Running Windows in a Network

You should load the network shell program and any network device drivers into your DOS computer before you run Windows. Then you can install the network into Windows and use the network's features through the Windows graphical operating environment.

The Setup program is where you tell Windows that you have a network installed and which one it is. Windows comes with drivers for many different network systems. They are not all alike, and Windows will operate differently depending on which one you have. The underlying concepts are the same, however, and although the commands and dialog boxes will reflect the characteristics of your network, the procedures are similar enough that this discussion, which uses the Novell NetWare network in its examples, should suffice to lead you through the procedures of other network products.

Installing the Network

You tell Windows that you are running on a network by running the Setup application. The Change System Settings dialog box includes the Network drop-down list box. You select from the various network systems in the list, and Setup asks you to mount certain Windows diskettes so it can install the Windows network driver programs.

When a network runs in a DOS system, it has its own driver and shell programs that run in every workstation. Some network products released new versions of their programs to operate correctly with Windows 3.1. You might need to acquire these new network drivers and shells before you can use Windows 3.1 on the network. Windows will tell you when you load it if the resident network driver is the correct version. If it is not, Windows will still operate, but it will not use any of its network capabilities.

Configuring the Network

You define the network configuration from the Control Panel. Figure 11.15 shows the Control Panel application window when Windows is installed with a network. Choose the Network icon on the Control Panel to see the Network dialog box shown in Figure 11.16.

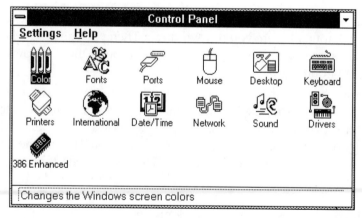

Figure 11.15   *The Control Panel with a Network Installed*

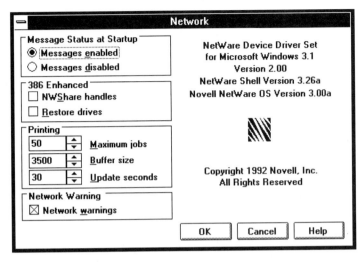

Figure 11.16 *The Network Dialog Box*

Figure 11.16 shows the Network dialog box for the network. The fields in the Network dialog box that you see will depend on the network you are using. Your network documentation and the Windows online Help will describe their meaning.

Broadcast Messages

Occasionally another user on the network will broadcast a message to you or a group of users. These messages interrupt whatever you are doing and you must acknowledge them to continue working. The Messages Disabled option button disables those messages. The Messages Enabled option button enables them again.

Drive Management

Programs in the workstation have access to the shared disks on a network through a system of pseudo-drive mappings. The network assigns a drive letter to a subdirectory on the volume. You will learn later how to assign your own drive mappings. If you are running Windows in 386 enhanced mode, you can tell Windows that any drive mappings you change in one session will apply to other sessions that are currently running. Select the NWShare Handles check box to select this option.

When you exit Windows, the drive mappings that were in effect when you started Windows will be restored if you select the Restore Drives check box. If not, the changes you make when Windows is running will be in effect when you exit Windows.

Print Queue Parameters

Two of the three values in the Printing control group modify how the Print Manager will display network print queues. The Maximum Jobs value specifies how many print queue jobs the Print Manager can display. This value does not limit the number of print jobs that the network print server can manage. The network print server is running without concern for what any particular workstation is displaying with respect to the print queue contents. The Print Manager must periodically refresh its displayed list of jobs in the queue, and the Update Seconds field tells the Print Manager how often to refresh its list.

The Buffer Size value specifies the size of the Print Manager's print job buffer size. This size can affect the performance of a program that prints. The bigger the buffer, the fewer times the Print Manager must send print data packets to the network. If you routinely print large graphics files, you should try setting this value to larger numbers to see how performance might be improved.

Network Warnings

Leave the Network Warnings check box turned on. It allows the system to advise you when things related to the network are not quite right.

Login/out

Users on a network are known to the network by their user identification or user name. When you log into the network, you must specify the file server you wish to sign onto, your user name, and perhaps a password. You can be logged into more than one server at a time in a multi-server network, and you can do so under different user names. When you log in you have access to the network resources available to the user name that you use. When you log out, those resources are no longer visible to you.

Logging In

You log into the network from DOS before you run Windows, or else from the File Manager. To log in from the File Manager, choose the Network Connections command on the File Manager's Disk menu. You will see the Network - Drive Connections dialog box shown in Figure 11.17. This dialog box has other uses, which you will learn later.

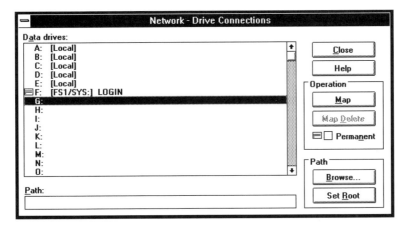

Figure 11.17   *The Network - Drive Connections Dialog Box*

Choose the Browse command on the Network - Drive Connections dialog box. You will see the Browse Connections dialog box shown in Figure 11.18. Choose the Attach command. You will see the Attach File Server dialog box shown in Figure 11.19. Select the File Server drop-down list box on the Attach File Server dialog box to see the list of file servers in your network, as shown in Figure 11.20.

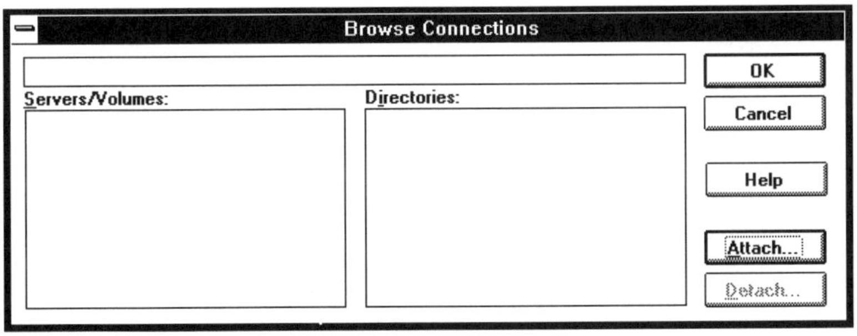

Figure 11.18   *The Browse Connections Dialog Box*

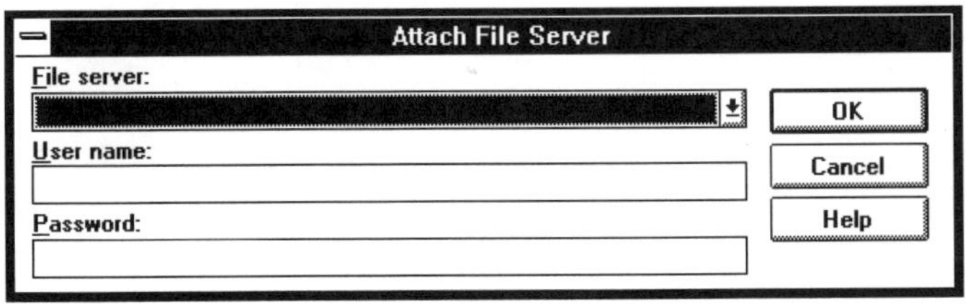

Figure 11.19   *The Attach File Server Dialog Box*

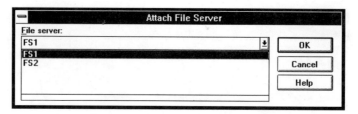

Figure 11.20 *List of File Servers in the Network*

Select a file server and fill in a user name and, if one is assigned to that user name, a password. When the dialog box is filled out as shown in Figure 11.21, choose OK. The server name and its volumes will be added to the Servers/Volumes list in the Browse Connections dialog box. Choose OK, and you are now logged into the network.

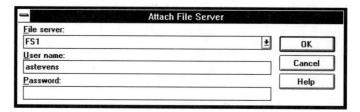

Figure 11.21 *Selecting a File Server and User Name*

N O T E

Some networks (Netware is one of them) have a system login script and a user name login script that execute when you use their DOS Login command. The login procedure that Windows provides does not execute these login scripts. If you need them executed, you must log onto the network from DOS before you run Windows.

A typical login script establishes drive mappings. You can get the same effect by defining permanent drive mappings in the File Manager. That procedure is described later in this chapter.

Logging Out

From the Browse Connections dialog box, choose the Detach command. You will see the Detach File Server dialog box shown in Figure 11.22. Select a server name from the File Server drop-down list box and choose OK. You will be logged out of the file server, and its name and volumes will be deleted from the Servers/Volumes list in the Browse Connections dialog box.

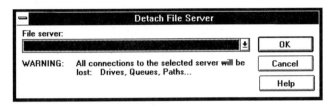

Figure 11.22 *The Detach File Server Dialog Box*

Network File Management

Drives on a network file server are organized into *volumes*. Users must address these drives as volumes rather than by their actual drive letter on the server, because there is the possibility that a workstation can have a local disk drive with the same drive letter. Within volumes, data files on the network are organized into a directory structure just like the DOS directory structure, except that the network usually imposes a certain defined set of directories where the network files and programs themselves exist.

DOS applications address disk files through the drive letters on which the files exist. The user of a DOS program running data files on a network must be able to translate the network's volume address into a drive—in this case a pseudo-drive—that DOS programs, including Windows, understand.

Pseudo-Drive Mapping

You assign pseudo-drive letters to subdirectories on the network file servers. The workstation can address a pseudo-drive letter in the same context that it would address a real disk drive in its own configuration. When you run the File Manager with a network installed, the network drives have a network drive icon, as shown for the F: and G: drives in Figure 11.23.

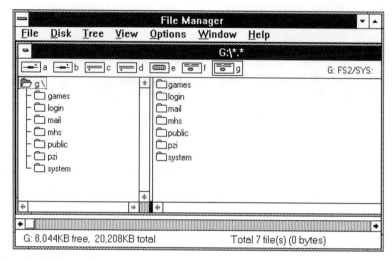

Figure 11.23   *The F and G Network Drives Added to the File Manager*

Mapping a Network Drive

Use the Network Connections command on the File Manager's Disk menu to assign network drive mappings. You will see the Network - Drive Connections dialog box that you saw in Figure 11.17. The Data Drives list box displays all the drives that are available to be mapped. You can add or change a mapping by selecting an entry from this list.

First you need to establish a network path to map the drive to. You can type a path into the Path field, or you can build it by choosing the Browse command, which displays the Browse Connections dialog box, as shown in Figure 11.24.

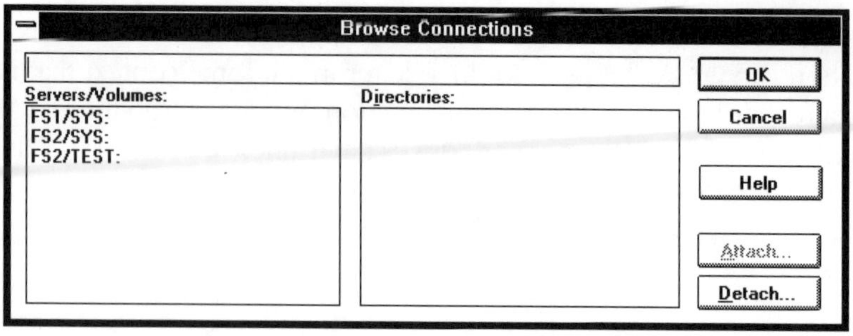

Figure 11.24   *The Browse Connections Dialog Box*

There are two file servers attached in Figure 11.24. When you select one, its name displays in the edit box at the top of the dialog box, and its subdirectories display in the Directories list box. Select a subdirectory, and its name will be appended to the path you are building in the edit box at the top of the dialog box. Double-click a subdirectory or select it and press the Space bar to view its subdirectories. The [..] entry at the top of the Directories list represents the parent directory of the current subdirectory.

When the edit box at the top of the dialog box shows the subdirectory path that you want to map, choose OK. The Network - Drive Connections dialog box will return with the path you defined displayed in the Path field. Choose Map. The path will be added to the selected drive in the Data Drives list. If you select the Permanent check box, the File Manager stores the mapping so that the next time you run Windows the mapping is in effect again. Permanent drives are marked in the Data Drives list with a disk drive icon. In Figure 11.17, the F: drive mapping is permanent.

Deleting a Drive Mapping

To delete a drive mapping, select it in the Data Drives list on the Network - Drive Connections dialog box, then choose the Map Delete command.

Printing on a Shared Network Printer

To print to a network's shared printer, you send your print output to a print queue on the file server. The file server manages the queuing, and the print server manages the printing of the job in a manner very much like that of the Windows Print Manager.

To tell Windows to send print output to the network printer, you must connect the network print queue to one of your printer ports. When an application prints to that printer port, the network shell intercepts the print output and sends it to the server's print queue.

The Print Manager assigns printer output to network print queues. Run the Print Manager and choose the Network Connections command on the Options menu. You will see the Network - Printer Connections dialog box shown in Figure 11.25.

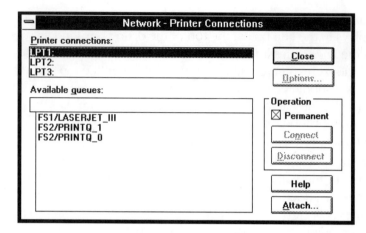

Figure 11.25 *The Network - Printer Connections Dialog Box*

Select a printer port from the Printer Connections list box and a network print queue from the Available Queues list box. Then choose the Connect command. The queue name is added to the port name and the association is made. Any subsequent printing to that port will be sent to the selected network print queue. You can use the Disconnect command to remove a port-to-queue association.

The Attach command allows you to attach to a file server by using the same procedure that you learned earlier in this chapter.

Viewing Print Queues

If you run the Print Manager with jobs queued to a network print queue, you will see a display similar to Figure 11.26. The list of jobs that shows in the Print Manager's workspace for a network printer are jobs that you submitted.

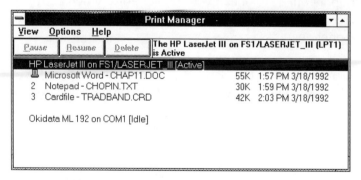

Figure 11.26 *Print Jobs Queued to the Network Printer*

The same print queue might have other jobs submitted by other users. To see the entire list of print jobs select the appropriate printer/queue entry in the Print Manager workspace and choose the Selected Net Queue command on the View menu. You will see a display similar to the one in Figure 11.27, which shows all the jobs queued to the selected network queue.

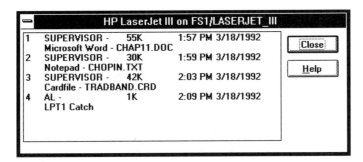

Figure 11.27 *Jobs Queued to the Selected Net Queue*

To view the contents of another network print queue, choose the Other Net Queue command on the View menu. You will see the Other Net Queue dialog box shown in Figure 11.28.

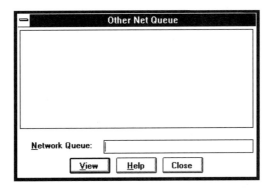

Figure 11.28 *Jobs Queued to the Other Net Queue*

To use the Other Net Queue dialog box, you must know the server and queue name of the network queue you want to view. You can find all the queue names and paths by choosing the Network Connections command on the Print Manager's Options menu. The Network - Printer Connections dialog box displays all the queues in its available queues list box. Return to the Other Net Queue dialog box and type the server and queue name into the Network Queue field.

Choose View, and the jobs queued to the selected queue will be displayed in the dialog box's list.

Setting Network Options

The Network Settings command on the Print Manager's Options menu displays the Network Options dialog box shown in Figure 11.29.

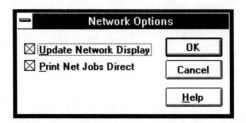

Figure 11.29   *The Network Options Dialog Box*

The Print manager updates the list of queued jobs in its workspace periodically. The Update Network Display check box allows this. Turn this box off to prevent the Print Manager from periodically reading the queue status and perhaps adversely affecting network traffic loads. To get a current display of the status of the network queues, select the Update Net Queues command on the View menu.

As a default, jobs printed to a network queue bypass the Print Manager and print directly to the network queue. To force network print jobs to go through the Print Manager, turn the Print Net Jobs Direct check box off.

Object Linking and Embedding

Windows 3.1 introduces the object linking and embedding (OLE) feature to the graphical operating environment. When Windows applications are OLE-capable, your work is made easier because OLE integrates the various applications you use to create your documents.

Embedded Objects

In Chapter 10 you wrote a letter with the Write application that included a letter-head logo that you designed with the Paintbrush application. Graphics pictures such as the logo are "objects." By using the Clipboard to transfer an object from the Paintbrush to Write, you "embedded" the Paintbrush object in the Write document. Figure 11.30 is the letter you wrote.

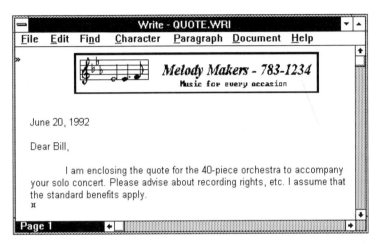

Figure 11.30 *A Notepad Letter*

If you wanted to change the text in the letter, you would simply position the cursor where you wanted to make the change and type the corrections. But suppose you wanted to change the logo. If Write and the Paintbrush did not support OLE, you would need to go to the Program Manager, execute the Paintbrush, open the logo's picture file, modify it, copy the modified picture to the Clipboard, return to the Write application, and paste the new logo into the letter.

Write and Paintbrush do, however, support OLE, and it simplifies the task considerably. In the lexicon of OLE, as applied to this example, Paintbrush is a *server* application and Write a *client* application. To modify the embedded logo letterhead object, you can double-click the picture, or move the keyboard insertion cursor to the beginning of the picture, hold the Shift key down, press the down arrow key to select the picture, and choose the Edit Paintbrush Picture Object on the Edit menu. The Paintbrush application will open with the logo object ready to be changed, as shown in Figure 11.31.

Figure 11.31   *Updating an Embedded Object in the*
Paintbrush Server Application

Perhaps you want to change the phone number. Make that change and choose Update on Paintbrush's File menu. You will see the change take effect in the Write document, as shown in Figure 11.32.

Figure 11.32   *An Embedded Object Updated in the Write Client Application*

Linked Objects

Changing an embedded object such as the logo letterhead in the example you just used changes only the client application's copy of the object. If other documents contain the same embedded object, their copies do not change. A linked object, on the other hand, is not stored in the client application's document. The client application stores a link to the original object's file and to the application that created it. When you modify the object, the new rendering automatically takes effect in all the documents that contain a link to the object.

In Chapter 10 you built a Cardfile database that described musical instruments. The picture of a cornet that you included in that database was, in fact, an embedded object. Suppose, however, that you were writing a report about those instruments, and you wanted to include the pictures in the report. So that the Cardfile database and the report would benefit from any subsequent changes you make to the pictures, you decide to implement the pictures as linked objects. Paintbrush will be the server application, and the Cardfile and Write applications will be the client applications. Figure 11.33 shows a picture of a trombone you will insert into the Cardfile database as a linked object.

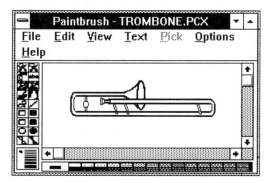

Figure 11.33   *A Paintbrush Object Ready to be Linked*

Copy the trombone's image into the Clipboard and then open Cardfile with the TRADBAND.CRD database and the trombone card selected as, shown in Figure 11.34.

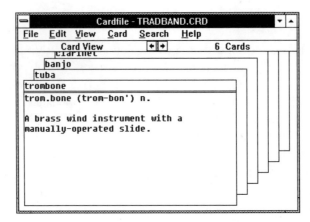

Figure 11.34 *The Cardfile Client Application Waiting for Linked Object*

Choose the Picture command on the Cardfile's Edit menu to change into the picture mode. Then choose Paste Link to insert the linked object into the card. Move the new picture so that it does not obscure the text. The Cardfile now has a picture of a trombone, as shown in Figure 11.35, and that picture is a linked object. The Paste Link command inserts a linked object while the Paste command inserts an embedded object.

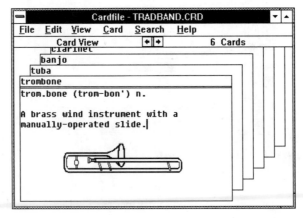

Figure 11.35 *A Linked Object in the Cardfile Client Application*

Open the Write application and begin your report. Figure 11.36 shows the report about the trombone. The same procedure inserts the linked object into the Write document. Position the insertion point cursor between the text and the figure caption. The trombone is still in the Clipboard from before, so choose Paste Link on the Write application's Edit menu. Use the Move Picture command on the Edit menu to position the picture where you want it. The document now appears as shown in Figure 11.37. Save the Cardfile database and the Write document and exit from these applications.

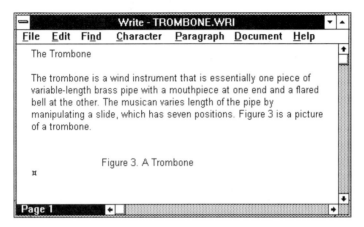

Figure 11.36   *The Write Client Application Waiting for a Linked Object*

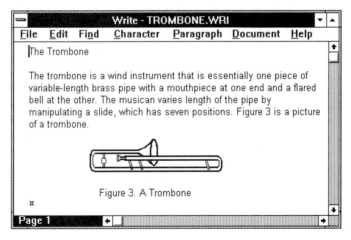

Figure 11.37   *A Linked Object in the Write Client Application*

Suppose you decide later to modify the picture of the trombone. Run Paintbrush and open the TROMBONE.PCX file. Modify the picture to add a spit valve to the slide and to improve the picture's perspective, as shown in Figure 11.38. Exit Paintbrush.

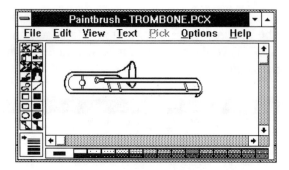

Figure 11.38   *A Linked Object Changed in the Paintbrush Server Application*

Run Cardfile and open the TRADBAND.CRD database. You will see the message shown in Figure 11.39. Choose OK. Select the trombone card, and you will see that the picture is still in its original form. Note that if you had not exited from Paintbrush, the picture would display in its modified form. In either case, you need to update the link. Choose the Picture command and then the Link command on the Edit menu. You will see the Link dialog box shown in Figure 11.40.

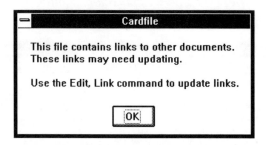

Figure 11.39   *The Cardfile Client Application Needing a Link Update*

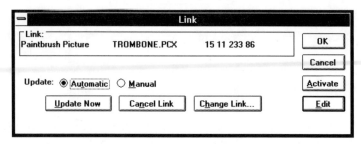

Figure 11.40   *The Link Dialog Box*

Choose the Update Now command on the Link dialog box. If the Cardfile database is still in view on the screen you will see the picture change to the modified trombone. Choose OK on the dialog box, and the Cardfile application now appears as shown in Figure 11.41, with the updated picture.

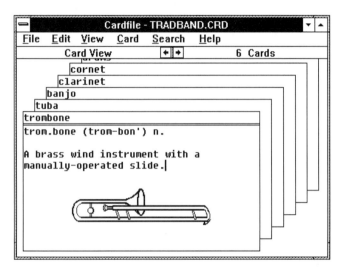

Figure 11.41   *The Linked Object Updated in the Cardfile Client Application*

Run Paintbrush again and open TROMBONE.PCX. Now run Write and open the trombone report document. You will see the Write dialog box displayed in Figure 11.42. Choose Yes and the link will be updated.

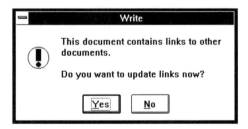

Figure 11.42   *The Write Client Application Needing a Link Update*

Figure 11.43 shows all three applications with the modified rendering of the trombone picture.

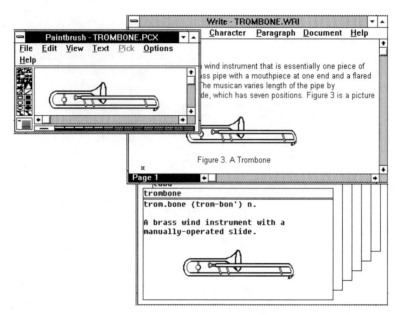

Figure 11.43 *One Server and Two Client Applications: One Linked Object*

The significance of this relationship is that the graphical representation of the object's picture occurs in only one place—the TROMBONE.PCX file maintained by the Paintbrush server application. The server applications—Cardfile and Write—store links to the object in their respective documents. This approach saves storage space because it eliminates redundant storage of the same object. It also preserves object integrity. When the server application changes the object, all the client applications can get the updated rendering. Finally, the user's interface to the object is streamlined.

Multimedia Windows

Windows includes the Media Control Interface, which specifies the control protocols for multimedia devices such as audio recording and playback, videotape players, digital video cards, and CD-ROM devices. To use the multimedia features, you must have the associated hardware devices and their software drivers installed. Windows includes some accessory programs that will drive these devices, and the vendors of the devices usually supply Windows applications that use the devices to best advantage.

Media Player

Figure 11.44 shows the Media Player application window. This application plays multimedia files into multimedia devices such as videodisk players, VCRs, compact disc players, etc. The Device menu allows you to select the device you are going to play. The File menu allows you to select the file you are going to play on the device. The Scale menu allows you to select whether the scroll bar control on the application window registers in time or in tracks on the device medium. The buttons control the device itself.

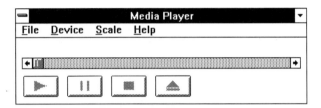

Figure 11.44   *The Media Player Application Window*

Sound Recorder

Figure 11.45 shows the Sound Recorder application window. It controls devices that record and playback sound. To use it, you need the device and its software driver installed in your system.

Figure 11.45   *The Sound Recorder Application Window*

Playing Sound Back

To play back sound, you must open a .WAV sound file from the File menu's Open command and choose the playback button, which is marked with a single right-pointing arrowhead. The double-pointing arrowheads are for fast-forward and rewind. The button with the square icon is the stop button.

Recording Sound

The button with the microphone icon is the record button. To use it, your device requires recording capabilities. The sounds you record will be added to the file.

Editing Sound

The rectangle in the center of the Sound Recorder application window is the wave form display. The scroll bar indicates the position of the wave form display in the sound file. Figure 11.46 shows the CHIMES.WAV file about half way through.

Figure 11.46 *The CHIMES.WAV File Being Played Back*

The Effects menu allows you to control the volume and playback speed and to add an echo effect to the sound. It also allows you to change the playback direction to reverse.

The Edit menu lets you insert other sound files into the current file at the current location and to blend the contents of other sound files with the current one. You may also copy the sound file to the Clipboard to insert it as an object into another application.

Summary

This chapter brings your self-taught Windows 3.1 course to an end. But it is a beginning, too. Windows 3.1 is the second in a series of Windows releases that is rapidly becoming the user interface of choice for the users of AT-class PCs. You will see improvements and added features to Windows in the next few years, and you will see many powerful applications come to market that take advantage of the full graphical operating environment of Windows 3.1.

Glossary

386 Enhanced Mode   The mode that Windows can run in if you have a 386 or 486 and at least 2MB of memory. Allows multitasking of DOS and Windows applications.

Active window   The active window is the one into which user inputs go. The active window has its title bar highlighted.

Application window   The first window that displays for an application. An application has only one application window. See also "Document window."

Arrow keys   The up, down, right, and left arrow keys on the keyboard. They are typically used to move a text cursor.

Bitmap

The internal representation of a graphics image. Wallpaper is stored in bitmap format. Paintbrush can work with bitmap files with the extension .BMP. See also "PCX Files."

Cascading windows

An arrangement of document windows that displays them in an overlapping cascade. See also "Tiled windows."

Check box

A square box in a dialog box that you can set to on or off. When on, it contains an X. When off, it is blank.

Choose

To activate a selected command or window. See also "select."

Click

Press and release the left mouse button once with the mouse cursor pointed at the screen item you wish to select. See also "double-click."

Clipboard

The Windows application to which you cut and copy text and graphics from applications and from which you paste text and graphics to applications. The method by which most Windows applications can share information.

COM port

See "Communications port."

Command button

A rectangular box in a dialog box that has a command label in it. When you click the command button you execute the command.

Communications port

A hardware device to which you can connect a modem, a terminal, a plotter, or a serial printer.

Control menu

The menu that accompanies most windows. It allows you to restore, close, move, size, minimize, and maximize the window. Minimized applications icons have Control menus as well.

Copy	Write text or graphics from an application to the Clipboard.
Cursor	A pointing icon associated with the keyboard or mouse. The cursor takes different forms depending on its current purpose.
Cut	Write text or graphics from an application to the Clipboard and delete the text or graphics from the application.
Default	The initial setting for a parameter usually established by the system. You can change the default setting for many parameters.
Desktop	The portion of the screen that holds application windows and icons.
Dialog box	A window with various kinds of control fields with which the user enters data and commands.
Directory	A group of files organized together in a structure of a root directory and subdirectories.
Directory window	The window in which File Manager displays the contents of a directory.
Disk	A mass storage medium. See also "Diskette" and "Hard disk."
Diskette	Removable disk medium. Also called "Floppy disk." See also "Disk."
Document window	The window or windows in which an application displays data. An application can have multiple document windows, all of which remain within the borders of the application window. Some applications use the work space of the application window for data display and do not have document windows.

DOS	The Disk Operating System under which Windows operates.
Double-click	Click the left mouse button twice rapidly to choose an item on the screen. See also "Click."
Drag	Press and hold the left mouse button while you move the mouse cursor across the screen. The object under the mouse cursor follows the cursor if the object is subject to being dragged. When the object is at its destination, release the mouse button.
Drop-down list box	A list box that has only one visible entry, which displays the current setting. When you click its down-arrow, the box opens to reveal a list of settings from which you can choose.
Extension	The one to three-character extension to a file name. The file name and its extension are separated by a period. See also "File name."
File	A collection of information stored into one logical file on a disk.
File name	The one to eight-character name of a file. See also "Extension."
Fixed disk	See "Hard disk."
Font	A complete assortment of type of one size and face, containing all of the characters needed for ordinary composition. See also "Point size."
Footer	A body of text that is printed at the bottom of every page in a document. See also "Header."
Format	Prepare a diskette for use.

Group   A logical grouping of pointers to executable pro-
                             gram files, maintained by and accessible through
                             the Program Manager.

Hard disk   A high-capacity, non-removable mass storage
                             medium. See also "Disk."

Header   A body of text that is printed at the top of every
                             page in a document. See also "Footer."

Hidden file   A file with the "hidden" attribute set. Such files
                             do not display in a normal file directory.

Highlighted   An item is highlighted when you have selected it
                             and it is ready to be activated or acted upon by a
                             command.

Icon   A small picture that represents an application.
                             When an application is inactive and minimized,
                             it appears as an icon at the bottom of the desk-
                             top.

Inactive window   An application window that is displayed while
                             another window is active. The inactive window's
                             title bar is displayed without highlighting.

List box   A text box on a dialog box that contains a list of
                             selections. You can select and choose one of the
                             selections. If the list is longer than the box, the
                             box has a vertical scroll bar.

Macro   A recorded sequence of keyboard and mouse
                             actions that you can play back by pressing a
                             shortcut key.

Mark   Select a block of text or part of a picture to delete
                             or to cut or copy to the Clipboard.

Maximize   Cause a window to occupy the entire screen.

Menu   A vertical list of commands from which you se-
                          lect. A menu displays in its own small window
                          that pops down from the menu bar.

Menu bar   A horizontal display of menus names. The menu
                          bar appears at the top of an application window
                          under the title bar. When you select a menu
                          name, its menu pops down.

Minimize   Reduce an application window to an icon.

Mode   One of the Windows operating modes. See "386
                          Enhanced Mode" and "Standard mode."

Network   A configuration of computers organized into a
                          file server and work stations. The work stations
                          support users. The file server is unattended. The
                          users share files on and printers connected to the
                          file server.

Non-Windows DOS   DOS program that Windows runs either in a
application   Window or by giving the entire screen to the ap-
                          plication.

Option buttons   A set of two or more selections in a dialog box.
                          Only one of the set may be selected at one time.
                          The buttons are represented by small round
                          circles. The selected option button has a dark
                          circle inside the button. The others are empty.
                          Also called "radio buttons."

Parameter   A value that controls or affects the operation of
                          an application and that appears on the applica-
                          tions command line following the application's
                          executable file name.

Paste   Write a block of text or a picture from the Clip-
                          board into an application.

Path
The DOS path that leads from the root directory to the file name. Expressed as a string such as C:\WINDOWS\SYSTEM\filename.

PCX file
A graphics file format that Paintbrush can read and write.

PIF
Program Information File. A file that describes a non-Windows DOS application in a way that allows Windows to run it.

Pixel
The smallest item of information in a graphics picture. A picture is made up of rows and columns of pixels, each one being a single dot of color.

Point size
The size assigned to the characters in a font.

Print queue
A queue of jobs waiting to be printed by the Print Manager.

Protocol
The method by which the two ends of a communications link coordinate the connection. Protocols exist at several levels, from the hardware protocols that physically connect the two computers to the data protocols that the two computers use to synchronize the transfer of data files and perform error detection and correction.

Radio buttons
See "Option buttons."

Read-only file
A DOS file that has the read-only attribute set. Users can read the file but they cannot modify or delete it.

Real mode
The mode that the processor runs in if you have an 8086 or 8088 processor. Windows 3.1 will not run in real mode.

Root directory	The top directory in the directory structure of a disk device.
Scroll bars	Horizontal and vertical bars that appear on the bottom and right side of a window when its contents do not fit in the visible work space.
Select	Point to and highlight an item before choosing it for an action.
Serial port	See "Communications port."
Shortcut key	A keystroke that provides a shortcut to what is otherwise a more complex action. Many menu commands have shortcut keys. Fields in dialog boxes can have shortcut keys. Recorder macros can have shortcut keys.
Standard mode	The mode that Windows runs in if you have a machine with a 286 processor and at least 1MB of memory. Multitasks Windows applications and swaps DOS applications.
System file	A DOS file that has the system attribute set.
Text box	A box in a dialog box into which you enter text data.
Tiled windows	Windows arranged so that each one is fully visible, their borders abutting each other. The windows are all the same size and shape. See also "Cascading windows."
Title bar	The top bar of a window where its title appears. When the window is active, the title bar is highlighted.
Tree	The File Manager's display of a disk drive's root directory and the subdirectories under it and each other.

Wallpaper   The bitmap pattern that displays on the Desktop. Users select wallpaper patterns to personalize their Windows operating environment.

Wildcard   A component in a file name to make it ambiguous so that a file selection function will find multiple matching files. Wildcards are asterisks and question marks.

Word wrap   The ability of a text editor or word processor to automatically move the word and the cursor to the next line when the word you are typing goes past the right margin.

Work space   The area in a document window where the application displays the document data and where the user makes changes.

Index